Daily Reflections for Recovering Adults

0422

NEW CLOTHES FROM OLD THREADS

By Sally Hill
with
Valerie Deilgat

Illustrations by
Kathleen Robb Parks

Published by

Recovery Publications, Inc.
1201 Knoxville Street
San Diego, CA 92110
(619) 275-1350

Illustrations by Kathleen Robb Parks

Cover Design by James Q. Millard

Printed in the United States of America

Library of Congress Catalog Card No. 90-53450

Recovery Publications, Inc.
    New Clothes From Old Threads: Daily Reflections for Recovering Adults.

ISBN 0-941405-10-9

For

Aquarius

ACKNOWLEDGMENTS

Writing this book has reminded me that recovery is a cooperative venture. I am especially indebted to:

Karen Casey, whose *Each Day A New Beginning* (Hazelden, 1982) provided the model for this book; and the late Bruno Bettelheim, whose *The Uses of Enchantment* (Vintage Books, 1977) revived my childhood interest in fairy tales.

The many people in twelve-step programs and therapy groups who shared their experience, strength and hope with me.

My friends, old and new, who supported my recovery and encouraged me in my efforts to write this book.

All those involved in the book's production, especially Valerie Deilgat, who has been more of a co-author than an editor, Darla Dougherty and Nan Cox, who edited the manuscript, Pam Nielsen, who designed the format, and Kathy Parks, who provided the illustrations.

My two fairy godmothers, Carolyn Dalphon and Dr. Florence Wiedemann, friends and mentors who have been a source of wisdom and inspiration to me, both personally and professionally.

TABLE OF CONTENTS

everal years ago, I was re-introduced to fairy tales through Bruno Bettelheim's book, *The Uses of Enchantment*. He describes these stories as magic mirrors that reflect aspects of our inner world and the stages involved required to reach maturity. Reading these childhood tales from a new vantage point deepened my appreciation for the twelve-step process and how it has contributed to my own development.

For me, the Twelve Steps address many of the same issues that fairy tales do: lack of faith in our own intuition and inner wisdom, the belief that we are small and helpless in the face of the witches and giants created by our self-defeating thoughts and attitudes, and the happy endings that follow when we have the courage to stop and look at what we are doing and who we really are.

I discovered the Steps at a time when my life was falling apart at the seams. The fabric of my relationships and activities had unraveled, leaving me with a tangled mass of threads that offered me little protection. Like the emperor, I felt I had to go on with the procession by maintaining a brave facade for others. I was under the illusion that they would somehow fall apart if I let my insecurity and vulnerability show. What I really wanted to do was throw away my tattered garments, run away to a place where no one knew me and adopt a totally new identity.

I feel differently today. Working the Steps has given me the "makeover" I wanted without requiring that I throw myself out in the process. I have learned that recovery is not a matter of discarding the past, but of reinterpreting it and incorporating it into the present. The Steps are tools I have used to comb through the threads of my life and separate the strong fibers from the weak ones.

Today I no longer feel a need to be so perfect. I can see parts of myself in all the characters in the stories that are included in this book—princes and princesses, witches and giants, children and beasts. I know what it feels like to think I am Rumpelstiltzkin and work compulsively through the night, driven to achieve superhuman tasks to prove I am worthy of love. I relate to Snow White in her glass coffin, waiting to be rescued by a handsome prince, forgetting that she is the only one who can unlock her feelings and open the lid. Envy has driven me to dance in red hot shoes like those the jealous queen wore at Snow White's wedding.

Like the Ugly Duckling, I know the joy of discovering that I am beautiful, after years of believing I was somehow defective. I can identify with the young prince, who, in the midst of his busy journey through life, hears Rapunzel's lonely song and discovers that feelings have value. In the course of my daily activities, I am often reminded of Cinderlad, who had to go back for another horse before he could climb the glass hill, and of the young woman in "East of the Sun and West of the Moon," who had the courage to cast new light on her behaviors and relationships.

Most of the quotations that appear at the top of each page have been abstracted from Andrew Lang's 19th century editions of fairy tales. Exceptions to this are found in "The Ugly Duckling," based on several translations of Hans Christian Andersen's story, and "The Selfish Giant," taken from a collection of Oscar Wilde. A list of references is given on pages 420-423 of this book.

I hope that you will discover your own personal meanings for the poison apples, golden spinning-wheels and other objects that are mentioned throughout this book. Part of the joy of these tales is the personal thoughts, feelings, memories and responses that they evoke in each of us—old threads with which we can weave new clothes on the loom provided by the Twelve Steps.

Rapunzel

RAPUNZEL

nce upon a time there lived a man and wife whose house overlooked a beautiful garden owned by a powerful witch. One day the wife spotted some rapunzel, a variety of salad green, in the garden and longed to have some. Her desire increased day by day until she became pale and wretched. Convinced that his wife would die if she didn't get some, the man began stealing it from the garden. The witch caught him, and instead of punishment, agreed to furnish the woman with as much rapunzel as she wanted in return for their first-born child. The man agreed, and when his daughter was born, the witch named her Rapunzel and carried her away.

When Rapunzel was twelve years old, the witch shut her up in a tower that had no door. When the witch wanted to get in, she stood below the tower and called, "Rapunzel, Rapunzel, let down your golden hair," and then climbed up the tower on the girl's long braids.

One day a prince was riding by and was attracted by Rapunzel's singing. Seeing how the witch scaled the tower wall, he returned that evening, called to Rapunzel and climbed up her hair. He visited her every evening, finally asking her to marry him. She requested that he bring a skein of silk each time he came so that she could weave a ladder to escape from her tower. Unfortunately, she betrayed her plan to the witch by mentioning the prince's visits. In her wrath, the witch cut Rapunzel's hair and banished her to the desert.

The witch then fastened the cut-off braids to the tower window. When the prince visited that evening, she told him that Rapunzel was lost to him forever. In despair, he threw himself from the tower and fell into thorns which blinded him. Years later, wandering miserably through the woods, he came upon the desert and recognized Rapunzel's voice. She embraced him and wept for joy. When her tears touched his eyes, he regained his sight. Then he took her to his kingdom where they lived happily ever after.

Once upon a time there lived a man and his wife who were very unhappy because they had no children. These good people had a little window at the back of their house, which looked into the most lovely garden, full of all manner of beautiful flowers and vegetables; but the garden was surrounded by a high wall, and no one dared to enter it, for it belonged to a witch of great power, who was feared by the whole world.

*I*t is difficult to feel content when our lives are at a standstill. If we are unable to experience growth and initiate positive changes, we may become unhappy with the world around us. When we lose our vitality and enthusiasm for daily living, relationships with ourselves and others begin to wither and die. Creating opportunities for growth and new life is important if we are to flourish.

The beauty around us is a potential source of pleasure. It adds richness to our lives and refreshes our spirits. Viewing beautiful gardens can be inspiring to us. It can also be painful if it only reminds us of what we can't have. We need not spend our lives looking out the back window of our soul at riches beyond our reach. We can learn to build gardens of our own to serve as personal sources of nourishment and pleasure.

I can create, cultivate and maintain my own garden. I will experience beauty and new life if I am willing to take certain steps.

One day the woman stood at the window overlooking the garden, and saw there a bed full of the finest lettuce: the leaves looked so fresh and green that she longed to eat them. The desire grew day by day, and just because she knew she couldn't possibly get any, she pined away and became quite pale and wretched.

Many of us know how it feels to be trapped by an obsession. Like the woman in this story, we often grow pale and wretched over feelings of longing for people or things. How quickly we lose sight of the priorities we have established when we're presented with something we want but can't have—especially if it happens to be something we think we deserve!

It doesn't matter whether we're obsessing over new relationships, power or money. Compulsive behavior may satisfy us temporarily, but eventually it adds to our emptiness and diminishes our self-worth. We begin to solve our problems when we stop running from one obsession to another and directly confront our fear and anger. Until we take Step One and admit our powerlessness and the unmanageability of our lives, we continue to be vulnerable to any new fad or fancy that comes our way. Coming to terms with our behavior helps prepare us to welcome more permanent, less-costly solutions.

Pining for things I can't have keeps me stuck in the problem. I will take a fresh look at what I want from life today.

Her husband grew alarmed and said: "What ails you, dear wife?"

*I*t's alarming when people we care about become depressed. Their behavior seems to change suddenly and they become like strangers to us. They seem to look the same—perhaps a bit thinner or a bit grayer—but they may move more slowly, speak less often and their eyes may lose their luster. We want the old person back, but we don't know where they've gone. We sometimes blame ourselves and think it's our job to fix things. Isn't it immoral to be happy when someone you love is miserable?

"Maybe if I smile at her more, plump her pillow in the morning and bring her breakfast in bed, she'll cheer up," we say to ourselves. "Maybe if he watches more television or hears some new jokes, he'll recover his interest in life." How many of us still fall into fantasies like this, fueled by the illusion that we have the power to make people around us happy? Learning to look at our part in relationships is important. We learn in recovery that there is a difference between being responsive to others—being available to them—and taking responsibility for their lives and feelings.

I help others when I take time to listen and
share my experience, strength and hope.
I can respond to others without
trying to control their lives.

"Oh," she answered, "if I don't get some lettuce to eat out of the garden behind the house, I know I shall die."

Some of us become so consumed by our desires that we think we will die if they are not fulfilled. Ignoring the positive aspects of our lives, we convince ourselves that we cannot be happy unless we possess a certain thing, are involved with a certain person or feel a certain way. Like the wife in the story, we know we are in need of new energy—fresh green lettuce—but we look for it in all the wrong places.

No matter how we try to fill our emptiness, we won't be truly satisfied until we begin cultivating our own garden. When we realize that material objects and mood altering substances cannot satisfactorily solve our problems, we are ready to make positive changes in our lives. With the help of our recovery program, we can put our self-destructive behaviors behind us and begin to bring our own garden of possibilities to fruition.

***I can find healthy ways to fill
my inner emptiness.***

The man, who loved her dearly, thought to himself, "Come! rather than let your wife die you shall fetch her some lettuce, no matter the cost."

*T*he statement "no matter the cost" implies a strong commitment. At first glance, it appears that this man truly loves his wife because he's willing to risk facing the wicked witch in order satisfy her need. But making personal sacrifices for someone else's well-being can be a sign of serious addiction.

Becoming so dependent on others that we are willing to sacrifice ourselves in order to take care of their needs makes us part of the problem. Taking responsibility for other people deprives them of the opportunity of learning how to take care of themselves. If we continue to take care of them in unhealthy ways, they have no reason to search for their own Higher Power and discover the joy of recovery.

Looking honestly at the consequences of supporting someone else's ineffective behavior helps us understand that we must become more self-sufficient if we are to be of help and assistance to the people we love. Working the Steps leads us to a spiritual awakening that allows us to "carry the message to those who still suffer." When we do so, we offer them the hope of replacing destructive, temporary solutions to their pain with lasting happiness, joy and freedom.

*I can show my love for the people close to me by allowing them to make their own decisions.
I will neither encourage nor allow
others to be dependent upon me.*

So at dusk he climbed over the wall into the witch's garden, and, hastily gathering a handful of lettuce leaves, he returned with them to his wife. She made them into a salad, which tasted so good that her longing for the forbidden food was greater than ever.

*W*hen satisfaction is followed by greater longing, the stage is set for addiction. If the cycle is not broken, our craving only grows in intensity until it becomes the major focus of our lives. This prevents us from keeping our material, emotional and social needs in balance. We cannot grow emotionally and spiritually if our happiness depends on a single substance or on our ability to satisfy someone else's obsessions.

In the process of recovery, we learn to stop reacting to the constant crises that result when we center our attention on meeting addictive needs. Hastily planned solutions may temporarily quiet the problem, but they do not provide permanent answers. Exploring possible alternatives with sponsors or other program members who understand the situation helps us obtain a broader perspective. We develop the courage to stop using false pretenses to get what we want and begin to find better ways to get our needs met.

When I can openly discuss my needs with others, my small cravings are less likely to become addictions.

If she were to know any peace of mind, there was nothing for it but that her husband should climb over the garden wall again, and fetch her some more.

*B*asing our peace of mind on a single outcome and looking to someone else to fulfill our needs can lead to unhappiness and frustration. Assuming responsibility for meeting someone else's needs is just as self-defeating and can also lead to problems. We limit our opportunities for satisfying experiences when we focus all of our attention on one object or goal. We lose sight of the pleasures around us when we become obsessed with objects in other people's gardens. We cannot be serene if we allow our lives to be constantly disrupted by single-minded longings for things we cannot have.

Being restored to sanity as Step Two states involves an adjustment in the kind of black and white thinking that traps us in cycles of perpetual discontent. We learn to think about the consequences before leaping into gardens and taking things that don't belong to us. When we ask ourselves if there is another way to accomplish our goal, we often find a more effective solution. We may be surprised at the creative answers that spring up within us when we remember to ask for help and then listen to the response.

*Peace of mind is within my reach when
I look away from other people's
gardens and find the Higher
Power within me.*

So at dusk over he got, but when he reached the other side he drew back in terror, for there, standing before him, was the old witch.

Sneaking into gardens at dusk increases our chances of going undetected, but it also prevents us from seeing things clearly. Our thinking becomes blurred when we are caught in a conflict between seizing what we think we need and hesitating to take something we know is not rightfully ours.

It is easy to put ourselves in the husband's place. He might have rationalized his actions by thinking, "She's probably a greedy old lady who'll set an unfair price on her lettuce if she knows I need it. She probably won't even miss it. It didn't cost her anything anyway—all she had to do was clear a tiny patch of soil. My wife needs it or she'll die. It's my duty to get it for her."

When we engage in similar rationalization, we risk falling into the hands of a witch. There is always a price to be paid for violating our own principles. Rather than victimizing ourselves in this manner, we can take a few moments and recite Step Three. This may put us back in touch with our true values and keep us from making a choice we will later regret.

*Am I compromising my values in order
to get something that will cost
me dearly in the end?*

11

"How dare you," she said, with a wrathful glance, "climb into my garden and steal my lettuce like a common thief? You shall suffer for your foolhardiness."

*W*henever we're unable to act naturally and spontaneously, it feels like we have fallen under some kind of spell. Our instincts go awry, and we find ourselves in the presence of witches who have the power to lock us up and stifle our growth. Suddenly, we become helpless children again, bearing the brunt of an adult's anger because we invaded forbidden territory in an attempt to satisfy our needs.

Although we still fall into these traps, we don't have to remain in them. We no longer need to play the part of helpless children in a world dominated by powerful witches. Working the Steps helps us develop healthy relationships with ourselves and those around us. We discover a loving Higher Power who supports our growth and development. We learn how to meet our needs honestly in ways that benefit others as well as ourselves.

I am on a journey and I am leaving my help-lessness behind so that I can experience the benefits of healthy adulthood.

"Oh!" he implored, "pardon my presumption; necessity drove me to the deed. My wife saw your lettuce from her window, and conceived such a desire for it that she would have died if her wish had not been gratified."

Sometimes we say to ourselves, "It's not my fault. I had no choice. I had to fill my wife's emptiness—to satisfy her craving—no matter what the cost." What a terrible place to be—caught between the neediness of a spouse and the vengeance of a witch! This is a logical consequence of allowing someone else's needs to become as important to us as our own. When panic over losing someone we love pushes us to try to satisfy them no matter what the demand, we find ourselves acting in demeaning ways—pleading, manipulating, begging—even stealing, if that's what it takes to quiet them.

Working the Steps restores us to sanity. We discover that we can rely upon our Higher Power to direct our lives. We recover our faith in our own inner authority and become less willing to participate in destructive games with others. Coming to know our own limits helps us give the responsibility for other people's lives back to them without withdrawing our support and encouragement. This gives them a chance to develop a relationship with their own Higher Power that will set them free.

My Higher Power does not seek vengeance
or control. I can trust the power
of the Steps to set me free.

When the Witch's anger was a little appeased, and she said: "If it's as you say, you may take as much lettuce away with you as you like, but on one condition only—that you give me the child your wife will shortly bring into the world. All shall go well with it, and I will look after it like a mother."

*A*ll of our choices carry consequences of some kind. We can find addictive ways to ease our pain and fill our emptiness, but they affect our ability to inject new life into our relationships. We put our opportunities for growth and development into the hands of a witch who promises to care for us but cannot give us what we really need.

If we were raised in homes where addiction was present or our caregivers were emotionally unavailable to us, we may have serious difficulties as adults. Our needs for food, clothing and shelter may have been met but our emotional needs were not. As a result, we may not have developed the inner security and skill that fosters our capacity for productive work and positive relationships.

The program gives us a chance to fill in the missing pieces and our development wherever it stopped. We are among people who understand what it's like to feel possessed, controlled and dominated by outside circumstances. We no longer have to suffer alone. We can look to others for help and support in working the Steps that will set us free.

*I am finding ways to meet my
needs for love and security.*

*The man in his terror agreed to everything she asked,
and as soon as the child was born the Witch appeared,
and having given it the name of Rapunzel, which is a
kind of lettuce, she carried it off with her.*

*W*hen we are caught up in addiction—our own or
someone else's—images of new life hold little attraction for us. Our development stops when all our energies are devoted to survival—to simply hanging on to
what little security we have. We may conceive or even
give birth to new ideas, but we cannot nurture them
to grow and prosper.

Many of us grew up in homes where one parent was
lost to addiction and the other was absent or involved
in responding to the problems this created. We may
have repeated the same pattern in our lives by marrying addicts or becoming addicted ourselves.

When we become aware of our addictions and make
the decision to initiate corrective action, we take the
first step toward recovering the valuable child that
was lost. By attending meetings and working the
Twelve Steps, we free ourselves from our obsessions.
Step Four gives us an opportunity to examine old
attitudes and behaviors that may still hold us captive.

*Am I still suffering from the effects of addiction
in my life? I can use Step Four to uncover
the things that hold me captive.*

Rapunzel was the most beautiful child under the sun.

*J*ust imagine what it would feel like to be the most beautiful child under the sun! We could be ourselves—spontaneous, curious and interested in the people around us. We wouldn't be afraid to reach out and be loved or to love in return.

All children are beautiful because they are filled with life. They know how to laugh and how to cry. They love the sun and rain, barking dogs and mewing kittens. When children are healthy and active, they rejoice in running, playing, dancing and singing. Children delight in being themselves and exploring what it means to be part of a constantly changing world.

The process of recovery slowly restores life to our beautiful inner child. We gradually lose our inhibitions and drop the unnatural behaviors we developed to make ourselves look good. As we regain our sense of self-worth, our enjoyment spills over onto our families, our careers and our relationships. We discover that life is good, that we can love and be loved and that there really are happy endings.

> *Today I will look at the world through the*
> *eyes of the beautiful child that I am. If*
> *I haven't yet discovered my beauty,*
> *I'll practice looking at the*
> *world as if I had.*

When Rapunzel was twelve years old the Witch shut her up in a tower, in the middle of a great wood, and the tower had neither stairs nor doors, only high up at the very top a small window.

Sometimes it seems as though our lives are being run by an old script—that we are actors in a play we didn't write. We suddenly realize that we are in the same situation as Rapunzel's mother—condemned to long for things beyond her reach. Instead of developing our potential to become confident, outgoing adults, we may feel like we are locked up in a tower.

Most of us know what it feels like to isolate and withdraw at times when we would like to reach out. Sometimes the causes are external, but more often we are held back by our own insecurity, shyness or fear of rejection. Participation in a recovery program helps alleviate our discomfort with people and new situations. Examining our behavior in Step Five helps us to identify old patterns that interfere with our relationships with others. This Step throws light on our motivations and behaviors and puts us in contact with someone else who also had the courage to do so.

Today I will be a participant in life instead of a spectator. I have everything I need to break loose from my lonely tower.

When the old Witch wanted to get into the tower she stood underneath and called out: "Rapunzel, Rapunzel, Let down your golden hair," for Rapunzel had wonderful long hair, and it was as fine as spun gold. Whenever she heard the Witch's voice she unloosed her plaits, and let her hair fall down out of the window about twenty yards below, and the old Witch climbed up by it.

*I*f our parents were addicted, depressed or emotionally unavailable to us, we may have felt obligated to take care of them. If they seemed to be incapable of meeting their own needs, we may have felt responsible for maintaining their fragile lifelines. Unless we find some way to escape this misplaced responsibility, we may spend our lives playing parts in other people's dramas instead of creating a world of our own.

Like Rapunzel with her golden hair, we all possess strength and energy. Many of us come into the program unaware of this fact. Our attention has been distracted by the daily demands of helping others survive in a world we don't feel adequately prepared to face. When we are able to get in touch with our own resources, we are less apt to let our hair—a symbol of our power, strength and vitality—be used as a ladder in self-destructive ways.

I am learning to be responsive, responsible
and free. I can choose to be of service
to others, but I owe allegiance
only to my Higher Power.

After they had lived like this for a few years, it happened one day that a Prince was riding through the wood and passed by the tower. As he drew near it he heard someone singing so sweetly that he stood still spell-bound, and listened. It was Rapunzel in her loneliness trying to while away the time by letting her sweet voice ring out into the wood.

*A*t some point in our recovery, we become aware of being pulled in two directions: outwardly to the world of spontaneous activity, represented by the Prince's free movement through the wood, and inwardly to the realm of feeling that Rapunzel expresses with her songs. Expressing our innermost thoughts and feelings can be frightening if we're not accustomed to doing so, but as we learn to verbalize them, we become more comfortable with ourselves.

Like Rapunzel, we may feel isolated and unable to communicate with others, but a healthy, outgoing part of us is looking for help and resists being silenced. This is the voice that guides us to the program, where we develop the courage to begin communicating with our inner child and sharing our feelings, thoughts and stories with others. There is no guarantee that we will be heard each and every time we speak; indeed, the story of Rapunzel reminds us this will probably not be the case. But giving voice to our feelings is a necessary step in finding the joy that comes from knowing and being known by others.

I am grateful for the voice that brought me into the program. I will continue to give expression to my innermost self.

The Prince longed to see the owner of the voice, but he sought in vain for a door in the tower.

*T*here are many ways of keeping people from getting too close to us—not listening attentively when they speak, not looking directly at them or not responding honestly to what they say and do. We can also try to protect ourselves from possible disappointment or rejection by not taking anything seriously. This only prevents us from experiencing the fun that spontaneity can bring to our lives.

Many of us stay locked in our towers, fearing that others will dominate us, abuse us or persuade us to do something we'd prefer not to do. We may be concerned about hurting someone's feelings or afraid we'll be laughed at for the way we behave. Becoming entirely ready to have these fears and behaviors removed in Step Six is a major milestone on the road to recovery. We prepare ourselves for Step Seven when we become willing to have these defects removed and find ways to let others share in our experiences.

*I am becoming ready to let go of behaviors that
are harmful to me. I trust that my Higher
Power will remove them and that I
can develop more effective
skills to replace them.*

He rode home, but he was so haunted by the song he had heard that he returned daily to the wood and listened.

*E*ach of us has a song within us that cries out for self-expression. Sending it forth—allowing our true feelings to be heard—strengthens our connection with others. If we are out of touch with our own emotions and disconnected from our Higher Power, we may need to stop and listen to the songs of other people, like the Prince, before we can make contact with our own. When we attend meetings and realize the benefits that others receive by sharing their feelings, we become less frightened of getting in touch with the way we feel.

Daily periods of meditation give us an opportunity to listen to the song which is sung by the lonely child in all of us. Developing a relationship with a sponsor or someone else we can trust gives us an opportunity to practice singing and voice our wants and needs.

For many of us, the ability to improve our relationships is a primary goal in recovery. If asked what shortcoming we most desperately wanted removed in Step Seven, we might reply "fear of intimacy." Discovering our true selves and allowing our thoughts and feelings to slowly emerge is a major step in overcoming this lifelong fear.

*I will listen to the song inside me and
learn to express my true feelings.*

One day, when he was standing behind a tree, he saw the old Witch approach and heard her call out: "Rapunzel, Rapunzel, Let down your golden hair." "So that's the staircase, is it?" said the Prince. The following day, at dusk, he went to the foot of the tower and cried: "Rapunzel, Rapunzel, Let down your golden hair," and as soon as she had let it down the Prince climbed up.

*W*hen we think of princes, we often think of people who are successful and free—able to roam wherever they want to in search of fame and fortune. We may forget that this orientation to life also has its drawbacks. If we become overly involved in material success and activity, we may lose touch with our feelings, locking them in towers like Rapunzel.

If we are patient and committed to restoring our relationship with ourselves and others, we will eventually find a way to reach our feelings. The idea of letting our hair down—releasing our inhibitions—may frighten us. We may feel embarrassed about what we might do or how it will be perceived by others. We can use Steps Six and Seven to let go of some of the attitudes that limit our freedom: our concern over with what others think of us, the need to be perfect or the fear of allowing others into our narrow, controlled world. Releasing these anxieties and concerns opens up new opportunities for personal fulfillment and relationships with others.

I am prepared to ascend the staircase of my feelings and discover the many rewards that are waiting for me.

At first Rapunzel was terribly frightened when a man came in, for she had never seen one before; but the Prince spoke to her so kindly, and told her at once that his heart had been so touched by her singing, that he felt he should know no peace of mind till he had seen her.

*C*ertain aspects of recovery may seem as foreign to us as the Prince did to Rapunzel. Part of the process involves developing parts of our personalities that we may have been afraid to acknowledge before. If we tend to be passive individuals, the thought of taking a more active part in things may intimidate us. If we've kept ourselves busy, the idea of spending time alone may make us uncomfortable.

It helps if we experiment gradually with these new ways of behaving. We can neither change old behaviors nor become different people overnight. We slowly find the freedom to acknowledge and experience our own true nature. Working the Steps helps to draw our inner and outer worlds closer together so that we can give full expression to all parts of ourselves—the contemplative, feeling side as well as the creative, active side. When we are patient with ourselves and willing to experiment with new options, our view of ourselves and others broadens, and new life begins to unfold.

Today I will prepare myself for the new life stirring within me. I welcome change, no matter how frightening it may first appear.

Very soon Rapunzel forgot her fear, and when he asked her to marry him she consented at once. "For," she thought, "he is young and handsome, and I'll certainly be happier with him than with the old Witch." So she put her hand in his and said: "Yes, I will gladly go with you, only how am I to get down out of the tower?"

*T*he program provides a bridge between our inner and outer worlds. In the beginning we may not be able to reach out to people easily and it may be difficult for us to speak in meetings. Fortunately, we are not required to share until we are ready to do so. We are free to listen until we feel comfortable talking and revealing a little of ourselves.

Many of us are like Rapunzel when we enter recovery. As we work the Steps, we begin to see that certain things make us happier than others. When we are willing to follow our inclinations, we start the process of improving the quality of our lives. During the first stages of recovery, we may have a desire to get down out of our tower, but be unclear about how to do it. As we develop trust in ourselves and others, our ability to think positively and realistically improves. We realize that our Higher Power will guide us, if only we take the time to ask for the help we need.

I can trust myself in the world again. My Higher Power gives me the inner security I need to confront life's challenges.

"Every time you come to see me," Rapunzel said, "you must bring a skein of silk with you, and I will make a ladder of them, and when it is finished I will climb down by it, and you will take me away on your horse." They arranged that, till the ladder was ready, he was to come to her every evening, because the old woman was with her during the day.

*O*ur longing for relationships cannot be satisfied until we unite two aspects of ourselves: our inner need for security and dependability, and our outer ambition to develop our potential in an uncertain world. Our ability to achieve healthy relationships is enhanced when we interact with people and things outside ourselves. Like Rapunzel, who needed silk for her ladder, we cannot leave the safety of our inner world without learning to work with material from the external one.

We have everything we need to construct a secure bridge between our inner and outer worlds. The Steps provide us with a basic blueprint for doing this. Working with others in the program gives us the material to build a framework that is strong enough to support our return to health and wholeness.

Each time I apply one of the Steps to a problem in my life, I add a stair to the ladder that allows me to reach my full potential.

The old Witch, of course, knew nothing of what was going on, till one day Rapunzel, not thinking of what she was about, turned to the Witch and said: "How is it, good mother, that you are so much harder to pull up than the young Prince? He is always with me in a moment."

*T*here comes a moment for all of us when we feel like we're half in and half out of the program. We are caught between a new and unfamiliar way of life and the old habits to which we are accustomed. We may even be tempted to leave the new world behind and return to our former way of life. Despite its clear limitations, it may seem to offer more security. If we cannot consciously resolve this issue, we may unwittingly sabotage our progress, just as Rapunzel did when she mentioned the Prince to the Witch.

There are numerous reasons why we might sabotage our progress. Security is important to us, and we may be overwhelmed by the thought of leaving the protected tower, where we are in control of our own space. For this reason, we may unconsciously impede our progress for fear of making a move. Recovery gives us a chance to look beyond our tower and discover a new world, full of joy, energy and freedom. Faith in the process gives us the courage to continue despite occasional lapses into fear.

My burden is lighter than when I came into the program. I am becoming less dependent on others and am overcoming my fear of the unknown.

"Oh, you wicked child!" cried the Witch. "What is this I hear? I thought I had hidden you safely from the whole world, and in spite of it you managed to deceive me."

*A*t the root of many of our difficulties is the lack of confidence in our ability to make wise choices. We often feel like wicked children for wanting to leave our current environment and create new lives for ourselves.

When we were growing up, some of us were hidden safely from the world and deprived of the opportunity to experience things for ourselves. Like Rapunzel, our natural desire is to achieve our potential, rather than remain in situations that imprison us. Our entry into the program is a sign that our Higher Power is pushing us toward further development. Our desire to be fully-functioning, independent adults is neither selfish nor deceitful. When we can free ourselves from the guilt and fear that hold us in destructive relationships, we can experience the joy of giving and receiving in mutually beneficial ways.

I am grateful for a Higher Power that helps me overcome the spells and enchantments of the past. I can reach out for help from a friend or sponsor if I feel threatened.

In her wrath she seized Rapunzel's beautiful hair, wound it round and round her left hand, and then grasping a pair of scissors in her right, snip snap, off it came, and the beautiful plaits lay on the ground.

*M*any of us know what it feels like to be cut off from our instincts, thoughts or dreams. When our desire for self-expression is repressed, hope of growth and development is stifled. We become afraid to move out into the wider world, imagining that people will ridicule us and consider us inadequate. Fears and distorted thinking like this interfere with our ability to form healthy relationships. We will be unable to relate equally with others if we allow our suspicions to dominate us.

It is also true that we cannot form mutually beneficial relationships if our insecurity and lack of confidence prevent us from allowing other people to develop in their own way. Making amends to others in Step Nine includes being respectful enough of their journeys to let them travel in their own directions. It helps to remember that all of us have access to a Higher Power who will guide us through our lives.

*I am learning that I cannot make hostages out
of the people I love by trying to deprive
them of their strength and power.
When I free others, I
free myself.*

And, worse than this, she was so hard-hearted that she took Rapunzel to a lonely desert place, and there left her to live in loneliness and misery.

No matter how much progress we have made in our recovery, we go through periods of loneliness and misery when it seems as if we cannot keep our hopes alive. "What have I done?" we wonder. "How did I end up being banished to this lonely and deserted place? Why did I ever leave my safe tower for this barren wasteland?"

Sometimes we find that feelings of neediness are still at the root of our problems. We may have given up one unhealthy way of coping with our problems only to replace it with another. Perhaps if Rapunzel had not been separated from her Prince, she'd have begun looking at him instead of the Witch to meet all her needs. Careful attention to our Step Ten daily inventory provides us with an opportunity to keep track of our actions. When we acknowledge and forgive ourselves for our mistakes as they occur, we no longer need to feel guilty for making them. We can continue to progress in our recovery and maintain healthier relationships with others when we pay close attention to our own motives and actions.

Today I will keep moving forward, no matter how difficult it seems. I will have faith in my own happy ending.

The Witch fastened the plaits on to a hook in the window, and when the Prince came and called out: "Rapunzel, Rapunzel, Let down your golden hair," she let them down, and the Prince climbed up. There he found the old Witch, who fixed her evil eyes on him, and cried mockingly: "Ah, ah! you thought to find your lady love, but the pretty bird has flown and its song is dumb; the cat caught it, and will scratch out your eyes too. Rapunzel is lost to you forever—you will never see her more."

*U*nchecked anger can be a powerful and destructive force. Unless we find ways to express and dispel it, we risk being possessed by a rage so intense that it could lead to violence against ourselves or others. Thoughts of vengeance may provide temporary relief, but they also prolong our turmoil and compound our feelings of being victimized and alone in towers of depression and resentment.

In recovery, we learn to deal with anger constructively. Rather than seeking revenge and causing harm like the Witch did, we find safe ways to "blow off steam" so that we can talk openly in a non-threatening manner to the people involved. Writing about our negative feelings or discussing them with sponsors before we communicate with those we are angry with relieves our internal tension and helps us have a more objective view of our problems.

*I do not need to fear being trapped by my anger.
I can find safe outlets for its expression.*

The Prince was beside himself with grief, and in his despair he jumped right down from the tower, and, though he escaped with his life, the thorns among which he fell pierced his eyes out. Then he wandered, blind and miserable, through the wood, eating nothing but roots and berries, and weeping and lamenting the loss of his lovely bride.

*L*ife is difficult when we lose our vision and can no longer see the way. Many of us felt like this when we came into recovery, although we may have tried to hide our handicaps from others. Our first impression may have been that the program would give us instant relief. It is true that the Twelve Steps can restore us to wholeness, but the transformation does not occur overnight. Our progress is enhanced when we begin to understand and communicate our feelings. Releasing them can be painful, and we may sometimes feel like we are still wandering, blind and miserable like the Prince, lamenting our losses without finding a solution.

Maintaining conscious contact with our Higher Power in Step Eleven helps us through these periods of grief and discontent when we mourn our past. If anger and despair make it difficult to maintain our conscious contact, honestly expressing our grief and anger can restore our connections. Then we can see that there is purpose and meaning to our lives.

When old losses cause me grief, I will ask my Higher Power for the courage to explore my feelings and communicate them to someone who understands me.

So he wandered about for some years, as wretched and unhappy as he could well be, and at last he came to the desert place where Rapunzel was living.

Many of us wander aimlessly for years, as wretched and unhappy as we can be, before discovering the program. We enter recovery blindly, tired of the struggle for existence, hardly daring to believe happiness could ever be restored to us. We may be familiar with the pain of living in lonely, barren places. Like Rapunzel, we know how it feels to face a hostile world alone.

As we become stronger and more attentive to working the Steps, we begin to restore balance to our lives. If we've been blind to our feelings like the Prince, we learn to experience our emotions. If we have been overly-dependent on others like Rapunzel, we begin to develop some independence.

There are occasions when it is wise to take action and others when it is best to do nothing; times to use our heads and times to use our hearts, moments to enjoy bodily pleasure and others to nourish our spirit. One of the program's greatest gifts is the ability it gives us to discover, explore and develop the wide range of possibilities that are available to each of us and integrate them into a working whole.

I am closer to being whole than I realize. I will move forward no matter how frustrated I feel.

Of a sudden he heard a voice seemed strangely familiar to him. He walked eagerly in the direction of the sound, and when he was quite close, Rapunzel recognised him and fell on his neck and wept. But two of her tears touched his eyes, and in a moment they became quite clear again, and he saw as well as he had ever done.

It can be overwhelming when we reconnect with lost parts of ourselves—a forgotten dream we abandoned years ago, the childlike wonder of play and laughter or the joy of succeeding at something we thought we could never accomplish. We are often overcome by conflicting emotions—we begin by laughing and end up crying. We delight in our present happiness, but feel saddened by the realization of lost time and opportunities. Both are natural and necessary aspects of the spiritual awakening that helps us see the part that past experiences have played in bringing us to our present level of happiness.

When we discover a twelve-step program, we stop wandering and searching, and eventually find peace within ourselves. When we can release our feelings like Rapunzel, our tears of joy and sorrow can restore the full vision that is possible when we make use of our intellect and our intuition. By remaining true to our thoughts and feelings and becoming willing to act on them, we bring healing and wholeness to ourselves and our world.

**Happiness, joy and freedom are possible
when I work the Steps and trust
in my Higher Power.**

Then he led her to his kingdom, where they were received with great joy, and they lived happily ever after.

*F*inally the happy ending: after years of pain and suffering, love triumphs as we persevere in our attempts at restoration. Although our journey toward growth and wholeness is sometimes interrupted by events and circumstances we can't control, we do have control over our commitment to working the Steps. This can bring us safely through the turmoil that accompanies our development.

The desire to be with those we love is natural. It can be a healthy sign when we express our ability to nurture and protect relationships that are important to us—a sign that we like ourselves enough to let some of the love we've found spill over into the lives of others. It's only when we become like the Witch—so needy that we cannot let other people lead their own lives or be who they want to be that the trouble begins.

When we cannot find security within ourselves, we become dependent on others to provide it for us. Finding and following our own path frees us to love others without turning them into hostages.

Basing my inner security on a Higher Power instead of other people frees me to love and be loved.

Rumpelstiltzkin

RUMPELSTILTZKIN

There was once a poor miller who told a king that his daughter could spin straw into gold. The king summoned her to the palace, gave her a spinning wheel and put her into a room full of straw. He then commanded that she spin all the straw into gold by the next morning or she would die.

The girl's tears of despair were interrupted by a tiny man who offered to do the work in exchange for a gift. The girl agreed to give him her necklace, and he spun all evening until the bobbins were full of gold. The king was delighted, but the sight only increased his obsession for more gold. The miller's daughter was told to spin increasingly large amounts of straw into gold, and was again helped secretly by the little man in exchange for a gift.

On the third day the king offered to marry the miller's daughter if she spun for one more night. The poor girl had nothing left to give the strange little man in exchange for his efforts. "Promise me when you are queen to give me your first child," he said. Not seeing any other alternative, she agreed.

So the miller's daughter became queen and gave birth to a son. The little man reappeared and demanded that she keep her part of the bargain. She was so distraught that he took pity on her and told her that if she guessed his name in three days, she could keep her child. She sent a messenger throughout the kingdom to search for exotic names. On the third day the messenger returned and announced that he had seen a little man dancing around a fire, proclaiming that his name was Rumpelstiltzkin. When she guessed his name correctly, the little man's rage was so intense that he tore himself in two.

There was once upon a time a poor miller who had a very beautiful daughter. Now it happened one day that he had an audience with the King, and in order to appear a person of some importance he told him that he had a daughter who could spin straw into gold. "Now that's a talent worth having," said the King to the miller; "if your daughter is as clever as you say, bring her to my palace to-morrow, and I'll put her to the test."

*I*t is natural for parents to want their children to lead fuller and more rewarding lives than they did. If our parents suffered from low self-esteem, they might have tried to turn us into superior students, athletes or artists so we would be more successful than they believed they were. If we were constantly pushed to achieve beyond our abilities, we may go through life thinking that we are always being put to the test. Our sense of pride, together with a need for approval, can sometimes lead us to place inordinately high expectations upon ourselves.

It is a relief when we find out that we are adequate the way we are. We stop expecting too much of ourselves and attempting to please others by always trying to be perfect. Life is more fulfilling when we accept our limitations and concentrate upon building our strengths. When we do this, we become who we really are instead of who we think we should be.

*I am learning to measure my success
by my own standards, rather than
the standards of others.*

When the girl was brought to him he led her into a room full of straw, gave her a spinning-wheel and spindle, and said: "Now set to work and spin all night till early dawn, and if by that time you haven't spun the straw into gold you shall die." Then he closed the door behind him and left her alone inside.

*F*eeling qualified to perform our tasks is important to our self-esteem. We may not be overly competitive, but we all monitor ourselves in some way to see how we measure up. We tend to set ourselves up to fail by trying to fulfill someone else's expectations. When we allow others to establish our performance standards, we may be coerced into working all night, spinning until early dawn. If we don't achieve our goal, we judge ourselves harshly. Many of us believe that we have to be perfect in order to receive appreciation for what we do.

Being in a twelve-step program helps us to resolve some of these inner conflicts. We become more comfortable with ourselves and others by taking control of our own lives and performing according to our actual abilities. There are no time clocks in the program and no one expects us to accomplish miracles overnight. But miracles can occur when we remember to work the Steps one day at a time, and rely on our Higher Power for inspiration and guidance.

I am not required to be perfect or expect more of myself than I can comfortably accomplish.

So the miller's daughter sat down, and didn't know what in the world she was to do. She hadn't the least idea of how to spin straw into gold, and became so miserable that she began to cry. Suddenly the door opened, and in stepped a tiny little man and said: "Why are you crying so bitterly?" "Oh!" answered the girl, "I have to spin straw into gold, and haven't a notion how it's done."

Sometimes there is no better way of releasing our frustrations than crying. Although tears cannot solve our problems, when we cry we often experience emotional release. The ability to cry helps us to admit defeat and become willing to explore new ways of dealing with our situation.

When we admit that we haven't a notion how to spin straw into gold, we have taken Step One and are ready to ask for help. Admitting our powerlessness exposes us to new possibilities for finding solutions to our problems. When we become willing to explore new alternatives with others who share some of our same experiences, the answers begin to appear. We no longer have to feel alone in the midst of seeming failure and defeat. We can share our feelings with others who understand the stress of trying to meet unrealistic expectations and thereby find a way to lighten our burden.

If I am faced with tasks that are beyond my present capabilities, I can ask for help in carrying them out.

"What will you give me if I spin it for you?" asked the manikin. "My necklace," replied the girl. The little man took the necklace, sat himself down at the wheel, and whir, whir, whir, the wheel went round three times, and the bobbin was full. So it went on till the morning, when all the straw was spun away, and all the bobbins were full of gold. As soon as the sun rose the King came, and when he perceived the gold he was astonished and delighted, but his heart only lusted more than ever after the precious metal.

*W*hen we become caught up in a whirlwind of activity, we lose the sense of balance that allows us to distribute our energies and interests evenly like beads upon the necklaces of our lives. If we think that people will love us because of what we do for them, we may work at a frenzied pace, attempting to achieve the impossible. Even when we accomplish what they have asked for, we may feel that they, like the King, only want more and more.

Through our recovery program, we learn that we don't have to work hard to be accepted. We become comfortable with ourselves and this helps us to maintain healthy connections with others. We meet people who are willing to accept us for who we are, and our relationships with them prosper as we let go of our need to be perfect.

If I feel pressured to accomplish the impossible, I will slow down and re-establish my priorities.

He had the miller's daughter put into another room full of straw, much bigger than the first, and bade her, if she valued her life, spin it all into gold before the following morning.

*O*n occasion it may be necessary to look at the commitments we make and see if we are being fair to ourselves. In our over-zealous attempts to please others, we sometimes set goals for ourselves that we cannot possibly meet. We find it necessary to invest extra energy into a project because of its magnitude. If this situation occurs frequently, it may be a sign that something is seriously out of balance. If the demands we place on ourselves or think others are placing on us become disproportionate or irrational, we need to re-evaluate our priorities.

Breaking this cycle of behavior is not always a matter of becoming more accomplished at what we do. Our Step Four inventory usually reveals that we are capable of high achievement when we are properly motivated. It is our goals and priorities that may require reassessment. There are no rewards for expecting too much of ourselves, but we do feel rewarded when we can set and attain realistic goals. We will always make the most progress when we take things one day at a time.

*When I establish realistic expectations
for myself, I can be successful and
still enjoy a balanced lifestyle.*

The girl didn't know what to do, and began to cry; then the door opened as before, and the tiny little man appeared and said: "What'll you give me if I spin the straw into gold for you?" "The ring from my finger," answered the girl.

*I*f we depend on others to complete our tasks for us, we might be forced to make personal sacrifices in order to pay the price. When we forfeit the rings from our fingers, we begin to lose our integrity and sense of competence. We may display a brave front and appear to be satisfied with the arrangement, but this usually hides feelings of inadequacy, guilt and helplessness. We may feel like the miller's daughter, and begin to cry because we don't know what to do.

At our deepest centers we know we cannot continue to accept unreasonable assignments, but the demands of the moment can make it difficult to be truthful. Beginning or ending each day with a Step Ten inventory that includes a list of priorities helps to curb our tendency to rush from crisis to crisis. This gives us a chance to find out what we really can do and helps us to develop a secure sense of self-esteem.

I can use Step Ten to look honestly at my behavior and evaluate the price I will pay for my present choices.

The manikin took the ring, and whir! round went the spinning-wheel again, and when morning broke he had spun all the straw into glittering gold. The King was pleased beyond measure at the sight, but his greed for gold was still not satisfied, and he had the miller's daughter brought into a yet bigger room full of straw, and said: "You must spin all this away in the night; but if you succeed this time you shall become my wife."

*E*ach time we complete an unreasonable assignment, we become more vulnerable to allowing unrealistic expectations to interfere with our serenity. Leading others to believe that we are capable of doing more than we really are makes us feel guilty and inadequate. We may then mask these feelings by pretending to be more capable and confident than we are. This begins a cycle of pretense designed to cover our mounting shame and self-doubt.

When we recognize our true capabilities and accept them as being good enough, our tendency toward over-achievement decreases. Frequent use of the Serenity Prayer can help us to reduce our work load to a more manageable size. When we are able to look closely at what we can and cannot change and develop the wisdom to know the difference, we find that our competency is not the problem. We discover that it is the expectations we have of ourselves or that we allow others to put upon us that can eventually defeat us.

I can set realistic and achievable goals for myself by closing the gap between my expectations and my capabilities.

When the girl was alone the little man appeared for the third time, and said: "What'll you give me if I spin the straw for you once again?" "I've nothing more to give," answered the girl. "Then promise me when you are Queen to give me your first child." "Who knows what mayn't happen before that?" thought the miller's daughter; and besides, she saw no other way out of it, so she promised the manikin what he demanded, and he set to work once more and spun the straw into gold.

*W*hen we are desperate, we sometimes make unrealistic promises just to ensure that we will be able to keep our commitment. We avoid thinking about the possible consequences and think to ourselves "Who knows what might happen before that?" In our state of panic, we fail to realize that our agreement may be damaging to our health and well-being.

When the compulsion to meet our commitments overwhelms us and we are driven to succeed no matter what the cost, it is time to stop and examine our behavior. We can calm the whir of the busy wheel in our mind by discussing our feelings with a sponsor or program friend and taking a more realistic view of the situation.

> *Communications with my Higher Power can provide the serenity I need to assess the commitments I make to myself and others.*

When the King came in the morning, and found every-thing as he had desired, he straightway made her his wife, and the miller's daughter became a Queen. When a year had passed a beautiful son was born to her, and she thought no more of the little man, till all of a sudden one day he stepped into her room and said: "Now give me what you promised."

*B*eing able to focus our energies on a single material project or goal can bring substantial rewards, but there are heavy prices to be paid for neglecting the rest of our lives. Frantic activity may distract us for awhile, but eventually our world begins to fall apart. When we discover how tired we are it some-times feels like a Rumpelstiltzkin has arrived to demand his price for helping us.

Supportive relationships and relaxing activities nourish us and help provide the balance we need. When we sacrifice our inner child to compulsive ac-tivities we lose opportunities for spontaneity and inner renewal. We will have fuller, richer lives if we allow ourselves time to enjoy the simple pleasures that bring us satisfaction and fulfillment. Learning to say "no" when we are tempted to prove ourselves by un-dertaking unrealistic tasks is a sign that our self-worth is being restored and that we no longer have to prove ourselves through performance.

I can stop paying the price of being an over-achiever by restoring balance to my life.

The Queen was in a great state, and offered the little man all the riches in her kingdom if he would only leave her the child. But the manikin said: "No, a living creature is dearer to me than all the treasures in the world." The Queen began to cry and sob so bitterly that the little man was sorry for her, and said: "I'll give you three days to guess my name, and if you find it out in that time you may keep your child."

*C*ompulsive activity and excessive time spent at work may bring us many riches, but it does not support new life. It interferes with our creativity and limits our ability to play by obscuring our childlike delight in the wonder of life. When we become aware of our condition, we are sometimes devastated to find that we have lost many of the things that were important to us.

Often the circumstances that make us feel most powerful and productive are the most likely to destroy our chances for true happiness. Substance abuse, workaholism and the "I-can-go-it-alone" approach to life are a few of the ineffective behaviors that distort our reality. When we name the problem and discover what prevents us from fulfilling our potential, we have a chance of creating a new life for ourselves. By attending meetings and working the Steps, we become aware of some of the wonderful opportunities that life has to offer.

I have named the problem and am on the road to recovery. I know that my Higher Power is there to guide me.

The Queen pondered the whole night over all the names she had ever heard, and sent a messenger to scour the land, and to pick up far and near any names he should come across. When the little man arrived on the following day she began with Kasper, Melchoir, Belshazzar, and all the other names she knew, in a string, but at each one the manikin called out: "That's not my name."

Usually our inner sense tells us that things are going wrong long before depression, anxiety or other signs of internal collapse appear. If we ignore these signals until we reach a crisis, we may put ourselves under unnecessary pressure to correct the problems.

In the beginning, we may search frantically for the possible causes of our discomfort by asking ourselves, "Is it my boss? Is it my spouse? Is it my kids? My mother? My brother?" If we feel no relief—if the answer we hear is, "That's not my name"—we may need to switch the focus to ourselves and look at what we are doing to perpetuate the problem.

It is an immense relief when we get to the root of the matter and are willing to make changes in our behavior. Once we have found the path to renewal, we can slowly regain our lost spirit and energy by getting in touch with our Higher Power and looking for signs of guidance.

Am I looking for excuses instead of solutions? No matter what the cause, my problems belong to me.

The next day she sent a messenger to inquire the names of all the people in the neighbourhood, and had a long list of the most uncommon and extraordinary for the little man when he made his appearance. "Is your name, perhaps, Sheepshanks, Cruickshanks, Spindleshanks?" but he always replied: "That's not my name."

When we realize the futility of blaming others for our difficulties and begin to honestly evaluate our situation, we might search in vain for fancy names to describe our condition. Some of us read medical books and employ doctors, hoping for a cure or a new insight that will correct the hidden defects that we think are causing our distress. If we fail in our search for a remedy, we may turn to self-help books and counselors, hoping for a therapeutic formula that will remove our discomfort and straighten out our lives.

Many of us can benefit from medical and psychological help as a supplement to our recovery. Professionals may be able to help us identify our problem and pose possible solutions, but they cannot actually do the work for us. Attending meetings and working the Steps with a supportive group of people who share our common problem is an important part of our recovery. It provides a nurturing environment where we can find constructive ways to implement the suggestions of doctors, therapists or other professionals with whom we may choose to consult.

Professionals can assist me in recovery, but the actual work is my responsibility.

On the third day the messenger returned and announced: "As I came upon a high hill round the corner of the wood, I saw a little house, and in front of the house burned a fire, and round the fire sprang the most grotesque little man, hopping on one leg and crying "To-morrow I brew, to-day I bake, And then the child away I'll take; For little deems my royal dame that Rumpelstiltzkin is my name!"

*C*ontinued failure to correctly identify and solve our problems heightens our anxiety and can lead to depression. We may gain temporary relief by escalating our compulsive behavior in an effort to escape reality, but we often burn up what little energy we have by springing around the fires of our anxieties. Any hope that we could have a peaceful and meaningful life seems to vanish.

At the very last minute, when we feel totally powerless, many of us experience a moment of clarity. Suddenly we see the true nature of the dance and become willing to give it up to save our lives. We can name the behaviors that *Rumpel* us, put us on *stiltz* out of the reach of others, and break our *kin*ship with family, friends and the human race. In recovery we have a chance to perform a different kind of dance that has twelve basic steps, and can lead us to serenity and a new life.

> *Today I will dance with the Twelve Steps*
> *instead of getting carried away by*
> *my ineffective behaviors.*

You may imagine the Queen's delight at hearing the name, and when the little man stepped in shortly afterwards and asked: "Now, my lady Queen, what's my name?" She asked first, "Is your name Conrad?" "No." "Is your name Harry?" "No." "Is your name, perhaps, Rumpelstiltzkin?" "Some demon has told you that," screamed the little man, and in his rage drove his right foot so far into the ground that it sank in up to his waist; then in a passion he seized the left foot with both hands and tore himself in two.

*N*aming our problem is the first step toward freeing ourselves from it. Acknowledging the power it has had over us helps us to recognize the damage we have done to ourselves. What we thought had been assisting us in overcoming our inadequacies has actually left us weak and hopeless. Once we have this revelation, we are ready to accept our condition and admit defeat.

Accepting Step One is not an overnight process. At the beginning of our recovery, we may be afraid that admitting our powerlessness will tear us in two. If we have the courage to stay in the program and look honestly at our lives from a new perspective, the very opposite will occur. Instead of tearing us apart, the Steps can heal our wounds and prepare us to enjoy the happiness, joy and freedom that we have denied ourselves for so long.

I am beginning to experience the happiness, joy and freedom that the program offers to me.

Cinderella

CINDERELLA

nce there was a gentleman who married a very haughty woman for his second wife. She had two daughters who were like her in all things. He also had a daughter, but she was of unparalleled goodness. The stepmother could not bear this girl's sweetness and employed her in the meanest work of the house. Her father, who might have been expected to come to her rescue, was too dominated by his wife to help his daughter. When the girl finished her work for the day, she would sit in the chimney-corner among the ashes. Because of this, they called her Cinderella.

When the king's son gave a ball, she was left behind after having spent many days helping her sisters prepare for the event. After watching them depart in all their finery, she collapsed in tears because she wanted to go with them. When her fairy godmother appeared, she had trouble telling her what was the matter because she was crying so hard. When she was able to speak, her godmother offered to help her go to the ball. She turned a pumpkin into a coach, a rat into a coachman and Cinderella's rags into beautiful clothes beset with jewels. She also warned her that she must leave the ball before the clock struck twelve, or all her finery would be as it was before.

The ball was magnificent. The prince was always by her side. She lost track of the time and hastened away just as the clock struck twelve, leaving a glass slipper behind. The prince sent a messenger to try the shoe on the foot of every woman in the kingdom. When Cinderella asked to try it on, her sisters ridiculed her, but the shoe fit as if it were made of wax. She married the prince and forgave her sisters, finding them suitable matches with two great lords of the court.

Once there was a gentleman who married, for his second wife, the proudest and most haughty woman that was ever seen. She had, by a former husband, two daughters of her own humour, who were, indeed, exactly like her in all things. He had likewise, by another wife, a young daughter, but of unparalleled goodness and sweetness of temper, which she took from her mother, who was the best creature in the world.

Depending on how we feel about ourselves at the moment, the people we encounter can seem as different to us as Cinderella was to her stepsisters. When we're feeling like helpless victims or indulging in self-righteousness, others may appear to be the haughtiest people we've ever met. But, when we're feeling badly about ourselves, these same people may appear to be paragons of virtue.

It helps to remember that we all have many different facets to our personalities. There are moments when we feel proud and times when we feel humble and sweet-tempered. These are all healthy qualities but each can become troublesome when carried to extremes. Being overly proud prevents us from seeing ourselves and others realistically, while being too sweet-tempered leaves us open to exploitation. By getting in touch with our own diversity, we can see others in a more realistic light and learn to avoid taking their behavior personally.

I will take pride in my accomplishments today and be gentle with myself.

No sooner were the ceremonies of the wedding over but the mother-in-law began to show herself in her true colours. She could not bear the qualities of this pretty girl, and the less because they made her own daughters appear the more odious. She employed her in the meanest work of the house; she lay up in a sorry garret, upon a wretched straw bed, while her sisters lay in fine rooms, where they had looking-glasses so large that they might see themselves at their full length from head to foot.

*W*hen we cannot bear the qualities of others, it's often because they remind us of something we lack or something we don't want to acknowledge about ourselves. One solution is to react harshly as the stepmother did and banish the offenders from our lives. Another is to turn them into objects of scorn so we can feel superior. These alternatives temporarily ease our envy and anxiety and minimize the threat to us.

When we can acknowledge our feelings of mediocrity or ugliness, we can stop projecting them onto others. Identifying the issues that underlie our feelings of inferiority helps us begin to deal with them honestly and stop using our false pride as a means of escape. When we realize that others no longer threaten our identity, we can let go of our attempts to dominate them and begin to relate to them as equals.

I acknowledge all aspects of myself today. When I feel inferior, I will find and correct the hidden messages that are causing this feeling.

The poor girl bore all patiently, and dared not tell her father, who would have rattled her off; for his wife governed him entirely. When she had done her work, she used to go into the chimney-corner, and sit down among cinders and ashes, which made her commonly be called "Cinderwench"; but the youngest sister, who was not so rude and uncivil as the eldest, called her Cinderella.

Many of us grew up in families where one or both parents were emotionally unavailable to us. They may have lacked parenting skills or been too involved with their own problems or addictions to give us the attention we needed. Their personalities could possibly have clashed with ours, which caused them to mistrust us, or they might have noticed behaviors in us they didn't like in themselves. Trying to change in order to meet their demands could have seriously limited our personal development.

These early experiences may have consigned us to chimney-corners of low self-esteem. Today we no longer have to listen to voices that speak against our healthy self-images. We regain our self-respect slowly by thinking of ourselves first as a Cinder*wench*, then a little more courteously as Cinder*ella*, until we finally reclaim our true name and identity.

If I am viewing myself through the eyes of an insecure child, I can develop the skills to parent myself.

It happened that the King's son gave a ball, and invited all persons of fashion to it. Our young misses were also invited. They were mightily delighted at this invitation, and wonderfully busy in choosing out such gowns, petticoats, and head-clothes as might become them. This was a new trouble to Cinderella; for it was she who ironed her sister's linen, and plaited their ruffles; they talked all day long of how they should be dressed.

*I*f we have fallen too far into depression, we may find it difficult to imagine the excitement of preparing for a special occasion—deciding what to wear, wondering who will be there and imagining what might happen when the big evening finally arrives.

It's exciting to look forward to special times when we can dress up and dance and enjoy ourselves. It can be fun wearing clothes that express our personalities and reflect the spirit of the occasion. If we have not learned to do this, we may be more comfortable playing Cinderella and getting others ready for the ball. When we focus all of our attention on providing pleasure for other people with no thought of pleasing ourselves, we may escape anxiety and depression temporarily. But, eventually the others will be off to the ball, and we will be left alone to face our feelings in dark chimney corners.

*I am finding a balance between taking care
of myself and doing things for others.*

Cinderella was called up to them to be consulted in all these matters and offered her services to dress their heads. As she was doing this, they said to her: "Cinderella, would you not be glad to go to the ball?" "Alas!" said she, "you only jeer me." "Thou art in the right of it," replied they; "it would make the people laugh to see a Cinderwench at a ball."

Many of us are quite familiar with the preparation involved in getting ready for the ball, but we don't always enjoy the evening once we arrive. Like Cinderella, years of hard work and effort may have had little positive effect on our self-esteem. Old habits may be so strong that we still take care of others and make them look good, then rush to the chimney-corner to smother our resentments in the cinders and ashes.

Sometimes it helps to identify the sources of our low self-esteem. We may have had parents who demeaned us because they felt inadequate, siblings who competed with us for attention and affection or peers who lashed out because they felt threatened by us. Sharing our inventory with another person in Step Five helps us to understand these feelings.

We can take decisive steps toward increasing our self-esteem by detaching from people who ridicule us and changing the way we talk to ourselves. Relying on the Twelve Steps to help us develop the healthy life skills we need enables us to get to the ball and join in the merriment.

I can take positive action to change the way I feel about myself and the way I allow others to treat me.

At last the happy day came; they went to Court, and Cinderella followed them with her eyes as long as she could. When she had lost sight of them, she fell a-crying. Her godmother, who saw her all in tears, asked her what was the matter. "I wish I could..." she was not able to speak the rest, being interrupted by her tears and sobbing. This godmother of hers, who was a fairy, said "Thou wishest thou couldst go to the ball; is it not so?" "Y-y-es," cried Cinderella, with a great sigh."

Sometimes it seems that people fall into two categories: the "haves" and the "have-nots." When we're overwhelmed with feelings of inferiority, we automatically assign ourselves to the second category. We ask ourselves: "Why does everyone else have so much when I have so little?", and then we cry and sob at the unfairness of it all.

Crying is a good way to vent our anger and frustration. It relieves our tension and allows our feelings to flow naturally. When we first expose these feelings, we may need help in identifying and understanding them. Though it may feel awkward, sharing with others is an essential part of our recovery. Talking to our Higher Power, writing in journals and sharing our dreams with others help to uncover our hidden aspirations. When we express our needs and desires honestly, we can discover long-term solutions to our problems and move forward in our recovery.

When I give myself permission to cry, I can experience the relief of expressing my feelings.

"Well," said her godmother, "be but a good girl, and I will contrive that thou shalt go." Then she took her into her chamber, and said to her, "Run into the garden, and bring me a pumpkin." Cinderella went immediately to gather the finest she could get, and brought it to her godmother, not being able to imagine how this pumpkin could make her go to the ball. When her godmother scooped out all the inside of it, she struck it with her wand, and the pumpkin was instantly turned into a fine coach, gilded all over with gold.

*A*s we begin recovery, the idea of working the Steps may seem to hold just as little relevance to solving our problems as the fairy godmother's request for a pumpkin. The things we want seem as far out of reach as Cinderella's desire to go to the ball, and the ways in which the Steps can help us get there are not always clear. But Cinderella trusted her godmother, and by following her advice, she ended up with a gilded coach to provide a way out of her cinder-filled corner.

We can experience success similar to Cinderella's when we learn to trust in our Higher Power. Coming to believe that we can be restored to sanity in Step Two restores our faith and prepares us to take action. Our belief in the power of the Steps comes gradually, as we begin to see the results of practicing the principles of the program in our lives.

I am willing to do what it takes to leave unnecessary pain and misery behind.

She then went to look into her mouse-trap, where she found six mice, and ordered Cinderella to lift up a little the trap-door, when, giving each mouse, as it went out, a little tap with her wand, the mouse was that moment turned into a fine horse. Being at a loss for a coachman, "I will go and see," says Cinderella, "if there is a rat in the rat-trap, we may make a coachman of him." "Thou art in the right," replied her godmother; "go and look."

When we follow the Twelve Steps, we may discover that we possess talents and abilities that we have not utilized before. Although we cannot perform magic like the fairy godmother and turn mice into horses, many of our accomplishments seem just as miraculous. Holding on to each positive experience and being willing to keep experimenting moves us forward toward a more fulfilling existence. Even one small success can inspire us to search for different ways to approach the next one.

As we progress in our recovery and learn to trust our instincts and intuition, we become willing to experiment with our own ideas. We can review our projects and plans with sponsors or friends when we need support or reassurance. Usually we find we are on the right track.

I trust the power of the Steps to free me from the cinders. I am developing the willingness to act on my inclinations and intuition.

The Fairy then said to Cinderella: "Well, you see here an equipage fit to go to the ball with." Then her godmother touched her with her wand, and her clothes were turned into cloth of gold and silver. This done, she gave her a pair of glass slippers. Her godmother commanded her not to stay till after midnight, telling her that if she stayed one moment longer, the coach would be a pumpkin again, the horses mice, her coachman a rat, and her clothes just as they were before.

*E*ven those of us whose self-images are severely tarnished have moments when we feel attractive, self-assured and full of confidence. It is important to hold on to these feelings, for they can provide the inspiration we need to become the person we wish to be.

Knowing that there are times when we feel special enough to go to the ball and others when we must labor by the fire helps to keep us centered in reality. The Steps do not transform us instantly like a magic wand, but our self-images may change rapidly if we are touched by others in the program. Being willing to experiment with new ways of being helps us to build well-balanced images of ourselves and embrace the many sides of life.

I am proud of the regal feeling within me and am willing to let others see this side of myself.

She promised her godmother she would not fail of leaving the ball before midnight; and then away she drives, scarce able to contain herself for joy. The King's son gave her his hand and led her into the hall. He never ceased his compliments and kind speeches to her; to whom all this was so far from being tiresome that she quite forgot what her godmother had recommended to her; so that she, at last, counted the clock striking twelve when she took it to be no more than eleven. She then rose up and fled, as nimble as a deer.

*I*t is easy for us to get so caught up in pleasurable activities that we lose track of the time. When we're enjoying ourselves, it's natural to want to push more serious responsibilities to the back of our minds.

It's especially difficult to return to reality if we are prolonging our excitement with mood-altering substances, compulsive behavior or daydreams. We learn in recovery to replace artificial highs with creative activity and healthy, responsible relationships. Accepting life on life's terms and finding a balance between work and play enables us to take satisfaction in all our activities.

I am learning to allow time for work and time for play. Embracing both aspects of life brings me joyful balance.

The Prince followed, but could not overtake her. She left behind one of her glass slippers, which the Prince took up most carefully. She got home, in her nasty old clothes, having nothing left of all her finery but one of the little slippers. The guards at the palace gate were asked if they had not seen a princess go out. They said they had seen nobody go out but a young girl, very meanly dressed, and who had more of the air of a poor country wench than a gentlewoman.

*F*inding a healthy middle ground between our feelings of self-contempt and grandeur takes time. We move through recovery in stops and starts—going forward and then regressing. Each time we fall back, we retain some of our new attitudes and feelings.

Sometimes it feels like we are right back where we started, but there have been some undeniable changes, even if they aren't always apparent. We can hold fast to the glass slipper that bears witness to our changing identity. Even if we temporarily lose sight of our progress, this small piece of evidence is a constant reminder of what we have accomplished. We can make use of it when the time is right.

*In order to protect and maintain the gains
I've made in recovery, I will continue to
attend meetings and work the Steps.*

What they said was true; for a few days after the King's son caused it to be proclaimed that he would marry her whose foot this slipper would just fit. They whom he employed began to try it upon the princesses, then the duchesses and all the Court, but in vain; it was brought to the two sisters, who did all they could to thrust their foot into the slipper, but they could not effect it.

No one else can wear shoes that are made especially for us. We all bear similarities to each other, but no one else has our unique personality or purpose in life. Our voice, our laugh, our personal taste may resemble someone else's, but they can never be quite the same. We may have shared many of the same experiences, but no one else can live our life.

Discovering who we are requires a willingness to try on many different shoes—to experiment with many roles and behaviors. We soon realize how futile it is to force our feet into shoes that don't fit. We only frustrate and cripple ourselves when we try to do so. Finding the shoes that fit us best is one of the benefits of recovery.

*I can avoid needless pain and
frustration by not trying to
force my feet into some-
one else's shoes.*

Cinderella, who saw all this, and knew her slipper, said to them, laughing: "Let me see if it will not fit me." Her sisters burst out a-laughing, and began to banter her. The gentleman who was sent to try the slipper looked earnestly at Cinderella, and said: It was but just that she should try, and that he had orders to let everyone make trial.

*W*e do not get ahead by staying quietly in our corners hoping that someday we will accidentally be discovered. When the right opportunities come our way, we must be bold enough to speak up and ask for our chance at the prize.

Others may laugh at us for trying, but this can't stop us if we hold on to our inner authority—our conviction that the shoe belongs to us. We can use the same intuition to tell us when the time is right for us to hold back and allow others to move ahead.

Recovery changes our sense of time. When we turn our lives over to our Higher Power in Step Three, we can let our lives unfold at their own natural pace. This releases us from the urgency of having to prove ourselves at every opportunity and gives us the serenity to wait until the time is right for us to act.

Recovery is not a race to a finish line. I am learning when to move ahead and when to wait peacefully.

He obliged Cinderella to sit down, and, putting the slipper to her foot, he found it went on very easily, and fitted her as if it had been made of wax. The astonishment her two sisters were in was excessively great, but still abundantly greater when Cinderella pulled out of her pocket the other slipper, and put it on her foot. Thereupon, in came her godmother, who, having touched with her wand Cinderella's clothes, made them richer and more magnificent that any of those she had before.

*B*y risking the ridicule of others and being willing to follow our inner voice, we have an opportunity to claim our missing treasure—to find the shoe that fits us best. We are no longer helpless. We have reclaimed our inheritance by making changes that encourage the positive forces for growth within us.

Part of the recovery process involves learning to focus on the positive aspects of our lives so that old negative images have less impact on us. Allowing constructive thoughts and attitudes to take precedence results in effective action that provides us with new shoes. The slippers we recover as a result of the spiritual awakening in Step Twelve fit naturally and comfortably, and ground us firmly in reality. Contact with our nurturing parent—the godmother within us all—makes our lives richer and more magnificent than ever before.

I can use the Twelve Steps like a magic wand to change my appearance, my outlook and my prospects.

She was conducted to the young Prince, dressed as she was; he thought her more charming than ever, and, a few days after, married her. Cinderella, who was no less good than beautiful, gave her two sisters lodgings in the palace, and that very same day matched them with two great lords of the Court.

*L*ike Cinderella, we must become comfortable both as servants and as royalty before we can find balance in our lives. If we have spent a great deal of time dancing at the ball, we must also learn to sweep the chimney corners. If we've spent most of our lives hidden away in the cinders, we must rise up and join the dance. Gradually, these two sides of us unite in a coherent whole.

Even the stepsister parts of ourselves—the inner negative voices that ridiculed us for so long—can be transformed. As we learn to understand and forgive ourselves for the negative thinking and behaviors that have limited our lives, the voices of defeat are silenced. When we find our true place in life, the past no longer has the power to hurt us. We can accept and forgive the imperfection in others, for they no longer have authority over us.

I am freeing myself from the spells of the past and am discovering the joy that comes from knowing how to give and how to receive.

Prince Charming

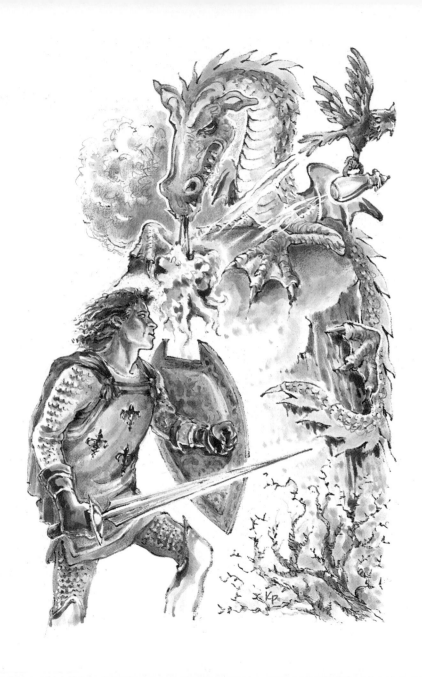

PRINCE CHARMING

here once was a king who fell in love with the portrait of a princess named Pretty Goldilocks. He sent an ambassador to her palace to ask for her hand and escort her back to the kingdom. When she declined the invitation, a member of the king's court, named Charming, said, "If I had been sent to Princess Goldilocks, I am sure she would have come back with me." Charming's enemies twisted his statement to make it seem as if he thought himself better than his monarch. Charming was imprisoned, but the misunderstanding was eventually resolved, and Charming was sent to ask the princess if she would marry the king.

When Charming presented the proposal, the Princess agreed on the condition that Charming carry out three tasks for her. He had to retrieve a ring that she had lost in the river, kill a giant who was threatening her kingdom and obtain water from the Fountain of Health and Beauty which was guarded by two dragons. He completed these tasks admirably with the aid of his dog, Frisk, and three creatures he had befriended on his way to the kingdom: a fish, a raven and an owl. The princess thanked Charming and made preparations for their departure.

During the journey she found Charming to be such an agreeable companion that she often wished they had stayed together in her kingdom. Charming felt obligated to carry out his mission and upon their return, Goldilocks and the king were married. Eventually, the king became jealous of the friendship between Charming and his wife, and again imprisoned him. Then, believing he was not handsome enough for Goldilocks, the king splashed water on his face which he thought to be from the Fountain of Health and Beauty. However, the flask contained a potion that put him to sleep forever. Goldilocks then freed Charming from the tower and they were married.

Once upon a time there was a princess who was the prettiest creature in the world. She was called Pretty Goldilocks. One of her neighbours was a young king who was not married. He was very rich and handsome, and when he heard all that was said about Pretty Goldilocks, though he had never seen her, he fell so deeply in love with her that he could neither eat nor drink.

*O*bsession is a familiar companion. Many of us can understand the plight of the King who was so in love that he could neither eat nor drink. We know what it's like to be so infatuated with someone that we find it difficult to function. At times we may feel consumed by a longing for people or things that we feel certain we cannot live happily without.

Working the Steps and learning to trust in a power greater than ourselves helps to minimize our obsessions. We stop looking to any one person or thing to make us happy and replace our visions of perfection with more realistic expectations. When we do so, we don't have to stay busy to distract ourselves or medicate ourselves with mood-altering substances to overcome our seeming inadequacies. We can turn our attention to the opportunities and challenges each day brings, following the guidance of our Higher Power and letting the true meaning of our lives unfold one day at a time.

Rather than allow images of perfection to interfere with my present happiness, I will take pleasure in the beauty available to me today.

He resolved to send an ambassador to ask her in marriage. The King felt so sure that the Princess would consent that he set his people to work at pretty dresses and splendid furniture, that they might be ready by the time she came.

There is certainly nothing wrong with planning for the future, as long as we maintain realistic expectations of what is possible. Preparing for opportunities that come our way increases our chances of success and gives us a confident, positive outlook on life. But when we base these arrangements on narrowly defined outcomes, we increase our chances of disappointment and resentment, should these plans fail to materialize.

Planning our lives around specific results restricts our vision, blocks our creativity and saps our strength. Turning our will over to the care of our Higher Power in Step Three makes it easier for us to take action. When we trust in a positive outcome, we are more willing to look for alternate routes when our pathway is blocked. As we progress in our recovery, we often find that what appear to be overwhelming barriers to self-fulfillment are actually only temporary detours.

I will prepare myself for tomorrow by enjoying what I have today, knowing that my happiness is not dependent on specific outcomes.

Meanwhile, the ambassador arrived at the Princess's palace and delivered his little message, but whether she happened to be cross that day, or whether the compliment did not please her, is not known. She only answered that she was very much obliged to the King, but she had no wish to be married.

*H*ow wonderful it must be to know clearly what we do and do not want and be able to respond quickly with a "yes" or "no" answer. It is difficult for many of us to imagine that we could make such a definite decision and respond politely without having to add an elaborate apology should the answer be "no." Learning that we have the right to accept or decline offers without justifying our choices adds to our new-found freedom.

"No, thank you. I appreciate the invitation, but I am unable to go out today." This simple response may seem unusually abrupt if we are accustomed to putting the needs of other people ahead of our own. If we believe that turning someone down will hurt their feelings, we often go along with them in spite of our desire to say "no." We then end up feeling trapped and resentful instead of fulfilled by the joy of shared pleasure. Determining what we really want and standing firm in the face of pressure to do something else leads to peace and serenity in our lives.

I will treat my own desires with the same respect
I show others. I can say, "No, thank
you" without feeling guilty.

When the ambassador reached the city where the King was waiting impatiently, everybody was very much annoyed with him for not bringing the Princess, and the King cried like a baby, and nobody could console him.

*H*ow frustrated the King must have felt when he realized that the ambassador was unsuccessful in his mission. When we place our happiness in the hands of others, we have no control over the outcome and risk being seriously disappointed. If we sit on the sidelines and chose not to participate, we cannot directly influence the course of our lives and must wait helplessly while others decide our fate. If the outcome is unfavorable, we feel angry and betrayed because our needs are not being met.

True contentment comes from knowing that personal happiness is our own responsibility and is not dependent on the actions of those around us. When we stop looking to others for fulfillment, we begin taking responsibility for finding our real purpose in life. By pursuing our own aspirations and finding a way around the obstacles that stand in our way, we become more courageous, less fearful of failure and more open to exploring opportunities for success. As our self-esteem improves, we can stop smothering those we love in order to escape our fear of being alone and incomplete.

I will stop relying on others as a source of fulfillment and recognize that I hold the key to my own happiness.

Now there was at the Court a young man, who was more clever and handsome than anyone else. He was called Charming, and everyone loved him, excepting a few envious people who were angry at his being the King's favourite and knowing all the State secrets.

*M*any of us know how painful it is to envy others, to feel bitter and resentful because they appear to have greater assets than we do. We go through life envying those who are smarter, better looking or have more money. To make ourselves feel better, we may resort to ridiculing those we envy or avoid our jealous feelings by seeking relationships with people to whom we feel superior. These tactics may provide temporary relief for our pain, but they ultimately compound the problem and prevent us from seeing how envy can destroy our self-esteem.

The more content we become with ourselves, the less threatening other people seem to be and the less we feel compelled to compete with them. When we no longer need to compare ourselves to others, we are rewarded with the satisfaction of mutual sharing in our relationships. Life becomes richer when we can respect our abilities and still revel in the talents and accomplishments of those around us.

Today I will take pleasure in who I am and
what I do. When I enjoy myself, I am
able to appreciate others.

One day Charming said rashly: "If the King had sent me to the Princess Goldilocks I am sure she would have come back with me." His enemies at once went to the King and said: "You will hardly believe what Charming has the audacity to say—that if he had been sent to the Princess Goldilocks she would certainly have come back with him. He seems to think that he is so much handsomer than you that the Princess would have fallen in love with him and followed him willingly."

*I*t is easy to twist the words of another person to suit our own purposes. Though it may make us feel better for a while, in the long run our dishonesty is very harmful. Our relationships suffer when people realize they cannot trust us. By changing what we say to make ourselves look better at the expense of someone else, we soon lose touch with the real truth.

Unlike Charming, some of us have difficulty being honest with ourselves. We may rationalize our behavior to eliminate guilt or shame and lower our self-respect instead. Being honest increases our self-esteem. When we are comfortable with ourselves, we can relax and enjoy our lives, knowing that we don't have to compete with others to find love and respect.

I can increase my self-worth today without distorting reality. Self-acceptance eliminates the need for deception.

The King was very angry when he heard this. "Ha, ha!" said he; "does he laugh at my unhappiness, and think himself more fascinating than I am? Go, and let him be shut up in my great tower to die of hunger."

*W*e usually become angry if someone laughs at our misfortunes. Most of us know the pain of being criticized by those who think they are more fascinating than we are. Yet, when we're feeling alone and miserable, it's difficult to rejoice in the happiness of others. We feel a little better knowing that we're not the only ones who are suffering.

It's painful to admit that we are jealous and that we sometimes take satisfaction in other people's misfortunes. If we were taught that feelings like this were unacceptable, we may repress them. It can frighten us when Step Four uncovers these emotions. It's a relief when we confess them in Step Five and find out that others have many of these same feelings. When we take a fearless inventory and then admit it to another person, we no longer have to banish the bad child in us to the tower to die of hunger. Allowing our feelings of inadequacy to emerge helps to free us from hate and envy and gives our inner child a chance to be cared for and loved.

*Today I will face my inner child's temper
tantrums fearlessly. Acknowledging
my anger and jealousy is a step
toward freeing myself
from their power.*

So the King's guards went to fetch Charming, who had thought no more of his rash speech, and carried him off to prison with great cruelty. One day when he was in despair he said to himself: "How can I have offended the King? I am his most faithful subject, and have done nothing against him."

*I*t can be devastating when we are betrayed, banished or punished for something we have not done or for some harmless action or word that has been misunderstood. The realization that others have the power to inflict such pain on us, especially when we are innocent of any misdeed, often leaves us determined never to lose control again. The discovery that disaster can fall upon us so unexpectedly often hardens our conviction to never let down our guard.

The constant struggle to maintain control and avoid being victimized is exhausting. Our fear of being exploited gradually disappears when we develop our own inner resources and become less dependent on those around us. We begin to understand that we are not as helpless as we once were. People and events slowly lose their power to dominate our lives as we learn that they cannot destroy us.

I am no longer a helpless victim, subject to the whims of people around me. I will develop my inner resources and become less dependent on others.

The King chanced to be passing the tower and recognised the voice of his former favourite. He stopped to listen in spite of Charming's enemies, who tried to persuade him to have nothing more to do with the traitor. Then he called to Charming, who came very sadly and kissed the King's hand, saying: "What have I done, sire, to deserve this cruel treatment?"

*H*ow wonderful to cry out and be heard! If our tears were ignored or discouraged when we were young, we may keep our emotions locked up in towers today. We may be afraid to show our true feelings to the world, thinking, "If I complain, they'll think I'm ungrateful. If I cry, they'll think I'm weak. If I'm depressed, they'll grow tired of me. If I tell them how I really feel, they'll go away and leave me by myself."

Voices like these inhibit our ability to express ourselves honestly. We betray ourselves and others when we hide our feelings from those who are close to us. If we allow them to persist, they can keep us locked in prisons of passivity and self-doubt. We can use the Steps to free ourselves from old beliefs that interfere with open communication.

*Today I will share my feelings with someone
I trust, knowing that it is safe to cry.*

"You mocked me and my ambassador," said the King, "and you said that if I had sent you for Princess Goldilocks you would certainly have brought her back." "It is quite true, sire," replied Charming; "I should have drawn such a picture of you that the Princess would have found you irresistible." The King could not see any cause for anger when the matter was presented to him in this light, and he began to frown fiercely at the courtiers who had so misrepresented his favourite.

*O*ur ability to settle past misunderstandings and prevent new ones begins to improve as our self-knowledge and self-acceptance grow. When we no longer have to disguise our feelings or hide our thoughts, we can be more direct in our communication with others.

We discover how our comments and actions can be misconstrued by examining how we interact with others. This is the purpose of Step Eight—to examine our part in relationships and recognize past harm and misunderstandings. We cannot change other people, but we can alter the way we treat them and respond to them. Taking responsibility for past actions by making amends in Step Nine does not always heal our relationships or resolve our conflicts, but our efforts are never wasted. By recognizing how we contributed to past misunderstandings, we become better prepared to develop healthy relationships.

I am learning to take responsibility for my actions. I will do my part to clear up past misunderstandings.

So he took Charming back to the palace with him, and after seeing that he had a very good supper he said to him: "I really should like to send you, to see if you can persuade Goldilocks to marry me." Charming replied that he was perfectly willing to go, and would set out the very next day.

Sooner or later we are all asked to reach out and help another program member. Someone may call us in the midst of a crisis, needing to talk to a friend or asking for help in working the Steps. If we've worked Steps Four and Five to the best of our ability, we may be surprised at how rewarding it is to share the strength and insight that we've developed through our own honest appraisal of ourselves.

We are grateful for our newfound ability to share our experiences honestly and listen to others in a caring and attentive way. Unlike Charming, we're not asked to carry other people's messages for them. We are encouraged, instead, to share what we've learned through our own struggles and triumphs. Reaching out to others in a loving and supportive way without taking responsibility for them demonstrates how far we've come and strengthens our confidence in our own recovery.

I will reach out to someone today with a smile. Helping others by sharing my own experiences is part of my commitment to recovery.

On a Monday morning he set out upon his errand, accompanied by his little dog, Frisk, thinking of nothing but how he could persuade the Princess Goldilocks to marry the King. He had a writing-book in his pocket, and whenever any happy thought struck him he dismounted from his horse and sat down under the trees to put it into the harangue he was preparing for the Princess before he forgot it.

*O*ur individual journeys through the Steps are unique. Though we share similar problems with other program members, they are never exactly the same, and parts of our journey must be taken alone. Some of us start out as Charming did, with a writing book in our pocket to record every thought that comes to us. Others find it easier to talk about their problems with a sponsor or friend. We each discover our own way and progress at our own pace.

Writing can be an effective way to get in touch with our thoughts and feelings. Some of us write gratitude lists, notes to ourselves and letters to others that we may choose not to mail. We maintain written Step Ten journals and compose letters to our Higher Power. Becoming familiar with our emotions through writing helps us to uncover the roots of our thoughts, feelings and behaviors. The solitary parts of our journey are not so frightening when we keep in contact with our Higher Power by recording our experiences and admitting and owning our true feelings.

*When I pick up a pencil, hidden thoughts
and feelings emerge. I will listen to
my inner child with love today.*

One day he had a capital idea and he sat down under a willow tree which grew by a little river. When he had written it down he saw a great golden carp lying gasping and exhausted upon the grass. In leaping after little flies she had thrown herself high upon the bank, where she had lain till she was nearly dead. Charming had pity upon her, and put her back into the water. She said "I thank you, Charming, for the kindness you have done me." "You have saved my life; one day I will repay you."

*W*riting gives us a chance to slow down and notice things we might ordinarily ignore in the course of our busy lives. It's amazing what opportunities for growth get thrown upon the banks of our waiting consciousness. Feelings that were repressed long ago emerge, bigger and stronger than ever before. As they surface, we are faced with a choice: to give them new life or let them die.

It may seem less painful to ignore our feelings, especially if we haven't learned to trust the seeds of joy, strength and fulfillment that lie in our forgotten past. When we seize the childlike hopes and fears that emerge and treat them with respect, we are often amazed at how quickly our weaknesses become powerful catalysts for change.

Today I will give life to my inner thoughts and feelings. I now have the courage to let my strengths and weaknesses emerge.

Another day, as he journeyed on, he saw a raven in great distress. The poor bird was closely pursued by an eagle, which would soon have eaten it up, had not Charming quickly fitted an arrow to his bow and shot the eagle dead. The raven perched upon a tree very joyfully. "Charming," said he, "it was very generous of you to rescue a poor raven; I am not ungrateful, some day I will repay you."

*W*hen we come to know and accept ourselves, it becomes easier to identify our eagles and our ravens—the things we do that cause us pain, and the parts of ourselves that are hurt in the process. We learn to recognize the situations and events that cause these inner conflicts so that we can take quick action to dispel them just as Charming did.

In recovery, we develop the self-esteem to quiet the critical inner voices that pursue us, saying, "You're ugly, weak, lazy, stupid, selfish and pitiful! Don't bother trying." We learn to shoot down these shrieking voices with arrows of positive thoughts which allows the hopes within us to grow. We work to provide the proper conditions for their survival. When our hopes grow stronger, they help motivate constructive action, and our joy and freedom increase.

I will detach from people whose criticism drags me down and stop listening to inner voices that exhaust me with constant demands.

Before the sun rose he found himself in a thick wood where it was too dark for him to see his path, and he heard an owl crying as if it were in despair. He began to hunt about, and found a great net which some bird-catchers had spread the night before. He took out his knife, cut the cords of the net, and the owl flitted away, and turning said, "Without your help I would have been killed. I am grateful, and one day I will repay you."

Sometimes we find ourselves on dark paths in thick woods, having lost our way inside forests of depression. It may seem impossible to sort through the thick wood of our own thoughts or the events that seem to close in around us. We may hear an owl—the wiser part of ourselves—crying out in despair because we are denying our feelings or ignoring our good judgment in order to survive.

The program gives us tools to cut through whatever net separates us from our lost wisdom. Working the Steps gives us the confidence to let go of old beliefs and broken dreams that keep us from flying free. Working Step Eleven and praying for knowledge of our Higher Power's will for us helps to free us from the snares of self-destructive thoughts and attitudes.

If parts of me are still crying out for help today, I will pay close attention and have the courage to set them free.

Then Charming was led in to the Princess, and was so struck with astonishment and admiration that at first not a word could he say. But presently he took courage and delivered his harangue. "Sir Charming," answered she, "a month ago as I was walking by the river I took off my glove, and as I did so a ring slipped off my finger and rolled into the water. As I valued it more than my kingdom, I vowed never to listen to any proposal of marriage unless the ambassador first brought me back my ring. So now you know what is expected of you."

No matter how much we prepare for important encounters, we sometimes find ourselves struck with astonishment and admiration or paralyzed by anxiety. We may experience confusion and feel inadequate in new situations where we're not sure what is expected of us.

By participating in a twelve-step program, we develop the courage to let others know who we are and what we want, even when the outcome is uncertain. We learn to accept the fact that we don't always immediately get what we think we need. Often we are faced with yet another task before we can achieve our goals. We avoid feeling overwhelmed by remembering that we don't have to get there all at once—that we experience recovery and life one day at a time.

I will not be intimidated by far-reaching goals today. I know that peace and serenity come from living one day at a time.

He went to bed without any supper, and Frisk couldn't eat any either. Charming sighed and lamented, "How am I to find a ring that fell into the river a month ago? The Princess must have told me to do it on purpose, knowing it was impossible." Frisk said: "My dear Master, don't despair; the luck may change. Let us go down to the river as soon as it is light."

At what point do we stop trying to achieve what we set out to do? When do we decide a task is impossible and stop making an effort to accomplish it? Do we brush off any promise of help the same way Charming ignored his little dog Frisk? We do ourselves an injustice when we fail to respond to the inner voices that urge us to try something new. Those tiny parts of us that dare to believe success is possible hold the keys to our recovery, if only we are willing to seek guidance from our Higher Power.

Picking some small task and accomplishing it gives our self-confidence a boost. We can bolster our self-esteem still more by patting ourselves on the back for being willing to try, despite our fear and insecurity. When we learn to acknowledge our successes and take pride in what we do, we begin to believe in ourselves and can often accomplish tasks we previously considered impossible.

Today I will push aside any feelings of despair that muffle the voice of hope in my heart. Faith in my Higher Power is essential to my recovery.

At the first glimmer of dawn Frisk began to jump about, and when he had waked Charming they went out together, first into the garden and then down to the river's brink, where they wandered up and down. Charming was thinking sadly of having to go back unsuccessfully when he heard someone calling: "Charming, Charming!" He looked all about him and thought he must be dreaming, as he could not see anybody. Then he walked on and the voice called again, "Charming, Charming!" "Who calls me?" said he.

*A*s we work the Steps, the voices of hope inside us grow stronger. When we confront certain difficult issues, we may spend time wandering up and down like Charming did, feeling uncertain about our lives and fearing failure. If we trust our Higher Power to show us the way, we will be gently urged toward logical solutions to our dilemmas.

If we are fearful of change or we anticipate failure, we may brush aside any suggestions as being impractical or choose to ignore them. If we continue to work Step Three and place our trust in our Higher Power, we discover that we possess the skills and ambition to search for and discover effective answers. When we work the Steps and discuss our problems openly, we see that they can be resolved in a myriad of ways.

I am learning that the answers to my problems are within me. Attending meetings and working the Steps improve my ability to accept and solve my problems.

Frisk, who was very small and could look closely into the water, cried out: "I see a golden carp coming." And sure enough there was the great carp, who said to Charming: "You saved my life in the meadow by the willow tree, and I promised I would repay you. Take this, it is Princess Goldilock's ring."

Working the Steps helps us to recover missing treasures. Many of us lost sight of our own goodness in the process of growing up. We became afraid to reveal our true selves to the world, believing that we were somehow damaged or worthless.

Learning to treat ourselves with respect is sometimes difficult. Each small courtesy we show ourselves returns like the golden carp to repay us with the ring of self-worth we lost but need so badly. Many of us are astonished to discover how it still shines in spite of our past despair and self-loathing.

By working the Steps and listening to the shared experiences of others, we are reminded of the buried treasures in all of us. We recover our self-worth, self-esteem and self-respect by having the courage to be open with other people who are also striving for honest relationships. What a joy and a relief it is when we finally retrieve our rings!

I will treat myself with respect, trusting that my self-worth will continue to grow.

When the princess saw her ring brought back to her unhurt she was astonished. "There is a prince not far from here whose name is Galifron, who once wanted to marry me," she said, "but when I refused he uttered the most terrible threats against me. I could not marry a frightful giant as tall as a tower. Before I can listen to your proposal you must kill him and bring me his head." Charming went out to arm himself suitably, and then, taking little Frisk with him, he mounted his horse and set out for Galifron's country.

Our search for self-knowledge takes courage and determination. We can arm ourselves suitably for this quest by trusting in our Higher Power and accepting encouragement from supportive friends. Our path may not be free of obstacles, but we can call on forgotten strengths along the way.

Some of our suppressed assets, like self-worth, lie quietly inside us like the ring at the bottom of the river, waiting to be recovered. Others, like our anger and resentment, have grown out of proportion and threaten to overwhelm us like the giant Galifron threatened Charming. When we confront our negative feelings, we begin to move towards establishing balance and stability in our lives.

I take a step forward when I have the courage to confront my rage and anger.

93

Everyone he met told him what a terrible giant Galifron was, and that nobody dared go near him; and the more he heard the more frightened he grew. Frisk tried to encourage him by saying: "While you are fighting the giant, dear master, I will go and bite his heels, and when he stoops down to look at me you can kill him." Charming praised his little dog's plan, but knew that his help would not do much good.

*F*ear is one of our worst enemies. The more we think about what we are afraid of, the more frightened we can become. Once unleashed, our fears tend to grow unchecked, fueled by the power of our own projections and fantasies. No matter how hard others try to encourage us, their suggestions will be ignored if we continue to hold on to the idea that nothing can be done to overcome the terrors from our past.

Coming to believe that a power greater than ourselves can restore us to sanity, as Step Two suggests, enables us to confront our fright. Having the courage to take action is the key to overcoming our fears. Any effort—no matter how small—is enough to motivate us and help build our confidence. We learn that even when it feels like we are facing the world alone, we have support. When we confront the giants we fear, we have our Higher Power to rely on, as well as the encouragement of other program members who have taken the same journey.

I will look to my Higher Power for the courage to face my fears. I can listen to the voices of hope in and around me.

At last he drew near the giant's castle. Galifron looked all about him, and saw Charming standing, sword in hand; this put the giant into a terrible rage, and he aimed a blow at Charming with his huge iron club. At that instant a raven perched upon the giant's head and so confused and blinded him that all his blows fell harmlessly upon the air. Charming cut off his head, and the raven croaked out: "You see, I have not forgotten the good turn you did me in killing the eagle. Today I think I have fulfilled my promise of repaying you."

*I*t is frightening to look back at the battles we have fought and lost, remembering how many of our blows seemed to fall harmlessly upon the air. We often say to ourselves, "I won't make that mistake again," or "This is the last time I'm going to do this." Statements or thoughts like these rarely get us very far. Our exhausted minds and bodies bear witness to the battles we have waged with our self-defeating behaviors.

When we come into the program, we begin to reverse the destructive process by giving the healthy parts of ourselves a chance to live. Working the Steps enables us to distract the negative thoughts that inhibit us until we can replace them with more positive ones. When we turn our will and our lives over to the care of our Higher Power in Step Three, the task becomes easier. We see that help is available when we require it. We need only to trust the process.

I will stop waging war on my destructive behaviors today. I will become ready to let them go and focus on developing my strengths.

"Behold the brave Charming, who has killed the giant!"
Their shouts reached the Princess's ear, but she dared
not ask what was happening, for fear she should hear
that Charming had been killed. Very soon he arrived at
the palace with the giant's head, of which she was still
terrified, though it could no longer do her any harm.

*L*ike the Princess, we sometimes close our eyes and
ears to the events around us to protect ourselves from
getting hurt. It keeps us from hearing what we don't
want to hear, or facing what we are afraid to face.
Ignoring reality muffles feelings of pain and confusion when we have no other way of dealing with
them. However, this behavior can ultimately stand in
the way of our happiness.

Participating in a twelve-step program provides us
with tools to meet life's challenges with our eyes wide
open. Yet there may still be times when we are
surprised by some reminder of our past fears. We may
see an old movie, hear a familiar song or walk into a
strange room and suddenly be overwhelmed with confusion. We tend to forget that we are not the same as
we were—that we have acquired new strengths and
skills. Our anxiety is lessened when we remember that
these are only temporary flashbacks to past times and
places—that today we have a program and friends we
can trust.

The farther I progress in recovery, the more I
am aware that the giants of my past
can no longer cause me harm.

"Princess," said Charming. "I have killed your enemy; I hope you will now consent to marry the King my master." "Oh dear, no!" said the Princess, "not until you have brought me some water from the Gloomy Cavern. The entrance is guarded by two dragons. You will find an immense hole full of toads and snakes; at the bottom of this hole rises the Fountain of Health and Beauty. It is some of this water that I really must have."

*W*e often wonder if there are a magical number of tasks we are required to accomplish before we can be happy, joyous and free. Isn't it enough that we've recovered lost treasures and confronted old giants? Is it only by wading through the toads and snakes of our deepest instincts that fountains of health and beauty can be found?

It takes courage to look honestly at our lives. When we do so, we may feel sad about where we have been and what we have been through. We may become discouraged when we discover that there are more monsters to confront. The fact that we are willing to examine our lives is a sign that we are ready to make positive changes. The Twelve Steps keep us moving through our despair toward the clear waters of health and beauty that symbolize the center of our being.

Today I will keep going no matter how gloomy my journey appears. Sadness and depression may accompany me, but they will not stop me from moving forward one day at a time.

When he was near the top of a hill he dismounted to let his horse graze. Looking about he saw one of the dragons with fire blazing from his mouth and eyes. Charming, quite determined to get the water or die, now drew his sword, and, taking the crystal flask which Pretty Goldilocks had given him to fill, said to Frisk: "I feel sure that I shall never come back from this expedition; when I am dead, go to the Princess and tell her that her errand has cost me my life. Then find the King my master, and relate all my adventures to him."

*A*ll of us have dragons inside us—unfulfilled needs that we fear will destroy us if we acknowledge their existence. We sometimes wonder if it would be easier and safer to avoid confronting them. Our reluctance to encounter these fiery desires prevents us from achieving health and happiness.

In Step One, we admit that we are powerless and that our lives are unmanageable. We may feel defeated by this powerlessness, but it is actually a sign that we are ready for recovery. When we acknowledge that our present ways of meeting our needs aren't working, we can come to believe that we deserve to drink from the fountain of life and become willing to take whatever steps we need to do so.

*When I willingly and honestly work the Steps,
I confront whatever dragons keep me
from enjoying the richness of life.*

As he spoke he heard a voice calling: "Charming, Charming!" "Who calls me?" said he; then he saw an owl sitting in a hollow tree, who said to him: "You saved my life when I was caught in the net, now I can repay you. Trust me with the flask, for I know all the ways of the Gloomy Cavern." After some time she returned with the flask, filled to the very brim with sparkling water. Charming thanked her with all his heart, and joyfully hastened back to town.

*T*he journey to the deepest parts of ourselves can be frightening, filled with our dreams as well as our fears. The reward at the end of this journey is worth striving for. At the center of our being we can find the lost child who wants to know the secret of happy and successful living.

As we journey toward wholeness and reconnect with our inner child, we discover many of the feelings that stand between us and our lost power. As we gain the courage to confront lost dreams and fears, we begin to make use of our inner wisdom. Like the wise owl, our intuition flies unerringly into the darkness and returns with water that revives the joy and sparkle of our inner child.

Today I will make use of my inner wisdom.

He went straight to the palace and gave the flask to the Princess. She thanked Charming and said, Everything this water touches becomes wonderful. The beautiful things will always remain beautiful, and the ugly things become lovely. If one is young, one never grows old, and if one is old one becomes young. You see Charming, I could not leave my kingdom without taking some of it with me."

*P*articipating in a twelve-step program and working the Steps can transform our world by awakening the spirit of life within us. Our view of reality changes. Where we once saw ugliness, we see beauty. We feel young again, no longer weighed down—made old before our time—by burdens of defeat and despair.

Developing a positive outlook on life revives a capacity for happiness we may have thought we had lost forever. We are able to stop behaving in ways that once protected us but now isolate us from others. We can reach out fearlessly to deepen our relationships, knowing that our security and well-being do not depend entirely on other people. We can look forward to a spiritual awakening, whereby we see the beauty in ourselves, and know that ugly things can also become beautiful.

I can change the way I view the world by looking for beauty even in the midst of ugliness.

The Princess ordered that preparations should be made for her departure, and they set out together. She found Charming such an agreeable companion that she said to him: "Why didn't we stay where we were? I could have made you king, and we should have been so happy!" But Charming only answered: "I could not have done anything that would have vexed my master so much, even for a kingdom, or to please you, though I think you are as beautiful as the sun."

*A*fter working Steps One, Two and Three, our lives can improve so radically that we are tempted to stay where we are and enjoy what we've gained. Why bother to move on when we are happy and things are much better already? Why go through more change and uncertainty when life is almost manageable just the way it is?

Sometimes we do stop at Step Three, but the pain of self-limitation usually inspires us to search for more serenity. We do not always understand why we feel a need to move forward, but we can do so confidently if we have placed the outcome in the hands of our Higher Power. The spiritual awakening we experience as the result of working the Steps comes within reach when we value ourselves enough to accept who we are and what we are. When we reach this point, the meaning of many of our previous struggles for identity becomes more clear.

I am learning to listen to the inner voice that pushes me forward, recognizing that this is a way to be true to myself.

At last they reached the King's great city, and the marriage was celebrated with great rejoicing. But Goldilocks was so fond of Charming that she was always singing his praises. Then Charming's enemies said to the King: "It is a wonder that you are not jealous. As if anybody you had sent could not have done just as much!" "It is quite true," said the King. "Let him be chained hand and foot, and thrown into the tower."

When we lay claim to affections not freely given to us, we become insecure about whether we are really loved or not. Our fear often distorts our honest appraisal of the situation and starts a chain of events in which we begin trying to control other people to protect our own interests. In the end we are the ones that are chained hand and foot and thrown into the tower, imprisoned by our own fears and jealousy.

When we are overwhelmed by the pressures of our busy lives and dissatisfied with ourselves, we can turn to the Twelve Steps to recover our balance and gain an understanding of the action we need to take to change the situation. Continued involvement with Steps Ten, Eleven and Twelve—personal inventory, conscious contact with our Higher Power and carrying the message—assures us that we will continue to enjoy our new-found freedom.

> *I will use Steps Ten, Eleven and Twelve*
> *to deal with my jealousy and envy.*

Then the King took it in his head that he was not handsome enough to please the Princess and thought he would bathe his face with the water from the Fountain of Beauty. One of the Princess's ladies had broken the flask and replaced it with one that was used for getting rid of troublesome people. Their faces were bathed with the water, and they instantly fell asleep. When the King sprinkled the water upon his face, he fell asleep, and nobody could wake him.

When old feelings of inadequacy return, it is a sign that we've lost contact with our Higher Power. We're afraid we're not handsome enough to please others. Our connection with our inner truth and goodness has been broken and we begin to search for something to make us look and feel better. We may look outside ourselves for something to restore our confidence—as the King bathed his face with what he thought was water from the Fountain of Beauty.

When we look to other people or return to old behaviors to fill our inner emptiness, we numb ourselves. Fortunately, we do not have to stay asleep like the King. Attending meetings and talking to others can revive us and renew our connection with our Higher Power.

I will resist the temptation to look for a "quick fix." I will ask my Higher Power for help in finding the source of my difficulty and then removing it.

Without saying a word to anyone, Princess Goldilocks went straight to the tower, and with her own hands took off Charming's chains. Then, putting a golden crown upon his head, and the royal mantle upon his shoulders, she said: "Come, faithful Charming, I make you king, and will take you for my husband." The wedding, which took place at once, was the prettiest that can be imagined, and Prince Charming and Princess Goldilocks lived happily ever after.

We become free to live happily ever after when we stop trying to be who we're not to please others and give up trying to manage them so they can please us. By discovering who we are and learning to remain true to ourselves, we take off our chains and let go of our need to dominate and control others. This frees us from being involved in relationships that are based on fear and obligation.

The program promises happy endings if we are willing to surrender to the process of recovery and accept life's challenges—one day at a time. We have survived the pain of self-confrontation and come to know and love ourselves. We have joined our inner and outer worlds—our feelings and our actions. We have learned to extend our love and understanding to others while respecting their freedom of choice and are building mutually satisfying relationships.

Today I will break the chains that isolate me from others and look for ways to love and be loved.

Snow White

SNOW WHITE

nce upon a time a queen wished for a child as white as snow, as red as blood and as black as ebony. Her wish was granted and she named her daughter Snow White. Soon after, the queen died. Her husband then married a woman who could not tolerate any rival to her beauty. She was constantly reassured by her mirror that she was the fairest in the land. When the mirror told her that Snow White had become the most fair, the queen flew into a rage and demanded that a huntsman take the girl into the forest and kill her.

The huntsman spared her life and Snow White found refuge in the home of seven dwarfs who worked in the mines in the heart of a mountain. They promised to take care of her if she would keep house for them. They warned her against letting anyone else into the house, suspecting that the queen would discover her presence and harm her.

When the queen learned that Snow White was alive, she disguised herself as an old peddler's wife and went to the dwarf's house. Playing on her vanity, she sold Snow White colored bodice laces and then laced them tight, suffocating her and leaving her for dead. When the dwarfs returned, they released the laces and revived her. The queen then gave Snow White a poison comb for her hair which the dwarfs were also able to find and remove. When the queen gave Snow White a poison apple, she fell down dead. Mournfully, the dwarfs put her in a glass coffin and watched over her day and night.

A prince saw Snow White in the coffin and fell in love with her. When the dwarfs refused to sell the coffin to him, he convinced them of his love for Snow White, and they gave him the coffin. As his men were carrying it down the mountain, they jolted it and the poisonous piece of apple was dislodged from Snow White's throat. She returned to life and married the prince.

Once upon a time, in the middle of winter when the snowflakes were falling like feathers on the earth, a Queen sat at a window framed in black ebony and sewed. And as she sewed and gazed out to the white landscape, she pricked her finger with the needle, and three drops of blood fell on the snow outside, and because the red showed out so well against the white she thought to herself: "Oh! what wouldn't I give to have a child as white as snow, as red as blood, and as black as ebony!"

Most of us come into the program in the middle of personal winters feeling lonely, depressed and discouraged. Our lives seem to be at a standstill, with no foreseeable hope for the future. We may intensify these feelings by numbing our minds with boring routines or isolating ourselves in solitary activities, thinking we are insulating ourselves from the possibility of change-induced turmoil.

Like the Queen when she pricked her finger, we are sometimes inspired by thoughts of colorful new possibilities. We can choose to pursue these opportunities or ignore them. Knowing we can move through disappointment makes it less frightening to consider new alternatives. Trusting in our Higher Power gives us the courage to look beyond our doubts and make choices that can effect positive change in our lives.

I will look beyond the fear that sometimes hinders my ability to pursue new possibilities in my life.

And her wish was granted, for not long after a little daughter was born to her, with a skin as white as snow, lips and cheeks as red as blood, and hair as black as ebony. They called her Snow White, and not long after her birth, the Queen died.

*B*elieving in new possibilities is the first step in bringing them to life. Often the things that first inspired them die, and we must look for new ways to foster their development. Recovery means saying goodbye to some of the attitudes and behaviors that protected us and learning new ways to nurture and care for ourselves.

Thinking that we will recover the purity and innocence of a newborn child like Snow White is unreal and self-defeating. Recovery involves recognizing and stopping our all-or-nothing thinking. Our chances of disappointment are lessened when we come to understand that life is not always all black or all white. We learn to find a balance in the midst of our love and hate, creativity and destructiveness, joy and despair. Contact with others who had the courage to risk disappointment and follow a new path can help us through the period of transition.

I will trust that there are new possibilities available to me. I want to recognize and utilize my potential.

After a year the King married again. His new wife was a beautiful woman, but so proud and overbearing that she couldn't stand any rival to her beauty. She possessed a magic mirror, and when she used to stand before it gazing at her own reflection and ask, "Mirror, mirror, hanging there, who in all the land's most fair?", it always replied: "You are most fair, my Lady Queen, none fairer in the land, I ween." Then she was quite happy, for she knew the mirror always spoke the truth.

*F*ew of us emerge from childhood feeling secure in the belief that we are beautiful. We may find it difficult to imagine a world in which just being ourselves would ever be good enough. Some of us work diligently at being the best in all we do to compensate for feeling inadequate.

Like the King's new wife, we may be driven by the fear that we don't measure up to others. When we begin to value ourselves and tie our self-esteem to who we are instead of how we look, we become less fixated on making comparisons. When we stop relying on the opinions of others to measure our self-worth, we can relate to them as people instead of mirrors through which we evaluate our own reflections.

I will base my self-esteem on who I am instead of how I look and will stop comparing myself to others.

One day when the Queen asked her mirror the usual question, it replied: "My Lady Queen, you are fair, 'tis true, But Snow White is fairer far than you." Then the Queen flew into the most awful passion, and turned every shade of green in her jealousy. At last she could endure Snow White's presence no longer, and, calling a Huntsman to her, she said: "Take the child out into the wood. Kill her, and bring me back her lungs and liver, that I may know for certain she is dead."

*P*lanning to eliminate our rivals to escape the pain of envy is certainly extreme. We may try to protect ourselves in more subtle ways by putting them down, allowing them to fail or pretending they don't exist. These solutions may offer temporary relief, but they don't work over the long term. They keep us focused on other people and leave us with no energy to fulfill the promise of our own lives.

When we base our self-esteem on how we measure up to others, we are inclined to drive all those who remind us in any way of our imperfections out of our lives. This leaves us alone and lonely. Learning to be comfortable with ourselves at whatever stage of life we have reached and to see the opportunities available to us makes us less vulnerable to envy and its suffocating effects.

> *By focusing on my own development, I am becoming less envious of others who appear to have more than I do.*

The Huntsman did as he was told and led Snow White out into the wood, but as he was in the act of drawing out his knife to slay her, she began to cry, and said: "Oh, dear Huntsman, spare my life, and I will promise to fly forth into the wide wood and never to return home again." The Huntsman had pity on her, and said: "Well, run along, poor child." For he thought to himself: "The wild beasts will soon eat her up." And his heart felt lighter because he hadn't had to do the deed himself.

*P*rior to recovery, we may have had no memory of how helpless we felt in the forest of turmoil and confusion. For many of us, recovery begins when the lost child within us says, "You are too beautiful to die. Life is too precious. Give yourself a chance." When we can admit our powerlessness and confusion, we have taken the first step toward freedom and happiness.

In the process of experiencing the monumental changes that recovery brings, we may feel like we're in the wild forest again. We may wonder if there will ever be a calm after the storm. Yet, when we listen to the hopeful voice within us and make a commitment to nurture it with the help of our Higher Power, we know we can survive whatever challenges confront us.

I no longer need to listen to the frightened voices of my past. I can give my inner child the same respect and care I extend to others who are close to me.

*And as he turned away a young boar came running past,
so he shot it, and brought its lungs and liver home to the
Queen as a proof that Snow White was really dead. The
wicked woman had them stewed in salt, and ate them,
thinking she had made an end of Snow White for ever.*

*T*here are many ways in which we can consume
ourselves and others through our negative behavior.
We may allow other people to drain our time and
energy because we do not set limits on our involvement with them. We can fail to develop our talents and
abilities by escaping into compulsive behaviors. Like
the Queen, who may have thought she could regain
her youthful vitality by eating Snow White's liver, we
may use alcohol or drugs to give us artificial energy.

We learn in recovery that using drugs or alcohol
burns us up, destroys our natural exuberance and
wastes our talents. We realize that we can lead healthy,
vital lives and have fulfilling relationships without
destroying others or ourselves, or allowing others to
consume us. The Steps help us to set limits and
priorities and make wise use of the resources we've
been given. Maintaining balance in our lives through
reliance on our Higher Power helps us to conserve our
energies and be productive in the process.

*I will stop giving all of myself to others, and
turn to my Higher Power for help in finding the best uses for my talents.*

Now when the poor child found herself alone in the big wood the very trees around her seemed to assume strange shapes, and she felt so frightened she didn't know what to do. Then she began to run over the sharp stones, and through the bramble bushes, and the wild beasts ran past her, but they did her no harm. She ran as far as her legs would carry her, and as evening approached she saw a little house, and she stepped inside to rest.

Although we may not be aware of it, many of us came into the program with a frightened child inside us. We may have been running from feelings or memories for a long time, tripping over sharp stones and rustling through bramble bushes. If anyone asked us where we were going, we probably wouldn't have stopped to answer them. We may not have even known. We had tried to take care of ourselves and were exhausted by the turmoil, fear and confusion brought on by the disorder of our lives.

The program gives us a safe place to stop and rest with others who know what the mad flight feels like. They help us to discover that it isn't other people we've been running from—it's ourselves. When we understand our self-defeating behavior and have the courage to change, we are less inclined to be frightened by our confused feelings and emotions. We do not have to face the task alone; we can reach out for help from others who have taken a similar journey and are able to give us support and encouragement.

*I can stop running today and rest from my flight.
I can reach out to new friends for help.*

Everything was very small in the little house, but cleaner and neater than anything you can imagine. In the middle of the room there stood a little table, covered with a white tablecloth, and seven little plates and forks and spoons and knives and tumblers. Snow White felt so hungry and so thirsty that she ate a bit of bread and a little porridge from each plate, and drank a drop of wine out of each tumbler.

*W*e don't always pay attention to the seemingly insignificant parts of our lives because we're too busy tidying up the big picture. We often concern ourselves with the major tasks we haven't finished or the big objectives we set out to accomplish. We forget that life moves in small segments, one moment at a time.

Getting caught up in the larger picture can be overwhelming. Like Snow White in the untamed forest, we rush from place to place, not knowing where to stop or what to do. This can keep us in a perpetual state of procrastination and discouragement. We say to ourselves, "I'll never finish it anyway. Why start?" Using Step Ten to establish priorities and remembering to focus on taking one small step at a time reduces our frustration and confusion. We don't have to have it all, eat it all or do it all in one day.

*I will take pleasure in small satisfactions today.
I realize that I can't have everything I want
or do everything I want in one day.*

Side by side against the wall there were seven little beds, covered with snow-white counterpanes. Feeling tired and sleepy, Snow White lay down on one of the beds, but it wasn't comfortable; then she tried all the others in turn, but one was too long, and another too short, and it was only when she got to the seventh that she found one to suit her exactly. So she lay down upon it, said her prayers like a good child, and fell fast asleep.

*H*ow many of us take the first bed we find when we're tired, not bothering to check whether or not it is suitable, or even remotely meets our special needs? Snow White refused to sleep in a bed that wasn't right for her. She remained true to herself and kept looking for a place to rest that would give her good support. When she was satisfied, she was able to fall fast asleep.

We follow Snow White's example when we decide to turn our lives over to the care of our Higher Power. We begin to discover things that are right for us and stop allowing ourselves to be pushed in directions we aren't meant to go. We develop the kind of faith that allowed this frightened child to say her prayers and go to sleep without worrying about what the next day would bring. The ability to rest at night without judging ourselves for what happened today or being anxious about tomorrow is one of recovery's gifts.

I am grateful for a way of life that lets me rest when I am tired. I will replace my fear with the kind of faith that allows me to sleep undisturbed.

When it got quite dark the masters of the little house returned. They were seven dwarfs who worked in the mines, right down deep in the heart of the mountain. They lighted their seven little lamps, and as soon as their eyes got accustomed to the glare they saw that someone had been in the room, for all was not in the same order as they had left it.

*W*hat is our typical reaction when the order of our lives is disturbed? Do we worry about signs of change and resist the idea that things may not always be the same? Do we welcome the thought that something new has arrived?

Like the Dwarfs' little lamps, the Steps throw new light on aspects of our lives that we may not be willing to face. Many of us are tempted to extinguish the light and pretend that nothing is amiss so that we don't have to worry about things that are strange and new. We may like the idea of quieting our anxiety and turning our lives over by taking Step Three, but then resist taking a good look at ourselves as required in Step Four. Trusting our Higher Power to guide us gives us the hope we need to look at our past and begin to deal with life as it unfolds.

I can use the light provided by the Steps in all aspects of my life. I will trust my Higher Power to help me deal with what- ever I discover today.

Then the first Dwarf looked round and saw a little hollow in his bed, and he asked: "Who's been lying on my bed?" The others came running round, and cried: "Somebody has lain on ours too." But when the seventh came to his bed, he started back in amazement, for there he beheld Snow White fast asleep. Then he called the others, who turned their little lamps full on the bed. And they were so enchanted by Snow White's beauty that they did not wake her, but let her sleep on in the little bed.

*T*he inventory suggested in Step Four helps to bring the childlike parts of us to light. It can be disturbing to discover that there's still a lonely and frightened child inside us who is in need of rest. We may be tempted to shout: "Wake up! Go away! How dare you disturb the calmness of my ordered world? I thought I'd finished with you years ago!"

If we turn our backs on our long-buried feelings of helplessness and confusion, we may not realize the beauty of the child who sleeps within us. Closing our eyes to that part of our lives prevents us from achieving wholeness and discovering our true identities. By taking our inventory in Step Four and admitting our wrongs to trusted friends in Step Five, we begin to achieve the self-acceptance we need to give the child we rejected long ago a chance to awaken and live.

*Today I will be patient with myself and
let the tired child within me rest.*

In the morning Snow White awoke, but when she saw the seven little Dwarfs she felt very frightened. But they were so friendly and asked her what her name was in such a kind way, that she replied: "I am Snow White." "Why did you come to our house?" continued the Dwarfs. Then she told them how her step-mother had wished her put to death, and how the Huntsman had spared her life, and how she had run the whole day till she had come to their little house.

*B*eing surrounded by supportive friends before we are ready can be overwhelming, especially if we are accustomed to keeping others at a distance. Rather than admit our fear of other people, many of us engaged in addictive behaviors to maintain the illusion that we were not alone. Our refusal to confront reality kept us in a deep sleep like Snow White, unable to develop healthy relationships.

Entering recovery marks a new beginning for those of us who are caught between the resentment of having no home to return to and the fear of venturing into the unknown. As newcomers to a twelve-step program, we may feel like strangers in an unfamiliar world, but we are no longer alone. Although we may be naive about the world outside like Snow White was, we now have a chance at survival. We have found kind friends who can show us a way through the forest.

I am grateful to have found a place to rest. I will stop running and know that I am safe.

The Dwarfs, when they had heard her sad story, asked her: "Will you stay and keep house for us, cook, make the beds, do the washing, sew and knit? and if you keep everything neat and clean, you shall want for nothing." "Yes," answered Snow White. "I will gladly do all you ask." And so she took up her abode with them.

*P*rogram members talk about "putting their houses in order" by taking action to clear their lives of chaos and confusion. Some of us take this literally and dig into desks and closets, uncovering unpaid bills and clothes in need of repair. Others start taking better care of our physical bodies by eating correctly, exercising regularly and resting properly. No matter what lifestyle we choose, we cannot put our lives in true order until we have become entirely ready to let go of chaotic thoughts and behaviors.

Many of us become so sick of the turmoil that we readily accept the Twelve Steps and quickly realize what they can do for us. When we approach Step Six, we spend time examining the function that chaos and confusion serve in our lives, so that we can become entirely ready to have these defects removed. We ask our Higher Power for help in removing our defects in Step Seven and move on to develop new habits and ways of doing things. The benefits that can be gained by working the Steps are similar to those that the dwarfs promised Snow White. If we keep our lives in order, we will want for nothing.

I intend to clear my life of disorder and confusion and prepare the way for serenity and balance.

Every morning the Dwarfs went into the mountain to dig for gold, and in the evening, when they returned home, Snow White always had their supper ready for them. But during the day the girl was left quite alone, so the good Dwarfs warned her, saying: "Beware of your step-mother. She will soon find out you are here, and whatever you do don't let anyone into the house."

Regular participation in a twelve-step program helps us put our intellectual and emotional house in order, but we also must allow it to help us sweep away the cobwebs from our spiritual space. Only then, like the gold nuggets dug from the mountain, can our spiritual treasure be brought forth.

Prayer and meditation can be valuable helpers to us like the dwarfs were to Snow White. They provide us with the inspiration and inner strength we need to make good decisions and avoid dangers that threaten our well-being. Building trust in our inner resources takes time; we cannot cast aside years of negative thought patterns overnight. Attending meetings and sharing honestly with others helps us stay focused on the positive aspects of our lives. When our faith in ourselves and our Higher Power has been restored, we can face the world with confidence. Until then we can take shelter and strength from the program.

I will take time to feed my spiritual hunger with daily prayer and meditation. I can rely on my Higher Power to guide me.

Stepping before her mirror one day, the Queen said "Mirror, mirror, hanging there, Who in all the land's most fair?" and the mirror replied: "My Lady Queen, you are fair, 'tis true, But Snow White is fairer far than you. Snow White, who dwells with the seven little men, Is as fair as you, as fair again." The Queen pondered day and night how she might destroy her, for as long as she felt she had a rival, her jealous heart left her no rest.

*H*ow painful it is to envy others so strongly that we feel they must be destroyed. Some of us have such poor hopes of our chances for success that we view others as a potential threat to us. We haven't yet discovered that there is enough love and support in the world for everyone.

Focusing on our positive qualities and noting the progress we have made increases our self-esteem and diverts our attention away from what we lack. Learning to appreciate the help and support of other program members is also beneficial. An "attitude of gratitude" and the knowledge that we are doing the best we can are the most useful defenses against the pain of envy.

I will measure my progress by recalling how I used to be instead of comparing myself to others.

At last the Queen hit upon a plan. She stained her face and dressed herself up as an old peddler wife, so that she was quite unrecognisable. In this guise she went over the seven hills till she came to the house of the seven Dwarfs. There she knocked at the door, calling out at the same time: "Fine wares to sell, fine wares to sell! Laces of every shade and description," and she held one up that was made of some gay coloured silk.

Many of us have trouble telling the difference between things that are seemingly harmless and those that are dangerous. Placing a high priority on honesty helps us to discover the areas in which we are vulnerable to deception. When we become willing to examine our past and present actions objectively, we can begin to understand why certain situations are dangerous to us. We cannot change the things that happened to us, but we can eliminate their influence on our present lives by exposing them to the light and dealing with them.

If we fail to examine our past behavior patterns, we may continue to be influenced by fine wares and laces which represent promises of instant happiness. With a more rational view of the world, fine wares may continue to attract us, but we will be able to consider the source and prepare to accept the consequences when we choose them.

I will watch for hidden motives and behaviors that color my view of reality. I will resist choosing easier ways of doing things knowing that they may harm me.

"Surely I can let the honest woman in," thought Snow White; so she unbarred the door and bought the pretty lace. "Good gracious, child!" said the old woman, "What a figure you've got. Come! I'll lace you up properly for once." Snow White, suspecting no evil, stood before her and let her lace her bodice up, but the old woman laced her so quickly and so tightly that it took Snow White's breath away, and she fell down dead.

*L*ike Snow White, we are sometimes lured into unsafe areas by appeals to our vanity. How can we help but be attracted to something we believe will make our lives better? There is nothing wrong with wanting to be prettier, more popular or more prized, but we can get into trouble when we let such desires override our good judgment.

Past efforts to develop our potential may have been thwarted by negative reactions from others or by our own self-conscious fear: "Don't say that—people will think you're foolish! Don't do that—people will laugh at you! Besides, you'll probably fail." We can use the program and the Twelve Steps to help us move beyond the voices that tend to stifle us. Looking within ourselves for approval, acceptance and affirmation helps us to breathe freely again and stop relying on others for validation.

I will try to silence the voices that discourage me and hinder my growth. Self-acceptance frees my spirit and allows me to develop my full potential.

In the evening the seven Dwarfs came home, and you may think what a fright they got when they saw their dear Snow White lying on the floor, motionless as a dead person. They lifted her up tenderly, and when they saw how tightly laced she was they cut the lace in two, and she began to breathe and gradually came back to life. When the Dwarfs heard what had happened, they said "Depend upon it, the old peddler wife was none other than the old Queen. In future you must be sure to let no one in, if we are not at home."

*O*ur reactions to people or situations may silence us temporarily and leave us breathless, but we needn't feel immobilized forever. We can recover our vitality and sense of self by expressing our thoughts and feelings whenever our breathing returns to normal.

Meetings provide us with an opportunity to come back to life. Having the courage to share our stories, even when frightened or depressed, frees us from the bondage of our self-consciousness. When we learn that it is safe to express ourselves freely, positive thoughts emerge to encourage and sustain us: "So what if I'm clumsy—that is part of learning something new." "Who cares if people laugh at me; I believe in this project and I know it will work!" Putting our newfound positive attitudes to use prepares us to offer hope and encouragement to others as they travel along the road to their recovery.

I can breathe more easily when I remember I am on the road to recovery. The past is losing its hold on me.

As soon as the wicked old Queen got home she went straight to her mirror, who answered as before: "My Lady Queen, you are fair, 'tis true, But Snow White is fairer far than you." When she heard this she became as pale as death. And by the witchcraft which she understood so well she made a poisonous comb; then she dressed herself up and assumed the form of another old woman. So she went over the seven hills till she reached the house of the seven Dwarfs, and knocking at the door she called out: "Fine wares for sale."

*O*ne way to sabotage our potential is by poisoning our minds with negative thoughts so that new possibilities don't have a chance to develop. What could be worse than having poisonous combs of despair and self-destruction lodged firmly in our heads?

We are fortunate to have found a program that addresses the problem of poisoned thinking. Although we may never be totally free from negative thoughts and feelings, we can neutralize our negativity before it paralyzes us. Learning to recognize pessimistic thinking helps us stop it before it stops us. Sharing our self-criticism with a sponsor or someone who understands the recovery process helps us put things in perspective. Attending meetings puts us in touch with more positive messages to balance the destructive thoughts that haunt us.

I will replace my poisonous thoughts with positive ones today. If I have difficulty doing this, I will call my sponsor or a close friend.

Snow White looked out of the window and said: "You must go away, for I may not let anyone in." "But surely you are not forbidden to look out?" said the old woman, and she held up the poisonous comb for her to see. It pleased the girl so much that she let herself be taken in, and opened the door. The old woman said: "Now I'll comb your hair properly for you." Poor Snow White thought no evil, but hardly had the comb touched her hair than the poison worked and she fell down unconscious.

Many of us tried to protect ourselves from painful experiences by shutting ourselves away like Snow White. We then found ourselves imprisoned in dungeons of our own making. In our solitude, our thoughts were often poisoned by our own negative inner voices: "You're not good enough. You don't deserve success. You'll never get it right. There's no use in trying. Anyone who really knew you would never want to be around you."

Locking ourselves away and avoiding contact with others is never the answer. We need positive outside influences in our lives in order to develop in a healthy manner. Our inner worlds are enriched and enlivened by interaction with people who foster positive thoughts and feelings. Participation in the program offers opportunities for us to meet others who are working to revise the ways in which they think about themselves and others.

*I don't have to shut myself away to feel safe.
I can choose to associate with people
who have positive attitudes.*

Fortunately it was now near evening, and the seven Dwarfs returned home. When they saw Snow White lying dead on the ground, they at once suspected that her wicked step-mother had been at work again; so they searched till they found the poisonous comb, and the moment they pulled it out of her head Snow White came to herself again, and told them what had happened. Then they warned her once more to be on her guard, and to open the door to no one.

*N*o matter how often we are warned, many of us seem to be drawn to potentially poisonous people. It can be difficult to withstand their negative influence, especially if we take no action against the self-defeating thoughts that occur to us in the course of a day. We are so accustomed to negative tapes continuously playing in our heads that we may not be aware of them. Allowing them to run endlessly reinforces thought patterns and attitudes that lead us to repeat self-defeating behaviors.

The program gives us tools to sort out these negative influences and make room for growth-producing thoughts and experiences. Daily time for reading and meditation adds immeasurably to the storehouse of positive messages we gather at meetings. Improving our conscious contact with our Higher Power in Step Eleven helps us to achieve the happiness, joy and freedom we seek.

I will not allow old beliefs and attitudes to poison me. I will ignore them and cultivate thoughts that contribute to my happiness.

As soon as the Queen got home she went straight to her mirror, and it replied as before: "My Lady Queen, you are fair, 'tis true, But Snow White is fairer far than you." "Snow White shall die," she cried; "yes, though it cost me my own life." Then she went to a little secret chamber, and there she made a poisonous apple. She stained her face and dressed herself up as a peasant, and went over the seven hills to the seven Dwarfs'.

*T*he potential for envy lies dormant in all of us. It can be activated when we compare ourselves to others and see ourselves as less fortunate than they are. This can plunge us back into feelings of resentment and intense self-pity. When this reaction becomes extreme, we may even entertain the thought of causing others harm to silence our envy. Thoughts like these take us to secret lonely chambers where it is extremely difficult to temper the forces of our anger and fear.

We often adopt disguises like the Queen did to cover our unacceptable feelings. We smile when we want to scream, or say "of course I don't mind," when we really do. Fear and envy cannot be silenced by hiding them away in secret inner rooms. We must be willing to admit their presence, accept them and deal with them honestly. Owning our negative feelings is the first step in diminishing their power over us.

*Today I will open the door of my fear and envy
and share their true nature with
someone whom I trust.*

The Queen knocked at the door, but Snow White put her head out of the window and called out: "I may not let anyone in, the seven Dwarfs have forbidden me to do so." "Are you afraid of being poisoned?" asked the old woman. "See, I will cut this apple in half. I'll eat the white cheek and you can eat the red." Snow White longed to eat the tempting fruit, and when she saw that the peasant woman was eating it herself, she couldn't resist the temptation any longer. But hardly had the first bite passed her lips than she fell down dead on the ground.

*I*t's hard to have confidence in our intuition if those we want to trust constantly disappoint us. Sometimes the fault lies not with our instincts, but in our failure to pay attention to them. We may say "no" to things we know are dangerous to us, but if our pride, our desire for love or our need to kill our pain wear us down, our resolve may begin to waiver. We end up saying "maybe" which soon becomes "yes." Our healthy instincts and emotions have been thrown off balance by denial, fear and distorted thinking.

This is part of the insanity that Step Two addresses. Coming to believe in a power greater than ourselves strengthens our resistance to temptation and helps us avoid eating tempting fruit. We are not so likely to override the danger signals our intuition provides us if we trust the power of the Steps to lead us in more positive directions.

*I am recovering my healthy instincts and intuition.
I will pay attention to my inner voices.*

When she got home she asked the mirror: "Mirror, mirror, hanging there, who in all the land's most fair?" And this time it replied: "You are most fair, my Lady Queen, none fairer in the land, I ween." Then her jealous heart was at rest—at least, as much at rest as a jealous heart can ever be.

*T*he problem with envious hearts is that they are never at rest. We may eliminate those we envy from our lives by making them look bad or erasing them from our minds, but we have no guarantee that someone else will not take their place. As long as we continue to base our self-esteem on external comparisons to other people, we must constantly be checking the mirror for reassurance that we are still the most fair.

The program helps to restore us to our rightful place in the world—an equal among equals. When we have built a solid base of self-worth, fear and envy no longer threaten us. We do not have to be better than others or "the fairest of the fair" to be accepted. In recovery, we learn to appreciate our differences without being threatened by their existence. When we are fully involved and committed to active participation in life, we find there is more than enough love for all of us.

I am becoming aware of the toll that negative feelings exact from me. I will be grateful for the opportunities I have and keep envy away from my door.

When the little Dwarfs came home in the evening they found Snow White lying on the ground, and she neither breathed nor stirred. They lifted her up, and looked round everywhere to see if they could find anything poisonous about. They unlaced her bodice, combed her hair, washed her with water and wine, but all in vain; the child was dead and remained dead. Then they placed her on a bier, and all the seven Dwarfs sat round it, weeping and sobbing for three whole days.

*O*ften, the voice of the young child within us was silenced before we entered the program, its spontaneity and spirit numbed by our negative feelings and behaviors. We may have looked everywhere for the poisonous thing that injured our child and tried in vain to put breath back into its lifeless body.

Recovery begins when we admit our powerlessness in Step One and come to believe in Step Two that we can be restored to wholeness. Although the grief we feel at having lost large parts of ourselves is natural and healthy, we now have the opportunity to renew our lives and revive our inner child. When we become open to a new way of being that has the power to resurrect us, we develop more positive ways of thinking and behaving and begin to restructure our lives.

I trust in the power of the Twelve Steps to restore the voice of my lost inner child.

At last they made up their minds to bury her, but she looked as blooming as a living being, and her cheeks were still such a lovely colour, that they said: "We can't hide her away in the black ground." So they had a coffin made of transparent glass, and they laid her in it, and wrote on the lid in golden letters that she was a royal Princess.

Some of us lived inside glass coffins, protected by our own defenses, able to see others but not allowing ourselves to be touched by them. We ignored our own good judgment to please those around us and set aside our own dreams, longings and aspirations in order to meet their needs. We hid from our true feelings, surrendered to our negative voices and turned away from life. We may have seen clearly through the glass walls, but were unable to respond emotionally to what we saw. Our appearance may have been lifelike, but we felt no life in us.

Entering recovery is a sign that we wish to return to life. Hiding is no longer an option for us. Our inner child has stirred and reminded us that we can shatter our glass coffin and achieve spontaneity and freedom. We may not become heavily involved in working the Steps immediately. Rather, we may choose to rest for awhile in the company of other program members who sustain us with their experience, strength and hope until we become comfortable with moving ahead on our journey through recovery.

I will not allow glass walls to cut me off from life. Life is meant for living, not for lying on display.

Then they put the coffin on the top of the mountain, and one of the Dwarfs always remained beside it and kept watch over it. And the very birds of the air came and bewailed Snow White's death, first an owl, and then a raven, and last of all a little dove.

*H*ow comforting to know that even when we feel as though we are dead, some surviving parts of us still stand guard like the Dwarfs, hoping that we may one day awaken to the fullness of life. Our healthy instincts, symbolized by the owl, the raven and the dove, wait with us too. The intelligent owl brings wisdom to illuminate our darkness; the raven carries the hope that clear thinking will be restored after this period of solitude; the dove represents the desire for peace and reconciliation with ourselves and others. They hope for our lost life to return, and do not desert us.

It is clearly our choice to continue to view the world from a coffin on top of the mountain peak or reconnect with ourselves and those around us. In recovery, we learn to move forward by listening to the voices of possibility and change within us and beginning to express them to people we trust.

I can choose to remain in darkness or to have my life restored to me. I will listen to the inner voices that push me forward.

Snow White lay a long time in the coffin, and she always looked as if she were fast asleep. One day a Prince came to the wood and saw the coffin on the hill, with the beautiful Snow White inside it. He said to the Dwarfs "Give me the coffin. I'll give you whatever you like for it." But the Dwarfs said: "No; we wouldn't part with it for all the gold in the world." "Well, then," he replied, "give it to me, because I can't live without Snow White. I will cherish and love it as my dearest possession." He spoke so sadly that the Dwarfs had pity on him, and gave him the coffin.

*F*ull involvement in life comes from joining both aspects of our humanity—the inner potential represented by Snow White in the coffin and the opportunity for external movement symbolized by the Prince. When the Dwarfs refuse to sell Snow White, the Prince discovers he cannot buy love.

When he realizes the importance of admitting his true feelings, the Dwarfs let Snow White go. They know the secret of the program—that the potential for love in each of us cannot be fulfilled until we bring it to life within our hearts and then search for ways to express it in the world.

Today I will guard my values as closely as the Dwarfs guarded Snow White. I realize how much my inner life influences the direction of my outer life.

The Prince made his servants bear the coffin away on their shoulders. As they were going down the hill they stumbled over a bush, and jolted the coffin so violently that the poisonous bit of apple Snow White had swallowed fell out of her throat. She gradually opened her eyes and lifted up the lid of the coffin. "Oh! Dear me, where am I?" she cried. The Prince answered joyfully, "You are with me," adding "I love you better than anyone in the whole wide world. Will you come with me to my father's palace and be my wife?" Snow White consented, and went with him.

*T*he jolt that dislodges the poisoned bit of apple from our throats has a different intensity for each of us. But whatever its size, its effect is the same—to lead us into Step One—the realization that our way of dealing with life is not working. We may feel like we have come to a standstill—that our life is over—but actually, we have just taken our first free breath. By admitting our powerlessness and recognizing the unmanageability of our lives, we can open our eyes and begin to see our way to a bright new future.

It is never too late to begin our journey toward wholeness. Whether our development was impeded by our own addiction or someone else's, we have the ability to lift the lid on the coffin of our isolation and enter into the fullness of life. Then we can begin to learn the meaning of love, growth, peace and serenity.

I have dislodged the poison bit of apple and discovered my own power and completeness. I am slowly and carefully uniting my inner and outer worlds.

Snow White's wicked step-mother was one of the guests invited to the wedding feast. At first she didn't want to go to the wedding at all, but at the same time she felt she would never be happy till she had seen the young Queen. As she entered Snow White recognised her, and nearly fainted with fear; but red-hot iron shoes had been prepared for the wicked old Queen, and she was made to get into them and dance till she fell down dead.

Some of us, like the wicked Queen, fail to recognize the opportunities for transformation within ourselves. Faced with the same problem again and again, we persist in trying to change or destroy the people or objects who cause us pain. We do not see that the difficulty is with us, not them. We must grapple with our own thoughts and actions, and with the shame and anger caused by our lack of self-worth.

The Queen shows us the consequences of failing to look at ourselves honestly. While Snow White and the Prince begin the dance of life, she begins her dance of death—the only power strong enough to wipe out the red-hot pain of her envy. She brought this unhappy ending on herself by asking her magic looking glass the wrong question. Mirrors of the self are meant to show us who we are, not how we compare to others.

Today I will choose the dance of life. I will accept myself the way I am and become free to live and love.

The Twelve Dancing Princesses

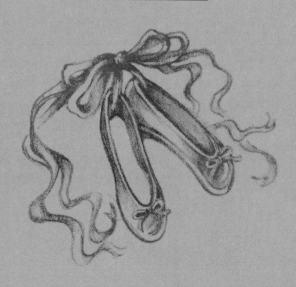

nce upon a time a poor cow herder named Michael had a dream in which a beautiful lady appeared and said, "Go to the castle of Beloeil, and you shall marry a Princess." His companions laughed at his aspirations, but he decided to follow his dream.

He traveled to the castle of the Duke of Beloeil and became a gardener's apprentice. One of Michael's duties was to make twelve flower bouquets each day and give them to the Duke's beautiful daughters. Lina, the youngest princess, was kind to the garden boy, but her sisters teased her for lowering herself to even look at him. The twelve princesses were locked into their bedroom every night, but mysteriously wore holes into the soles of their satin slippers before morning. The Duke offered to marry one of his daughters to anyone who could discover the secret.

Michael had a second dream in which he was told to cultivate two laurel trees which would aid him in his quest for the princess. He asked for the gift of invisibility so that he could discover the princesses' secret. He followed them to a lake, where they were met by twelve princes in twelve little boats. Together they crossed the lake and entered a castle. The twelve Princesses danced until they wore holes in their shoes, while a magic potion caused the princes to remember nothing but a love of dancing.

The next day, Michael added a branch from the laurel tree to Lina's bouquet. She realized he had discovered their secret and offered to pay him for his silence. He refused, and her sisters decided that he must drink the magic potion.

At the end of that night's dancing, the eldest sister gave Michael a golden cup. When he started to drink the contents, Lina cried, "Don't drink! I would rather marry a gardener." Her decision broke the spell. Lina married Michael, the princes returned to life and the princesses each chose one for a husband.

Once there lived in the village of Montignies-sur-Roc a little cow-boy, without either father or mother. His real name was Michael, but he was called the Star Gazer, because when he drove his cows over the commons to seek for pasture, he went along with his head in the air, gaping at nothing. While his companions round the fire saw nothing in the flames but everyday fancies, he dreamed that he had the happiness to marry a princess.

Dreamers are often ridiculed and seldom respected in today's production-oriented society. We tend to be uncomfortable with people who walk around with their "head in the clouds," dreaming of worlds seemingly beyond their reach. "Come down to earth with the rest of us," we're tempted to advise. "Life is hard, and the sooner you face up to it, the better for all of us!"

It's true that if we spend all our time in idle fantasies, we probably won't get very far. But if we never dare to dream, we lose many opportunities to enrich our lives. Thoughts of princesses—of worlds beyond our reach—can lighten a tedious routine and make driving the cows to pasture a little more interesting. There's nothing wrong with letting our imagination run far afield as long as we remain grounded in life's realities.

I am learning to dream without losing track of the cows and am regaining my childlike imagination.

One morning Michael ate his dinner of a piece of dry bread, and went to sleep under an oak. And while he slept he dreamt that there appeared before him a beautiful lady who said to him: "Go to the castle of Beloeil, and there you shall marry a princess." That evening the little cow-boy, who had been thinking a great deal about the advice of the lady, told his dream to the farm people. But, as was natural, they only laughed at the Star Gazer.

Some of us know what it feels like to share our dreams with people only to have them laugh at us. If we grew up in environments where we didn't "fit in," sharing our thoughts and fantasies with others may have been a risky thing to do. Talking about dream worlds to people whose attentions are captivated by life's harsh realities may provoke ridicule and scorn.

It's a relief when we find a group of people in recovery with whom we can share our dreams without exposing ourselves to contempt or shame. Finding people who understand how vulnerable we are when we reveal our thoughts and feelings helps us overcome our fear of doing so. Owning our dreams without feeling ashamed or apologetic is a sign of growing self-acceptance and recovery.

I am confident of finding a place where I can safely share my dreams with people who support me.

The next day at the same hour he went to sleep again under the same tree. The lady appeared to him a second time, and said: "Go to the castle of Beloeil, and you shall marry a princess." In the evening Michael told his friends that he had dreamed the same dream again, but they only laughed at him more than before. "Never mind," he thought to himself, "if the lady appears to me a third time, I will do as she tells me."

When inner messages begin pushing us in directions that cause others to ridicule or disdain us, we are forced to make a decision. Will we listen to people who discourage us, or will we follow our own instincts?

Sometimes we struggle for a long time before we can make a decision. We may set our dreams aside in order not to run the risk of failure. But if the voice persists, pushing us in new and unknown directions, we may eventually respond. Like Michael, we may say to ourselves, "If the lady appears to me a third time, I will do as she tells me."

We can look to others for help in evaluating our goals and visions, but we are the only ones who can make our dreams a reality. In recovery, we come to trust our own reactions again—the feelings, inner voices, intuition and physical sensations that put us in touch with our Higher Power who works for good in our lives.

I am learning to respect my feelings and reactions, knowing that my Higher Power is there to guide me.

The following day, to the great astonishment of all the village about two o'clock in the afternoon a voice was heard singing: "Raleo, raleo, How the cattle go!" It was the little cow-boy driving his herd back to the byre. The farmer began to scold him furiously, but he answered quietly, "I am going away," made his clothes into a bundle, said good-bye to all his friends, and boldly set out to seek his fortunes.

*W*hen we set out to follow our own path, we often find that it leads us away from those our friends and families are following. The people closest to us may feel angry or abandoned, thinking we are rejecting their way of life. They may worry about us, afraid that we won't find happiness on a road that is different from theirs, or that we may not survive the disappointment, should we fail. Trying to reassure them may exaggerate our own fear and provide them with opportunities to dissuade us from our chosen course of action. Politely saying good-bye and acknowledging their anxiety is a measure of our inner strength and determination.

We can be aware of other people's concerns for us without being influenced by them. We can let them know that following our own path doesn't mean that we don't care about them. Recognizing and trusting our own inner voice is the first step toward developing positive relationships with others.

I am developing the courage to follow my heart's desire and create a new path for myself.

There was great excitement through all the village, and on the top of the hill the people stood holding their sides with laughing, as they watched the Star Gazer trudging bravely along the valley with his bundle at the end of his stick. It was enough to make anyone laugh, certainly.

*L*aughter is a common response to grandiose, unrealistic dreams. To think that a cowherder could marry a princess can provoke a range of reactions, from pity to boisterous ridicule. It is our nature to believe that no one in their right mind would take such a dream seriously!

Many of us question whether our dreams are realistic, or if they are rooted in fantasy. We may be so ashamed of these aspirations that we never share them with anyone. Step Five gives us a chance to describe our dreams and discuss them with a trusted friend who will not ridicule or reject us. In the process, we often learn that it is not simply the opinions of others that prevent us from achieving our goals—it is our own insecurity. As we progress in recovery, we become more confident in our ability to follow the Star Gazer's example and trudge off bravely down the valley.

*I am learning to listen to my inner wisdom
and follow my own intuition.*

It was well known for full twenty miles round that there lived in the castle of Beloeil twelve princesses of wonderful beauty. It was whispered about that they led exactly the lives that princesses ought to lead, sleeping far into the morning, and never getting up till mid-day. They had twelve beds all in the same room, and though they were locked in by triple bolts, every morning their satin shoes were found worn into holes.

*I*t's hard to visualize how princesses could wear holes in their shoes if they go to bed at a reasonable hour and don't arise until noon the following day. We wonder what could be going on during the night to cause their shoes to be so worn by morning.

Some of us can relate to this topsy-turvy feeling, where our lives seem to be upside down. We may not have the luxury of sleeping until midday, but we might allow ourselves to settle into routines that seem to put our minds to sleep. If we are not stimulated and rewarded by our daily activities, we may have restless nights and wake up the next morning, already exhausted by the thought of another meaningless day.

In recovery, we become aware that a number of alternatives are available to us. When we are able to make better choices about how we spend our time, we experience a greater sense of purpose. When our lives are fulfilling, we sleep more peacefully.

I will stay awake and alert to the many opportunities that life has to offer me.

When they were asked what they had been doing all night, they always answered that they had been asleep. At last the Duke of Beloeil ordered a proclamation to be made that whoever could discover how his daughters wore out their shoes should choose one of them for his wife. A number of princes arrived at the castle to try their luck. They watched all night, but when the morning came they had all disappeared, and no one could tell what had become of them.

*W*hen someone asks us what we are doing to wear ourselves out, we don't always know what to tell them. Friends may try to determine what is wrong and end up being involved in whatever problem holds us in its deadly grip. Until we discover and overcome whatever is disrupting the normal course of our lives, others may also be affected by it.

In meetings we can discuss the things that are making us weary without worrying about the reactions of those present. We can release our anger and our fear, knowing that we are with people who understand our feelings. As we work the Steps, we develop a new kind of honest self-revelation that paves the way for us to have relationships in which no one has to present a false image in order to be accepted.

I am learning to be more honest with myself and others. When I am open about who I am, others are encouraged to be honest with me.

When he reached the castle, Michael went straight to the gardener and offered his services. Now it happened that the garden boy had just been sent away, and though the Star Gazer did not look very sturdy, the gardener agreed to take him. The first thing he was told was that when the princesses got up he was to present each one with a bouquet, and Michael thought that if he had nothing more unpleasant to do than that he should get on very well.

*W*hen we set out to follow a dream, the ways in which our present opportunities can help us achieve our final goals may not be immediately clear. Being hired as a garden boy if we want to marry a princess may seem far removed from what we really want. If we are following the Steps to the best of our ability, we can trust our Higher Power to lead us in the right direction.

Some of us are afraid to trust our instincts because of disappointment with our past choices. Learning to apply the principles of the program to our daily decisions helps us to make better choices. Being satisfied with meeting small challenges increases our self-esteem and gives us confidence in our ability to meet larger ones. When we learn to trust the recovery process, we can take our attention off the larger picture and begin enjoying whatever tasks we are given to do, no matter how insignificant they may seem.

I am learning to take pleasure in small achievements, knowing that they will help me obtain my final goals in due time.

Accordingly he placed himself behind the door of the princesses' room, with the twelve bouquets in a basket. He gave one to each of the sisters, and they took them without even deigning to look at the lad, except Lina the youngest, who fixed her large black eyes as soft as velvet on him, and exclaimed, "Oh, how pretty he is—our new flower boy!" The rest all burst out laughing, and the eldest pointed out that a princess ought never to lower herself by looking at a garden boy.

*A*llowing our lives to be defined only in terms of bouquets received from others limits our ability to reach our full potential. There is something uniquely satisfying about digging in the earth and cultivating our own flowers that we can't experience if we expect others to do the digging for us. When false pride—or the low self-esteem that often fuels it—takes away our connection with productive, self-supporting activity, our lives become meaningless.

Entering the program is a sign that something is drawing us toward a better life—that we are ready to examine our behavior and look for new opportunities to grow. By meeting new people and learning to love them for who they are, we correct our tendency to pretend we are princesses who should not lower ourselves by looking at a garden boy. Our lives become more meaningful when we treat others as equals and share our experience, strength and hope with them.

I can accept others as equals, knowing their talents are as important to them as mine are to me.

Now Michael knew quite well what had happened to all the princes, but notwithstanding, the beautiful eyes of the Princess Lina inspired him with a violent longing to try his fate. Unhappily he did not dare to come forward, afraid that he should only be jeered at, or even turned away from the castle on account of his impudence.

*I*f we have worked hard all our lives and felt obligated to tend the cows or hoe the garden, we may hesitate to acknowledge or enjoy the frivolous side of our nature. We are drawn to the idea of having fun—living free from cares and concerns like the princesses—but we may be afraid of losing control. If we give in to these anxieties, we may resent the tedious aspects of our lives even more and be tempted to stop working altogether!

Some of us feel unworthy like Michael and do not dare to come forward and try our fate, no matter how violent our longing may be. We convince ourselves that we will be jeered at for trying to better ourselves. When we enter recovery and start to attend twelve-step meetings, we don't have to come forward and share until we are ready. It takes time and patience to have our self-worth restored and to believe that we have a right to success and happiness.

I know that I have a right to enjoy life.
I can begin by allowing myself to
enjoy a small pleasure today.

The Star Gazer had another dream. The lady in the golden dress appeared once more, holding two young laurel trees, a little golden rake, a little golden bucket, and a silken towel. She thus addressed him: "Plant these two laurels in two large pots, rake them over with the rake, water them with the bucket, and wipe them with the towel. When they have grown, say to each of them, 'My beautiful laurel, with the golden rake I have raked you, with the golden bucket I have watered you, with the silken towel I have wiped you.' After that ask anything you choose, and the laurels will give it to you."

*W*hen we enter a twelve-step program and begin recovery, we are provided with the tools we need to cultivate and nurture the new life that stirs within us. Steps One through Three prepare the ground for us to create a healthier and more rewarding future.

We can use our Step Four and Step Ten inventories to rake the soil—sorting out the positive attitudes and behaviors that support us from the negative thoughts and feelings that do not. We can use Step Eleven to maintain conscious contact with our Higher Power and water our inner gardens, so that new ideas and solutions can grow.

By attending meetings regularly, we can gain the support and encouragement of other program members. The lessons we learn and the new relationships we develop are signs that our Higher Power is guiding us toward peace and serenity.

*It is my responsibility to work the Steps
that nurture me and give me new life.*

Michael thanked the lady in the golden dress, and when he woke he found the two laurel bushes beside him. So he carefully obeyed the orders he had been given by the lady. He said, "My lovely cherry laurel, with the golden rake I have raked thee, with the golden bucket I have watered thee, with the silken towel I have wiped thee. Teach me how to become invisible."

*B*eing invisible has its advantages. It protects us from the risk of being criticized or rejected. It helps us discover things that others might conceal if they were aware of our presence. Hiding from others also has its drawbacks. If we are afraid to show ourselves, we may do little to develop our own personalities.

Some of us begin to retreat into a world of daydreams as a poor substitute for reality. Our task in recovery is to begin moving outside of ourselves, making contact with others and developing the skills to communicate openly with them. Some of us remain invisible by paying such close attention to other people and what they want that we don't make our own needs known. Our task is to learn to express ourselves more openly.

In recovery we become more comfortable in both roles. Becoming aware of our own feelings increases our sensitivity to others. Making our presence known opens up new opportunities for relationships.

I am developing healthy new insights and cultivating positive behaviors.

153

That evening, when the princesses went upstairs to bed, he followed them barefoot, so that he might make no noise, and hid himself under one of the twelve beds, so as not to take up much room. The princesses began to open their wardrobes and boxes. They took out of them the most magnificent dresses, which they put on before their mirrors, and when they had finished, turned themselves all round to admire their appearances.

*W*hen we become familiar with our true selves through meditation, writing and exploring our dreams, we are often amazed at what we find. Instead of the drab, unimaginative person we expect to encounter, we find wardrobes full of magnificent apparel. Looking at ourselves through these new inner mirrors can be delightful, and we may turn ourselves all around like the princesses, admiring our newfound images.

If we do not become too absorbed by it, this kind of inner work can be useful to us in our recovery. Discovering the richness inside us bolsters our feelings of self-worth and helps us to overcome our shame. Gradually these images spill over into our external lives, and we begin to clothe ourselves in garments and behaviors that express our growing self-esteem. Being happy with who we are and how we look is a sign that we are becoming more comfortable with our true image.

In recovery, I can discover the beauty and delight of my inner wardrobe.

"Are you ready?" asked the eldest. "Yes," replied the other eleven in chorus, and they took their places one by one behind her. Then the eldest Princess clapped her hands three times and a trap door opened. All the princesses disappeared down a secret staircase, and Michael hastily followed them. As he was following on the steps of the Princess Lina, he carelessly trod on her dress. "There is somebody behind me," cried the Princess; "they are holding my dress." "You foolish thing," said her eldest sister, "you are always afraid of something. It is only a nail which caught you."

*S*ome of us used drugs and other substances to shut out reality and escape through trap doors into inner dream worlds. In recovery, we find other more natural ways of exploring these inner worlds. Doing so may cause us to feel uncomfortable, fearing that we might lose contact with reality.

What we find is that working the Steps in the company of others engaged in the same process helps protect us from retreating too far down the secret staircase of our fantasies. By confronting us and treading on our dresses, other members can help us to maintain our connection with the world. We gain insight into our dreams and ideas by sharing them with other program members. This keeps us on course and helps us translate our thoughts into positive action.

*If I behave like the eldest sister by trying to
ignore intrusions into my fantasies, I will
lose opportunities to engage fully
in the life around me.*

They went down, down, down, till at last they came to a passage with a door at one end, which was only fastened with a latch. The eldest Princess opened it, and they found themselves immediately in a lovely little wood, where the leaves were spangled with drops of silver which shone in the brilliant light of the moon. They next crossed another wood where the leaves were sprinkled with gold, and after that another still, where the leaves glittered with diamonds.

*I*n the process of recovery we encounter forgotten resources—inner woods whose sparkling leaves reflect the depth of our spirit. We discover that our lives are not as tarnished as we thought they were and that the silver still shines brightly on our inner trees. With the Twelve Steps we can access these treasures of insight and intuition and gain knowledge as valuable and durable as gold. Finally, we reach the most brilliant and ageless jewel of all—our Higher Power.

Some of us have difficulty with the concept of a power greater than ourselves. It helps to remember that we are meant to explore our own understanding of a Higher Power and that our comprehension grows and changes in the course of recovery. We may dig deep within ourselves before we find our Higher Power, but the door is never locked. It is only fastened with a latch, which we are free to open at will.

Contact with my Higher Power helps to take away my fear and renews my sparkling spirit.

At last the Star Gazer perceived a large lake, and on the shores of the lake twelve little boats with awnings, in which were seated twelve princes, who, grasping their oars, awaited the princesses. Each princess entered one of the boats, and Michael slipped into that which held the youngest. The boats glided along rapidly, but Lina's, from being heavier, was always behind the rest. "We never went so slowly before," said the Princess; "what can be the reason?" "I don't know," answered the Prince. "I assure you I am rowing as hard as I can."

*W*e all encounter points in our recovery when the journey becomes tedious and our progress seems to stop. When we're rowing as hard as we can and getting nowhere, it helps to review what is actually happening. Each of us grows and changes at our own pace. Periods of seeming inactivity when we think nothing is happening are a normal part of the process.

Sometimes we allow ourselves to become bogged down by external activities and needless concerns. Taking time out for some fun or quiet meditation can give us new energy and restore our spirit. Taking a daily inventory and examining our behaviors in Step Ten helps us maintain a balance between the time we give to ourselves and the time we give to others.

I can balance my responsibilities to myself and others by using Step Ten to monitor my progress toward my goals.

On the other side of the lake the garden boy saw a beautiful castle splendidly illuminated, whence came the lively music of fiddles, kettle-drums, and trumpets. In a moment they touched land, and the company jumped out of the boats; and the princes, after having securely fastened their barques, gave their arms to the princesses and conducted them to the castle.

*T*here is a difference between getting in touch with our feelings and deepest desires and losing ourselves in a world of fantasy. Our imagination can be of immense value. It can inspire us, make our lives richer and help us find creative and constructive solutions to life's challenges. But if we spend all our time in fantasy lands, we only hear the fiddles, kettle-drums and trumpets in the castles of our minds.

The Steps help us discover the music in the real world. Attending meetings exposes us to music other than our own. Our ideas are enriched when we can be silent and listen to the experiences of others. When we find safe places to share our dreams with other people, we gain new insight and confidence which helps to make them a reality.

By using the Twelve Steps in my life, I can blend the music of my dreams and the rhythm of reality into a wonderful harmony.

The poor boy envied those handsome young men with whom the little Princess with the velvet eyes danced so gracefully, but he did not know how little reason he had to be jealous of them. The young men were really the princes who, to the number of fifty at least, had tried to steal the princesses' secret. The princesses had made them drink something of a philtre, which froze the heart and left nothing but the love of dancing.

*M*any of us are familiar with the "dancing-as-fast-as-I-can" style of living. Some of us become involved in it by means of a philtre—some combination of drugs or alcohol that froze our hearts and left us with nothing but the love of dancing. Others were driven by low self-esteem or a lack of social skills into compulsive behaviors or activities that temporarily hid discomfort but left us feeling empty when the dance was over.

When there is nothing left in our hearts but love for one thing, we become blind to everything else and severely limit our potential. In recovery, our hearts open and take in more of life. We become comfortable with laughter and tears, with work and play, and with ourselves and others. Surrendering our endless struggle and learning to enjoy the quiet is the first step in restoring balance to our lives.

I can ask my Higher Power to center me when I find myself compelled to dance as fast as I can.

They danced on till the shoes of the princesses were worn into holes. When the cock crowed the third time the fiddles stopped, and a delicious supper was served. After supper, the dancers all went back to their boats. As a proof of what he had seen, the boy broke a small branch from the tree in the last wood. Lina turned. "What was that noise?" she said. "It was nothing," replied her eldest sister; "it was only the screech of a barn-owl."

When our shoes are full of holes and our mad dance slows to a stop, we have worn out the soles that protect us from injury. When we "hit bottom," we are often bankrupt—spiritually, emotionally, physically and financially. We then must leave our addictive worlds behind and return to reality.

We may disregard the sound of breaking branches in our lives and tell ourselves that we have the situation under control. "It was nothing," we say as we rest, preparing for the next dance. Some of us have to wear out pair after pair of shoes before we are willing to commit ourselves to a recovery program and take Step One. Although this can be a difficult transition for us, when we trust in the power of the Twelve Steps, we have unlimited resources available to help us.

When I feel drawn to participate in endless dances of madness, I will remember Step One and acknowledge my powerlessness.

That day, when he made up the bouquets, Michael hid the branch with the silver drops in the nosegay intended for the youngest Princess. When Lina discovered it she was much surprised. However, she said nothing to her sisters, but as she met the boy by accident while she was walking under the shade of the elms, she suddenly stopped as if to speak to him; then, altering her mind, went on her way.

*I*f we allow wishful thinking to guide us without taking steps to achieve our dreams, we may find ourselves acting as if we've achieved them when we haven't. In recovery we learn to recognize and appreciate the signals that warn us we are losing touch with reality. Like the subtle messages Michael gave to Lina when he put the silver-coated leaves in her nosegay, we receive signs from our Higher Power that we are in trouble. We become uncomfortable with the idea of spending money before we've earned it, behaving as if we're in charge when we're not or pretending to be experts at things about which we know very little.

We may resist believing these messages when we first hear them, fearful that they'll take away the temporary relief that short-sighted solutions often give us. But, having faith that our Higher Power will help us find constructive long-term answers to our problems gives us the courage to do what it takes to achieve them.

I will trust my Higher Power's warnings about behavior that is not beneficial to me.

The twelve sisters went again to the ball, and the Star Gazer again crossed the lake in Lina's boat. The Prince complained that the boat seemed very heavy. "It is the heat," replied the Princess. "I, too, have been feeling very warm." During the ball she looked everywhere for the gardener's boy, but she never saw him. As they came back, Michael gathered a branch from the wood with the gold-spangled leaves, and now it was the eldest Princess who heard the noise that it made in breaking. "It is nothing," said Lina; "only the cry of the owl which roosts in the turrets of the castle."

*E*ach day we spend in recovery we become a little more in tune with reality. We become more aware of the signals—the breaking branches our Higher Power sends to warn us of our ineffective behaviors. We may not always be happy with what is going on around us, but we recognize the value of giving up unrealistic expectations and working toward long-term rewards.

Discovering the richness of life is not a matter of abandoning our dreams, but of harnessing them. Using our imagination and feelings helps us find creative ways of achieving our highest aspirations. We can use Steps Six and Seven to let go of the fear that prevents us from making our dreams become a reality. We can also use them to remove the desire for instant gratification that pulls us away from reality into a fantasy world.

I can put my dreams to good use today without giving my life away in the process.

As soon as she got up she found the branch in her bouquet. When the sisters went down she stayed a little behind and said to the cow-boy: "Where does this branch come from?" "Your Royal Highness knows well enough," answered Michael. "So you have followed us?" "Yes, Princess." "How did you manage it?" "I hid myself," replied the Star Gazer. The Princess said: "You know our secret—keep it." And she flung the boy a purse of gold. "I do not sell my silence," answered Michael, and he went away without picking up the purse.

Some of us were fortunate to have people around us who refused to ignore the signs that we were in trouble. They helped us to recognize our problems and realize the price that we were paying to maintain our destructive behaviors. We can be grateful to them for refusing to remain silent and for helping us find a recovery program. Although it may seem easier to be quiet and turn a blind eye to self-destructive behaviors, it only traps us in more vicious cycles of despair. Selling our silence may temporarily keep us from painful confrontation with ourselves or others but it buys an uneasy peace.

Today we can count on finding people like Michael when we attend twelve-step meetings. They may recognize the emergence of old attitudes and behaviors even before we do. Although we are not always comfortable with their perceptive abilities, their insights help make us more aware of our actions.

I have the right to speak out when it's necessary. Selling my silence hurts both me and others.

For three nights Lina neither saw nor heard anything extraordinary; on the fourth she heard a rustling among the diamond-spangled leaves of the wood. That day there was a branch of the trees in her bouquet. She took the Star Gazer aside, and said to him in a harsh voice: "You know what price my father has promised to pay for our secret?" "I know, Princess," answered Michael. "Don't you mean to tell him?" "That is not my intention."

*W*itnessing someone else's destructive behavior does not mean we must confront that person immediately. Sometimes it is better just to let them know that we are aware of the situation. Choosing to wait until it becomes clear whether or not we need to take further action is not a sign of weakness. It is an acknowledgment that we can't make other people's choices for them. We can help them to open their eyes, but we cannot force them to see.

Talking to other program members can help us decide what action to take when people we love get into serious trouble. As we work through Steps Eight and Nine we begin to gain some insight into how our behavior affects other people. Eventually, as we begin to rely more heavily on our own instincts, applying the principles of the program to our relationships becomes second-nature.

There are times to speak out and times to remain silent. I can ask my Higher Power for help when I'm not sure which is best.

Lina's sisters had seen her talking to the little garden boy, and jeered at her for it. "What prevents your marrying him?" asked the eldest. You could live in a cottage at the end of the park, and help your husband draw up water from the well, and when we get up you could bring us our bouquets." The Princess was very angry, and when the Star Gazer presented her bouquet, she received it in a disdainful manner. Michael behaved most respectfully. He never raised his eyes to her, but nearly all day she felt him at her side without ever seeing him.

Many of us know the pain associated with sarcastic remarks that hurt our pride. We may become so accustomed to sarcasm that we fail to notice the devastating effect it has on us and everyone around us.

Learning to detach from the sarcastic remarks of others and not be offended by them takes time. If we are accustomed to defending ourselves against insulting remarks, treating others with respect despite their disdain is difficult. When we can do so, people can no longer provoke or manipulate us with their sarcastic behavior. Then it becomes easier to make choices based on our own set of values and hold fast to them despite the ridicule of others.

*I can remove myself from the presence
of people whose remarks are abusive
without returning their scorn.*

One day she made up her mind to tell everything to her eldest sister. "What!" said she, "this rogue knows our secret, and you never told me! I must lose no time in getting rid of him." "But how?" "Why, by having him taken to the tower with the dungeons, of course." For this was the way that in old times beautiful princesses got rid of people who knew too much. But the astonishing part of it was that the youngest sister did not seem at all to relish this method of stopping the mouth of the gardener's boy, who, after all, had said nothing to their father.

Repressing the inner voices that warn us of the danger of negative behaviors supports our denial system. Banishing people who know too much to the dungeon enables these self-destructive behaviors to thrive and flourish.

When we become conscious of our addictions or compulsive behavior patterns, they begin to have less influence on us. When we become uncomfortable with the idea of silencing our warning voices, like the youngest princess, we come closer to recognizing how denial has protected us from reality. Having the courage to acknowledge and address our behavior moves us further along the road to recovery.

I will respect the voices that call attention to my compulsive thoughts or behaviors. Becoming conscious of them is the first step in releasing them.

Then the youngest sister declared that if they laid a finger on the little garden boy, she would go and tell their father the secret of the holes in their shoes. At last it was decided that Michael should be put to the test; that they would take him to the ball, and at supper would give him the philtre which was to enchant him like the rest. They sent for the Star Gazer, and gave him the order they had agreed upon. He answered: "I will obey." He had made up his mind to drink of the philtre, and sacrifice himself to the happiness of her he loved.

*I*f we continue to obey our negative inner voices, we eventually reach a crisis point. Some of us continue to engage in behavior that provides temporary relief but isolates us from reality. Others come to terms with the fact that we are wearing out our shoes. When we commit to a program of recovery, we begin the process of restoring our connection with the real world.

These decisions often require that we be put to the test like the Star Gazer was. If we remain enchanted by our addictions, we continue to be left with nothing but the love of dancing. If we choose to return to the real world and sacrifice our short-term fixes for the happiness of a new beginning, we gain an opportunity to participate in the richness of life.

> *I am grateful for a new beginning*
> *and an opportunity to partici-*
> *pate in the richness of life.*

MAY

27

Not wishing to cut a poor figure at the ball by the side of the other dancers, he went to the laurels, and said "My lovely rose laurel, with the golden rake I have raked thee, with the golden bucket I have watered thee, with a silken towel I have dried thee. Dress me like a prince." Michael found himself in a moment clothed in velvet. Thus dressed, he presented himself that evening before the Duke of Beloeil, and obtained leave to try and discover his daughters' secret. He looked so distinguished that hardly anyone would have known who he was.

Many of us have trouble directly expressing our desires. We feel ashamed of saying, "I'm lonely," or "I'm unhappy, I want someone to cheer me up," or "I'm attracted to you." We're afraid these feelings mean there's something wrong with us—that people will look down on us if they find out what we're really thinking or what we really want.

When we can express our needs honestly, we develop the behaviors and attitudes that help us attain our goals. "I'd like to have a try at that," we say, presenting ourselves in clothes appropriate to the situation. We learn to do the footwork and leave the results to our Higher Power, knowing we have done our best to care for the tree of life we've been given.

I am learning to be open about what I want and am developing new behaviors that support my desires.

The twelve princesses went upstairs to bed. Michael followed them, and waited behind the open door till they gave the signal for departure. At last the time came for him to dance with the little Princess. When he was taking her back to her place she said to him: "Here you are at the summit of your wishes: you are being treated like a prince." "Don't be afraid," replied the Star Gazer gently. "You shall never be a gardener's wife."

We are not strangers to mockery, although we may attempt to camouflage the aspects of ourselves that we believe others would ridicule. We may become compulsive over-achievers to prove the chiding voices wrong. Even when we achieve princely feats, the mocking voices may continue in our own heads: "Here you are at the summit of your wishes: You are being treated like a prince." Despite whatever outer garments of success we accumulate, no matter how gracefully we have learned to dance, we still fail to measure up to our own grossly inflated expectations.

In recovery, we discover the anxieties that lie behind mocking statements. If we are wary of our achievements or feel insecure about our lives, we may continue to put ourselves down long after others have stopped. When we risk opening ourselves up to the pleasures life offers, we can begin to accept and enjoy our successes. We will not be ashamed, like Michael, of making a princess a gardener's wife.

*If I am still hiding my anxieties behind
a mask of mockery, I can ask for
help in confronting my fears.*

At last the eldest sister made a sign, and one of the pages brought in a large golden cup. He cast a lingering glance at the little Princess, and without hesitation lifted the cup. "Don't drink!" suddenly cried out the little Princess; "I would rather marry a gardener." And she burst into tears. Michael flung the contents of the cup behind him, sprang over the table, and fell at Lina's feet. Each of the princesses chose a husband. The charm was broken.

Making a decision to follow the gardener and return to reality breaks the spell that traps us in self-destructive behaviors. Leaving our fantasy world is not easy. It requires us to stop intellectualizing and get in touch with our feelings again. We have to quit pretending that things are okay when they're not, or that we have unlimited supplies of money when we don't. We must acknowledge the damage we do to ourselves when we stay in abusive relationships while pretending to love and be loved.

There is pain involved when we move away from denial and face reality for the first time, but there is also joy and relief. Working the Steps helps ease our pain and gives us a roadmap with which to find our way to a fulfilling life.

*Reciting the first three Steps each day keeps
me in touch with the reality of my life and
my commitment to a Higher Power.*

They went straight to the room of the Duke of Beloeil, who had just awoke. Michael held in his hand the golden cup and he revealed the secret of the holes in the shoes. "Choose, then," said the Duke, "whichever you prefer." "My choice is already made," replied the garden boy, and he offered his hand to the youngest Princess, who blushed and lowered her eyes.

*W*hen we are comfortable with all aspects of our-selves, our options increase and decision-making be-comes easier. If we have learned to trust in a Higher Power, we can make decisions confidently, knowing that whatever happens will turn out for the best.

When we take advantage of the Steps, we are less inclined to make mistakes for which we are sorry. We know that we can use Step Eight and Step Nine to become aware of our errors and make amends where necessary.

Confidently making our own choices and willingly giving others the freedom to make theirs is a sign that we have taken Step Twelve. We have experienced the spiritual awakening promised at the end of the Steps and have become responsible for our own lives. We are now ready to build healthy relationships in which others are free to take responsibility for themselves.

***Working the Steps brings balance
and wholeness to my life.***

Before the marriage ceremony the Princess insisted that her lover should tell her how he came to discover the secret. So he showed her the two laurels which had helped him, and she, like a prudent girl, thinking they gave him too much advantage over his wife, cut them off at the root and threw them in the fire. And this is why the country girls go about singing: "Nous n'irons plus au bois, Les lauriers sont coupes," [We will no longer go into the woods; the laurels are cut] and dancing in summer by the light of the moon.

*W*e feel invaded when someone gains access to our private space without our permission—when people find out things about us we don't want them to know or when they seem to know more about us than we know about ourselves. We may protect ourselves as best we can by trying to cut down whatever laurel trees appear to give them this advantage over us.

Until we come to understand that our Higher Power is "a part of us" and not "apart from us," this fear of invasion may prevent us from taking Step Three. When we begin to let our Higher Power direct our lives and discover that this strengthens our identity, we no longer feel so vulnerable to being taken over by other people. We can let go of our efforts to direct or dominate them and allow their own Higher Power to work in their lives.

> *Turning my life and will over to a Higher Power strengthens my identity and helps me let go of my need to control others.*

The Emperor's New Clothes

here once was an emperor who was so fond of new clothes that he spent most of his time in his wardrobe instead of the council-chamber. One day, two visiting weavers announced that they could manufacture the most beautiful cloth imaginable. Garments made from this fabric would be invisible to anyone who was not fit for his office or who was unpardonably stupid. The emperor gave them a large sum of money and commanded them to begin work immediately.

After they began weaving, the emperor sent an honored minister to judge the quality of the cloth for him. Although the minister could not see anything, he praised the quality of the material, not wanting anyone to know what he was really thinking. A second statesman sent by the emperor saw no more than the first, but he also tried to protect himself by complimenting the weavers' skill. When the emperor finally decided to pay them a visit and view their progress, he was frightened by his inability to see anything on the looms. He granted the cloth his gracious approval, lest the others should believe he was unfit for his office. He also agreed to wear his splendid new clothing in an upcoming royal procession.

On the day of the parade, the weavers went through the motions of dressing the emperor in his new clothes. When they were finished, his chamberlains put their hands to the floor as if they were lifting the train, and they began the procession. Everyone in the crowd praised the magnificence of the fabric until a small child said, "But he has nothing on." Then the people began to whisper this message to one another. "But he has nothing on!" the crowd called out at last, and it seemed to the Emperor that they were right. "I must go on with the procession now," he thought to himself, and his chamberlains walked along behind him, holding up the train which was not there.

Many years ago there lived an Emperor who was so fond of new clothes that he spent all his money on them in order to be beautifully dressed. He had a coat for every hour of the day; and just as they say of a king, "He is in the council-chamber," they always said of him: "The Emperor is in the wardrobe."

Clothes can be a wonderful way to express our personality and mood. Wearing bright colors can help to cheer us on a rainy day, while choosing drab colors instead may be a sign that we feel as dreary as the weather. Taking off a business suit and putting on something more casual usually signals a change of mood or activity. But changing clothes every hour is a sign that something's amiss. Becoming overly concerned with our appearance is likely to reflect more than a change in weather, mood or activity. It usually indicates that we are unsure of our true identity.

Image can be important—few of us would advocate parading through the streets naked, exposing ourselves to the scrutiny of those around us. Learning how to present ourselves appropriately in various situations helps us to achieve our goals. Changing our appearance to distract from our imperfections or meet someone else's expectations is futile and self-defeating. We lose touch with ourselves and others when we put appearances ahead of reality.

Do I choose clothes to present who I am or to hide my imperfections? Today I will wear clothes that appeal to me.

One day two impostors arrived who gave themselves out as weavers, and said that they knew how to manufacture the most beautiful cloth imaginable. Clothes which were made of the stuff possessed this wonderful property: that they were invisible to anyone who was not fit for his office, or who was unpardonably stupid.

*W*hen we abdicate the council-chamber for the wardrobe—when we stop communicating honestly with others and devote our energies to contriving false facades—we can easily fall prey to unrealistic promises. If we do not trust our intelligence and intuition, we become vulnerable to the wiles of dishonest people. We become concerned with our self-worth and competence. If we cannot trust our senses, how can we be fit for office? If events in our lives confuse us, how can we be wise?

We cannot always distinguish truth from fiction. Being disappointed by people we trust and enchanted by fantasies that appear to hold great promise is a part of life. Being afraid to trust our own good judgment makes us even more likely to be misled. Applying the principles of the program to our lives restores our faith in our ability to make intelligent and sensitive decisions. When we stop trying to hide our inadequacies under beautiful robes woven by deceivers, we prepare the way for strengthening our decision-making abilities.

I am learning to trust my inner wisdom. Today I will be confident and secure in my own strengths.

JUNE

3

"Those must indeed be splendid clothes," thought the Emperor. "If I had them on I could find out which men in my kingdom are unfit for the offices they hold; I could distinguish the wise from the stupid! Yes, this cloth must be woven for me at once." And he gave both the impostors much money, so that they might begin their work.

When we pay attention to developing our own intuition and intelligence, we don't need any powerful magic to separate the wise from the stupid. If we have confidence in our judgment and pay attention to messages from our Higher Power, we become less vulnerable to imposters.

Sometimes we stifle our intuition by refusing to acknowledge it. If we're involved in a situation that makes us uneasy, it may seem easier to turn our warning signals off than to confront them directly. Because many of our perceptions are affected by past experiences, we may react negatively to things that remind us of something that was painful for us. We can use Step Four to obtain a more realistic picture by identifying old fears and resentments that prevent us from distinguishing between the present and the past. Although others can help us examine our perceptions and experiences, we hold the threads of reality in our own hands.

I will pay attention to my intuition today, knowing that it is a message from my Higher Power.

They placed two weaving-looms, and began to do as if they were working, but they had not the least thing on the looms. They also demanded the finest silk and the best gold, which they put in their pockets, and worked at the empty looms till late into the night.

As newcomers to the program, many of us may have problems being honest with ourselves and others because we're frightened of what working the Steps might reveal about us. Being afraid to get to the root of our problem causes us to work furiously on empty looms like the weavers. We may seem to be working as hard as we can to put our lives back together, but our activity may only serve as a smokescreen, obscuring the reality of our buried pain and anger. We may carry the finest silk and best gold away from meetings in the form of experience, strength and hope that others share with us. But until we have the courage to be truly honest with ourselves, our looms will remain empty.

For many of us Step Three—turning our lives over to the care of our Higher Power—is the key to honesty. When we begin to see that doing the footwork and turning over the results are effective, we discover that the threads with which we weave the fabric of our lives are strong and beautiful.

I can weave with actual threads today. I don't have to cover up what I believe to be my defects with a smokescreen of activity.

J
U
N
E

5

"I should like very much to know how far they have got on with the cloth," thought the Emperor. He certainly believed that he had nothing to fear for himself, but he wanted first to send somebody else in order to see how he stood with regard to his office. Everybody in the whole town knew what a wonderful power the cloth had, and they were all curious to see how bad or how stupid their neighbour was.

Many of us have a special ability to see the weak points in others more clearly than we see our own. We go through life being uncertain about standards of normal behavior, constantly agonizing over whether or not we meet the criteria. Or, we may clearly understand what is proper behavior and what isn't, but still find it difficult to believe that we measure up. It quiets our anxieties when we discover that someone else isn't as good or as wise as we'd thought they were.

When we begin feeling better about ourselves, we don't have to take other peoples' inventories—we can leave that responsibility to them. Regaining our self-worth relieves us of the burden of constantly comparing everything and everybody. Letting go of our critical views frees us to be who we are and allows others to be themselves. Life is easier and a lot more fun when we surround ourselves with companions instead of competitors.

I do not need to tear others down to make myself feel better. Building my self-worth frees me to pursue enjoyable activities.

"I will send my old and honoured minister to the weavers," thought the Emperor. "He can judge best what the cloth is like, for he has intellect, and no one understands his office better than he." The good old minister went into the hall where the two impostors sat working at the empty weaving-looms. "Dear me!" thought the old minister, opening his eyes wide, "I can see nothing!" But he did not say so.

Keeping quiet when we don't really see things the way other people do has its advantages. We don't risk being ridiculed, ignored or rejected. If we suffer from low self-esteem, holding our tongues may seem the best way to protect our already fragile feelings. Often it appears that we have much more to lose than to gain by voicing our opinion.

When we do not express ourselves, we risk losing touch with our perceptions and begin to value other people's opinions more than we value our own. Eventually, we may even distrust our own judgment. Like the Emperor who relied upon his honored minister, we become dependent on outside authorities to make decisions for us about what is good or bad, or right or wrong. When we do this, we set the stage for a vicious cycle of distortion and denial in our lives.

When I speak honestly about my perceptions, I can begin to rebuild confidence in my own judgment.

"Dear, dear!" thought he, "can I be stupid? Can I be not fit for my office? No, I must certainly not say that I cannot see the cloth." "Have you nothing to say about it?" asked one of the men who was weaving. "Oh, it is lovely, most lovely!" answered the old minister, looking through his spectacles. "I will tell the Emperor that it pleases me very much."

*A*ll the insight, intellect and intuition in the world cannot help us if we allow fear to rule our lives. Wisdom is useless if we're afraid to speak the truth as we see it. Openly voicing our thoughts and perceptions is constructive; it increases our knowledge and helps us to uncover distortions in our views of reality. Keeping quiet, like the minister did, hinders our development and sets the stage for deceitful living.

One of the dangers in being dishonest is that we may eventually believe our own lies. Being unable to separate the real from the unreal makes us question whether or not we are even fit for office and capable of doing the job properly. We can use Step Five to help us acknowledge and change our self-defeating behaviors. Relief comes when we are able to shed the burden of guilt and shame we have carried with us for so long. When we become truthful with ourselves and others, we begin to discover our many strengths.

*Faith restores my ability to be honest.
Lying is only an expression of old
fear, and a way to disguise
my true feelings.*

The Emperor soon sent another worthy statesman to see how the weaving was getting on, and whether the cloth would soon be finished. It was the same with him as the first one; he looked and looked, but because there was nothing on the empty loom he could see nothing. "Stupid I am not!" thought the man, "so it must be my good office for which I am not fitted. It is strange, certainly, but no one must be allowed to notice it."

*I*t's not always easy to maintain our integrity if people we trust see things differently than we do. We look carefully, trying to see things their way, puzzling and fretting over what could be wrong with us. We sometimes conclude that, if intelligence isn't the problem, it may be our aptitude—that perhaps we're not fitted for the office we hold.

We may present a false image to the world by disguising our insecurities with a flashy external showcase: awards, promotions, fine homes, attractive spouses or new cars. We refuse to address our underlying anxieties, fearful that pulling any little thread will unravel the entire fabric that hides our low self-worth. Step Two—coming to believe in a power greater than ourselves—gives us the faith to begin tracing the lost inner threads of our lives. Our fear lessens as we discover that these threads lead us to an unending source of strength and renewal at the center of our being.

As I begin to see the extent of my own self-rejection, I recognize that finding a Higher Power can restore my self-worth.

J
U
N
E

9

Now the Emperor wanted to see it himself while it was still on the loom. With a great crowd of select followers, he went to the impostors, who were weaving with all their might, but without fibre or thread. "Is it not splendid!" said the old statesmen who had already been there. And then they pointed to the empty loom, for they believed that the others could see the cloth quite well.

*I*f we repeatedly discount our own perceptions, we soon believe that we are the ones with the faulty eyesight. When we allow others to determine reality for us, we lose touch with our own inner vision and truth. Sometimes we reinforce the charade by telling others that everything is fine and that things are splendid when that is far from the truth. We can also perpetuate these unhealthy patterns by continuing to remain silent, pretending that nothing is wrong.

We can't control other people's perceptions or behavior, but we can speak honestly about how we comprehend a situation. Being in a twelve-step program and attending meetings regularly helps us to correct our own distorted vision through sharing with others. There, we can safely discuss our viewpoint with people who have no vested interest in helping us weave false stories from artificial threads.

I will trust my own perceptions and stop relying on others to interpret reality for me.

"What!" thought the Emperor. "I can see nothing! This is indeed horrible! Am I stupid? Am I not fit to be Emperor? That would be the most dreadful thing that could happen to me!" "Oh, it is very beautiful!" he said. "It has my gracious approval." And then he nodded pleasantly and examined the empty loom, for he would not say that he could see nothing.

*B*eing thought of as inadequate is often one of our biggest fears. Like the Emperor, we may worry that if people know what we're really like they will surely know that we are unfit for office. We are often afraid that others will find out that we're actually not in charge of our lives—that things aren't as much under control as they appear to be. Sometimes we cannot even identify the fears that cause us to hide our feelings of inadequacy behind external achievements. We go from one compulsive activity to another, wondering why we are so driven to succeed, or why we tend to drop out and not even try.

When taking our inventory in Step Four, we discover that many of our fears and inadequacies have, in fact, no basis in reality—that they are but a remnant of our past. We can identify some of the factors that caused us to develop our distorted views of life. When we admit these behaviors in Step Five, we free ourselves from the tangled threads of deceit that we have woven into our lives.

I am making a sincere effort to disclose my true self to others. Exposing my fears to people who can admit their concerns helps to set me free.

His whole court round him looked and looked, and saw no more than the others; but they said like the Emperor, "Oh! It is beautiful!" And they advised him to wear these new and magnificent clothes for the first time at the great procession which was soon to take place.

*A*ttempting to protect ourselves or others by denying the true nature of things has a snowball effect. Like the Emperor, we set the stage for our embarrassment and failure. We may start out innocently by saying, "That doesn't seem quite right to me, but I guess he knows what he's doing." It becomes more serious when we deny reality and say, "It's not your fault things got so messed up. They just didn't understand what you were trying to do." Meanwhile, whatever we're protecting—violence, addiction or compulsive behavior—continues to grow unchecked.

We can break this destructive cycle by listening whenever we hear a small inner voice that says: "Wait! There's something wrong here." Respecting our warning signals as being messages from our Higher Power is the first step. The second step is to discuss our doubts with someone who understands. Examining our uncertainties strengthens our ability to make wise choices in our lives. When we ignore our inner voice, we may find ourselves in the midst of a great procession of false fronts and phony facades that we've created to protect ourselves from the truth.

Today I will stop rationalizing other people's behavior to protect myself from hearing the truth.

"Will it please your Majesty graciously to take off your clothes," said the impostors. "Then we will put on the new clothes, here before the mirror." The Emperor took off all his clothes, and the impostors placed themselves before him as if they were putting on each part of his new clothes, and the Emperor turned and bent himself in front of the mirror. "How beautifully they fit! How well they sit!" said everybody. "What material! What colours! It is a gorgeous suit!"

*P*utting on clothes that other people admire instead of those that we prefer is at the heart of many of our problems. Rather than trust our own thoughts and feelings, we rely on what others tell us. We allow ourselves to be controlled by impostors—the fraudulent identities we've adopted—as a way to prevent anyone from seeing the naked and vulnerable child within us. Eventually, these false facades isolate us from ourselves and others.

If we do not present ourselves truthfully, how can we trust the reactions of others? Faith in our Higher Power gives us the courage to be ourselves. When we become willing to give up the charade, we improve our chances that others will see us as we really are. Being able to accept and believe in the compliments we receive from others is one of the joys of recovery.

I will trust my own perceptions today and not rely on others to tell me how I look.

"They are waiting outside with the canopy which your Majesty is wont to have borne over you in the procession," announced the Master of Ceremonies. "Look, I am ready," said the Emperor. "Doesn't it sit well!" And he turned himself again to the mirror to see if his finery was on all right. The chamberlains who were to carry the train put their hands near the floor as if they were lifting up the train; they would not have it noticed that they could see nothing.

*I*t's difficult to imagine the depth of the Emperor's denial, when he could look in the mirror and actually convince himself that his finery was sitting well. Each time we close our eyes to what is really in front of us, we lose a little more faith in our perceptions and become more dependent on others to bolster our self-respect. When people around us are caught up in the same game, we often enter a fantasy world in which everyone acts as if things are the way they want them to be rather than the way they really are.

When we live in a fantasy world, we create an image of ourselves which may bear little resemblance to reality, and it can seriously affect the direction of our lives. We may suppress our natural traits and work at developing others that are compatible with our desired image. Working the Steps helps us to pull out the threads that unraveled in the course of our development and reweave them into a healthy and nurturing pattern of life.

> *I will stop displaying false finery and remember that I don't have to pretend that everything is "fine" when it isn't.*

So the Emperor went along in the procession under the splendid canopy, and all the people in the streets and at the windows said, "How matchless are the Emperor's new clothes!" No one wished it to be noticed that he could see nothing. None of the Emperor's clothes had met with such approval as these had.

*W*hen we pretend to see something that isn't really there and others pretend to see it too—whether out of fear or courtesy—everyone involved becomes trapped in an endless cycle of deception. The same thing happens when we pretend not to see what's actually going on around us. Everyone loses in these meaningless rounds of activity that are designed to cover up things that are too threatening to be confronted openly.

Usually the issue has its roots in fear—the fear that we'll be rejected if anyone discovers our true personalities—that we'll never find the love and security we desire if we reveal our true natures. We break the cycle of deception when we stop depending on other people to boost our self-esteem. We build a sense of our own well-being by remaining true to our own vision. Step Three—turning our will and our lives over to the care of a Higher Power—helps us to overcome our fear and find our own way.

*I do not need to pretend to be someone I'm not
in order to gain approval from others.
Self-respect comes from remaining
true to my own vision.*

J
U
N
E

15

"But he has nothing on!" said a little child at last, and each one whispered to his neighbour what the innocent child had said. "But he has nothing on!" the whole of the people called out at last. This struck the Emperor, for it seemed to him as if they were right; but he thought to himself, "I must go on with the procession now." And the chamberlains walked along still more uprightly, holding up the train which was not there at all.

Many of us remain caught in endless false processions because of an inflated sense of importance and responsibility. We believe that if we don't continue to maintain the illusion that we are in control, other people will suffer by falling into the same fear and insecurity we are trying so desperately to avoid. This kind of thinking places us in the same position as the Emperor, who ignored the voice of the honest child.

When we finally hear the message, we are on the threshold of taking the first step and recognizing that we have problems. Step One carries a message of hope. By acknowledging the dilemma, we prepare the way for finding a solution. Each of us has a choice: to accept reality or continue our allegiance to illusion. We can choose to follow the example of the Emperor and remain in denial, or take the lead of the innocent child and look at reality.

Taking responsibility for my problems is a step toward breaking their hold over me. Admitting my powerlessness is a sign that there is hope.

The Ugly Duckling

THE UGLY DUCKLING

here once was a mother duck who became concerned when the largest egg of her brood finally hatched. The young duckling that tumbled out was large and ungainly—different than his brothers and sisters. The mother thought he was awfully big for his age and didn't look like any of the others.

The little duckling swam well. Noticing the power of his legs and the straightness of his neck, his mother decided that he was actually quite handsome. However, the other birds in the yard called him ugly, pecking at him and teasing him without mercy until he ran away in grief and despair.

Life did not instantly improve for the young misfit. He tried living with a cat and a hen, who thought laying eggs and purring were essential for success. He continued his journey, searching for a sign that he truly belonged somewhere, until one day he ended up desperate and alone on a frozen lake in the middle of winter.

The duckling's efforts to find a place where he could be loved and accepted failed. Each new experience only confirmed his ugliness. The hardship and suffering the duckling experienced were horrible. When spring came, his wings were powerful enough to carry him out of the dismal swamp to beautiful gardens he never dreamed existed.

One day the duckling alighted on a lake and admired a flock of swans. He had seen these birds before, and had not known what they were, but had been drawn to them. Out of his loneliness, he turned to them in despair, preferring their rejection to the isolation and suffering of the only other world he knew. When they noticed him, the swans came near. He bent his head in shame and saw his own reflection for the first time. He, too, was a beautiful swan.

"Leave him alone!" the mother duck said fiercely. "He was not troubling you." "No, but he's big and he doesn't look like us," replied the duck who had bitten him. "That's enough reason to beat him."

*B*efore we become fully secure with our own identities, the ways in which we compare ourselves to others can be painful and confusing. Believing that differences alone somehow make us unworthy, we do our utmost to blend in with our peers and caretakers. We cater to the needs of others to avoid rejection or to get the approval we desperately require. This tends to lower our self-esteem and deepen our negative feelings about ourselves.

Having the courage to discover our true identities and what we are seeking in life lessens our tendency to put other people's values ahead of our own. The fearless moral inventory of ourselves suggested in Step Four helps us discover the roots of our low self-esteem. By understanding how old beliefs and images caused our present unhappiness, we can move beyond the ducks that bit us and find peace and joy in our lives. We can also respect and value the individuality of others when we let go of our expectations of how they should perform.

*I am learning to appreciate my unique-
ness. Life would lose its richness
if we were all the same.*

"What handsome children!" added the old duck who ruled the fowlyard. "They are all good looking except this one. It's too bad you can't make him over again!"

We may have spent a lifetime making ourselves over to satisfy what we thought other people wanted us to be. We see personal criticism as an indication that we are not beautiful enough. Many of us believe that we are somehow at fault for not turning out better. Even when we are praised, we find it hard to accept and appreciate our talents and abilities. Obsolete standards and unrealistic expectations continue to limit us, although we may not be consciously aware of them.

Letting go of our fear of disapproval frees us to accept our self-images. We all have human failings, but it is not necessary to make them the focus of our lives. Identifying negative self-talk and replacing it with positive affirmations are signs that Step Six is working in our lives—that we have become willing to release the character defects that impede our progress and are taking positive action to do so.

Are old negative voices interfering with my happiness? Turning them off gives my inner beauty a chance to shine through.

The poor little fellow dropped his head, and did not know where to look. He was mocked by everyone in the fowlyard when they thought his mother was not looking. How he grieved over his own ugliness!

*N*othing is worse than believing we are so ugly that we are unlovable. We assume disguises, hoping to hide who we really are. We put on masks of composure to make people think we don't care. We rush to meet the demands of others, fearful of being rejected if we express our own needs.

It's wonderful to discover that we don't have to stay in a fowlyard of mocking voices like the Ugly Duckling did. It is a relief to find other people who once believed they were unattractive, but who are now leading lives of peaceful serenity. Hearing the story of how they successfully discovered the beauty in themselves can give us the courage to risk revealing our own tattered images.

Step Five provides a means for setting aside our disguises. Sharing our personal inventory with another person promotes self-acceptance and renews our identification with others. Releasing our destructive preoccupation with real and imagined liabilities frees us to focus on developing our assets.

I choose to associate with people who accept and encourage me. I can take off my mask and let them know me as I am today.

His brothers and sisters soon became as rude and unkind as the rest: "If only the cat would catch you, you ugly thing!" At last he could bear it no longer. He ran and flew over the hedge, frightening the little birds so that they flew away. "That's because I'm so ugly," the duckling thought; and he shut his eyes, but kept on running.

*T*here was a time when survival meant running away from things that hurt us. Hiding from others protected us when we were powerless and shielded us from many of the harmful situations that we were unable to change.

Today, retreating when we feel uncomfortable or compromised no longer serves a good purpose. It maintains our isolation from others and separates us from our true feelings. Our habit of fleeing from other people or lashing out at them before they can reject us may provoke equally defensive behavior in others. Like the Ugly Duckling who misread the behavior of the little birds, we may interpret other people's reactions as indicative of our ugliness rather than as a learned defense.

As we come to trust in our Higher Power, we find fewer reasons to run away and hide. We develop the ability to see our true beauty instead of the ugly duckling we believe ourselves to be.

Am I still running from myself and others?
If so, I will stop and find a secure
place where I can be me.

He reached a small cottage where an old woman, her cat and a hen lived; and it was really they, and not she, who were masters of the house. "Can you lay eggs?" asked the hen. "No." "Then you'd better hold your tongue." "Can you arch your back and purr?" "No." "In that case, you have no right to have an opinion."

*H*ow relieved we are to find a place where we can be ourselves and feel safe, where we don't have to impress anyone in order to be accepted. No one cares whether we can lay eggs, purr, stretch or fly. Their only concern for us is that we be offered an opportunity to experience the peace of mind that our program of recovery can bring us.

In meetings we may encounter members who remind us of the hen or the cat. In our eagerness to carry the message, we sometimes become overly enthusiastic and forget that the Twelve Steps are only guides to recovery and not a set of fixed rules. Each of us has the freedom to interpret the Steps and apply them in ways that are beneficial to us. Even as newcomers, our stories are beneficial if we speak from our heart and resist the opportunity to give advice or criticize what others offer.

I will make an effort to listen with an open mind to what others say and take advantage of the opportunity to learn something new today.

The duckling was seized with a great longing to be floating in the water, and he could not help telling the hen. "What are you thinking of?" asked the hen. "You have nothing to do. That's why you have these fancies. Lay some eggs or purr, and such notions will disappear."

Many of us are in professions or relationships that have more to do with what other people want for us than what we want for ourselves. We spend our lives doing work for which we have no aptitude, and from which we derive no satisfaction. We keep trying to prove that we can do what we "should do" instead of turning our backs on what doesn't interest us and devoting our energy to things we enjoy.

Life often feels empty and meaningless when we are not being true to ourselves. These feelings can make us desperate to discover our true potential and to find the place where we belong. Talking to others who have successfully recovered their own identities helps us to pursue our own aptitudes.

The longings of my inner child are important clues to the meaning of life for me. I will dream and explore alternatives for achieving my heart's desire.

"You don't understand me!" wailed the duckling. "Well, if we don't understand you, who should? You are nothing but an idle chatterer. Get to work: learn to lay some eggs or purr." "I think I'll go out into the world," said the duckling. And he left.

*A*fter wailing, "You don't understand me!" many of us ran away, looking desperately for someone to whom we could relate. The fear that no one would ever understand us kept us running until our lives became unmanageable and we were forced to admit we were on the wrong track. We didn't realize that running away wasn't the answer—that we had to face our pain and make peace with ourselves before we could establish healthy relationships with others.

Taking Step One and admitting that our present ways of relating to others are not working does not solve our problems immediately. It simply helps us to acknowledge that we are unhappy with our present situation and are willing to consider new ways of looking at ourselves and our lives. Like the Ugly Duckling, we must risk leaving familiar situations and behaviors behind us if we are to find a better life for ourselves.

I am grateful for the opportunity to be with people who understand my feelings and who offer support and encouragement to me while I am finding my way.

The sun was setting one day when he heard a sound of whirring wings, and a flock of swans flew up from the rushes. He did not know what the birds were, but he was drawn to them as he had never been drawn to any other creatures.

Sometimes we are instinctively drawn to certain people or situations like the Ugly Duckling was drawn to the beautiful birds in the rushes. If we stop to look at what attracts us, we often find that some hidden longings have been awakened in us. These feelings may be important clues to what we can achieve if we uncover and develop the hidden aspects of ourselves.

Acknowledging and understanding the difference between people who model a healthy life and those who pull us toward self-destructive behavior are signals that we are growing. When we develop positive ways of relating to others, our lives begin to flourish. The daily inventory suggested in Step Ten helps us to identify negative patterns when they first appear so that we can avoid repetition of behaviors that create road blocks on the road to recovery.

With the help of my Higher Power I can release the beautiful bird within me. Then I will have the faith I need to rise above the rushes.

*Every morning it grew colder and colder, and the duck-
ling had to work to keep himself warm. He had to swim
around in the water to keep the ice from freezing around
him. He never could tell afterwards exactly how he had
spent the winter. He only knew that he had somehow
survived.*

*L*ike the Ugly Duckling, we are survivors, or we
would never have come this far. For some of us our
hardships are so deeply buried that we can't always
remember them. Though it may hurt to recall some
of the emotions we suppressed just to keep going, we
must do so in order to complete our restoration. Holding on to old feelings and resentments keeps us swimming around in circles in order to avoid being frozen
in the icy memories of our past.

We extend a life line to the freezing child within us
when we find a secure environment in which these
memories can safely emerge. We release them a little
at a time in the company of trusted counselors, sponsors or friends who can help us experience the pain
without being destroyed by it. We can trust our Higher
Power to reveal only as much of the past as we are able
to receive at any one time. It is up to us to seek an
environment where this is possible.

*I can stop treading water and find a safe
place to release the suffering child
within me from the frozen ice.*

*The duckling was lying out on the moor among the reeds
when the sun began to warm again and the larks to sing.
Beautiful spring had come. He spread his wings to fly.
They beat the air more strongly than before, and bore
him away.*

J
U
N
E

25

*W*e all go through periods when nothing seems to
be happening. We feel as though our lives are at a
standstill and our growth has stopped. Rather than
become discouraged, we can remind ourselves that
internal changes take time and often manifest themselves gradually.

When we reach a plateau, it helps to review the
progress we have made since we began working the
Steps. Taking advantage of a new challenge to test our
wings can be useful, provided we're careful not to take
on more than we can handle. We know that spring
follows winter, but the timetable for personal recovery
is not always self-determined. When we quit trying to
force unseasonable changes and make the decision to
be comfortable where we are, life becomes more
manageable. By attending meetings regularly, we
reinforce the reality that recovery is accomplished one
day at a time.

*Recovery takes time. I will rejoice in small
successes, knowing that my Higher
Power will guide me through
the difficult times.*

Then he saw a flock of the same beautiful birds he had seen so many months ago. "I will go to them," said the duckling to himself; "I would rather be killed by them than to be pursued by ducks and beaten by fowls."

*R*ecovery begins with surrender. We gain some immediate relief in Step One when we admit that we are powerless and recognize that our lives are unmanageable. We reason that if we cannot manage our own lives, we cannot hope to survive. It is not surprising that many of us wait until we hit the very bottom to enter the program. Often, we must face total defeat before we elect to take the first step toward regaining our personal power by admitting our powerlessness.

We have all been bitten by ducks of low self-esteem, pecked by hens of negative thinking and kicked by those who tend the fowlyards of rejection. Recovery begins when we accept ourselves as we are and the past as it was. This frees us to join a flock of beautiful birds and follow them, knowing that we will feel safest when we are where we belong.

I can overcome the negative influences from the past and accept myself for who I am.

It did not take him long to reach them. As soon as they saw him, they started towards him with outspread wings, which the duckling misunderstood.

Many of us don't expect to be greeted by cries of welcome when we first come into the program. Our self-image is sometimes so poor that it's hard to believe we would be wanted anywhere. We tend to misinterpret other people's offers of friendship and stay distanced from them. We see things the way we expect them to be instead of how they really are.

Learning to communicate with people more openly helps to clear our distorted sense of who we are and how other people see us. Talking about our feelings and problems and looking at events in our lives with someone else gives us a new perspective. We slowly begin to see their interaction with us as a gesture of friendship, rather than as an intrusion on our privacy. The acceptance we find in the program helps to change our negative expectations and we come to view potential enemies as friends.

I will be comfortable with myself today and not allow my low self-image to prevent me from reaching out to others.

He approached them trembling and said, "Kill me!" And as he spoke, he bowed his head and looked down into the water. He was no longer a clumsy, gray bird. He had become a swan!

*I*t takes courage to let down our defenses and allow our inner self to shine through. The transformation from the ugly ducklings we think we are to the swans we can't imagine becoming happens slowly. The changes that occur when we cast aside our fears and insecurities take time and effort. The joy we experience by seeing ourselves as we really are is our reward.

Through our spiritual awakening, we become aware of the miracles in our lives and recognize the power within us. We realize that we are no longer bankrupt—physically, emotionally or spiritually—but are blessed with fullness of meaning and purpose. We recover our identity and become capable of sharing our happiness with others. We are prepared to lead balanced lives and carry the message to others as Step Twelve suggests.

I will see myself as I am today, and not allow old images to interfere with my true reflection.

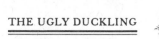

The duckling thought that all the persecution and loneliness that he had passed through had been worthwhile, for it made him value his present happiness all the more.

Unbearable pain drives most of us into the program—pain so deep that it is hard to imagine we could ever be healed. We aren't looking for peace and serenity in the beginning; we are looking for a way to stop hurting. When the pain begins to subside, we are grateful. If we are asked to define what happiness, joy and freedom mean to us, we may be content to reply "release from constant pain."

As we work the Steps, we find many more reasons for gratitude. We revel in the security that allows us to take productive risks, knowing that our Higher Power will see us through any pain, loss or disappointment that results. We value the freedom of choice that comes from knowing when to speak and when to be silent or when to accept and when to disregard someone else's opinion.

Knowing who we are and having confidence in ourselves allows us to get close to others without assuming responsibility for them or their feelings. We learn to appreciate the persecution and loneliness we have been through, for it makes us value our present happiness even more.

I accept the hurts of my past and no longer need to run from them. I can use them as a measure of my present happiness.

J
U
N
E

30

He ruffled his feathers, lifted his slender neck, and cried joyously from the depths of his heart: "I never dreamed of such happiness when I was still the ugly duckling."

*T*he twelve-step process leads us to a spiritual awakening—an awareness of the power within us and around us. When we learn to use that power wisely without abusing its privileges, we discover our own beauty and talents and find happiness we never dreamed existed.

The negative voices that inhibited our self-expression gradually fade away, giving us an opportunity to discover our true limits and capabilities. We experience a sense of oneness with other people while appreciating and retaining our individuality. Knowing and liking who we are and allowing other people to be themselves leads us to deeper levels of intimacy.

As we grow in the program, we learn more about how to live in the present and to relate to others as equals. We are not afraid to ruffle our feathers along the way and show pride in the changes that are happening in our lives. We carry the message by sharing our successes and our disappointments with others.

I am aware of the power within and around me.
I will stop dreaming about perfect worlds
and work with my Higher Power to
free the joyful spirit within me.

Cinderlad

CINDERLAD

nce upon a time a farmer discovered that his crop was being destroyed every St. John's Eve, at the height of its vigor. He decided to send one of his three sons to discover what was cutting down the meadow. His oldest boy was frightened away by the violent earthquakes that ensued when he reached the field. The same thing happened the following year, when he sent his second son to watch the field.

The third year, it was Cinderlad's turn. Each time an earthquake commenced, he calmly assessed the situation and decided that if the shaking got no worse he could manage to stand it. When the tremors ceased, the boy discovered a huge horse with a shiny suit of armor on its back grazing in the field. He subdued the animal by throwing his tinder box over it, and then hid it in a secret place and returned home. The next two years, the situation repeated itself. Each time Cinderlad tamed the horse, led it away to his hiding place and saved the crop.

The king of the country decreed that whomever could ride to the top of a steep hill and take three golden apples from his daughter's lap could marry her. Every prince and knight in the land failed to ascend the hill until a knight in gleaming armor rode his powerful horse part of the way up and then turned back. The princess threw one of the golden apples into his shoe, and then he disappeared as quickly as he had come.

The events were repeated, and each time the mysterious knight rode farther up the hill. On the third day, he reached the top, took the last golden apple from the lap of the princess and disappeared. The king ordered everyone in the kingdom to appear before him and produce the apples if they had them. Cinderlad was the last to appear. Standing before the king, he threw off his rags, revealed his shining armor and presented the golden apples. The king was delighted, and everyone made merry at the wedding.

Once upon a time there was a man who had a meadow which lay on the side of a mountain, and in the meadow there was a barn in which he stored hay. But there had not been much hay in the barn for the last two years, for every St. John's eve, when the grass was in the height of its vigour, it was all eaten clean up.

*W*hat a familiar story for many of us! We invest large amounts of time and energy on major projects and find the profits vanish into thin air. We try to save money for something important, yet cannot stop spending it on foolish things. We diet faithfully, then lose our incentive just short of the goal. Or we get involved in relationships which seem to flourish and then end for no apparent reason.

Disappointments like these are often caused by a lack of self-esteem. We think we don't merit the rewards that come with accomplishment, or that other people or causes deserve to have our time and money more than we do. Taking our inventory in Step Four makes us aware of our self-defeating attitudes. In this process, we acknowledge that we have thoughts and behaviors that hamper our growth. When we look at these in Step Five, we lay the groundwork for making changes that will lead us to more satisfying lives.

I will ask for help in identifying unproductive attitudes and unrealistic expectations that sap my strength and energy.

The man got tired of losing his crop, and said to his sons that one of them must go and sleep in the barn on St. John's night. The eldest was quite willing to go to the meadow; he would watch the grass, he said, and he would do it so well that neither man, nor beast, nor even the devil himself should have any of it.

Many of us believe we have to be perfect in all we do—that we have to do things so well that no one will be able to do a better job. We put on a brave front to mask our weaknesses and insecurities. We plunge blindly into projects, afraid we will be humiliated if we ask for help or direction. If we need assistance, we see it as a sign of weakness—a signal that we are not capable of performing in a satisfactory manner.

This way of thinking undermines our understanding of our circumstances and capabilities. If we stubbornly insist on doing everything our own way, we can not get the help we need to handle new challenges successfully. It inhibits our ability to learn and increases the stress we inflict upon ourselves.

When we finally discover that our way isn't working, we are ready for change. Step One encourages us to put aside our brave facades, admitting that we are powerless and that our lives are unmanageable. When we do this, we begin a journey that leads to healing and wholeness.

I don't have to be superhuman today. Doing the best I can with what I've been given is all that is required of me.

So when evening came he went to the barn, and lay down to sleep, but when night was drawing near there was such a rumbling and such an earthquake that the walls and roof shook again, and the lad jumped up and took to his heels as fast as he could, and never even looked back, and the barn remained empty that year just as it had been for the last two.

*W*hen we set out to put our lives in order with vain boasts and unrealistic expectations as guidelines, we set the stage for certain failure. Even the slightest shaking of the earth can plunge us into a pattern of compulsive behavior and cause us to lose control.

Step Three helps us contain our inner panic by assisting us to connect with our Higher Power—our true source of strength. Stopping in the midst of confusion and asking for guidance can quiet our minds. We can also rely on sponsors or other program members to help us explore new ways of managing our fear and pain. Revealing our feelings to people we trust helps to relieve anxiety and allows the security of the present moment to comfort and reassure us.

If I am in a situation that causes me to panic today, I will remember to stop and ask for help.

Next St. John's eve the man again said that he could not go on in this way, losing all the grass in the outlying field year after year, and that one of his sons must go there and watch it, and watch well too. So the next oldest son was willing to show what he could do. But when night was drawing near there was a great rumbling, and then an earthquake, which was even worse than the former, and when the youth heard it he was terrified, and went off, running as if for a wager.

Periods of emotional turmoil are often followed by interludes of peace and tranquility. Then the pressure builds again and we experience another explosion. We muster our courage and set out to arm ourselves against the devastating effects of another emotional earthquake. With no one to turn to and nowhere to go for help, we often end up right back where we started.

Admitting our fear allows us to approach it with a different attitude. By calming our terror, we become able to explore new ways of managing out-of-control drives and emotions. Step Two, coming to believe in a power greater than ourselves, helps us realize that we do not have to be in control to have control. Trust in our Higher Power helps us gain and sustain sanity in our lives.

I will meet fear head on today. I can rely on my Higher Power and the wisdom of other people in the program to guide me through any crisis.

The year after, it was Cinderlad's turn, but when he made ready to go the others laughed at him, and mocked him: "Well, you are just the right one to watch the hay, you who have never learnt anything but how to sit among the ashes and bake yourself!" said they. Cinderlad, however, did not trouble himself about what they said, but when evening drew near rambled away to the outlying field.

*T*hose of us who grew up with criticism and shame can easily understand how Cinderlad must have felt when his brothers ridiculed him. We are often unable to quiet the inner voices that say: "Whatever gave you the idea you could possibly do that? Don't even try it—people will know what a fool you are."

Before we can turn off these old tapes we must be conscious of when they play and what they say. Replacing them with new affirmations that include the experience, strength and hope of other program members helps to erase them. Coming to trust that we can be productive, joyous and happy helps us turn away from negative influences. Then we are free to take advantage of opportunities that support healthy recovery.

*I will doing something in a new way today. Then
I will praise myself for taking the risk,
no matter what the outcome.*

When he got there he went into the barn and lay down, but in about an hour's time the rumbling and creaking began, and it was frightful to hear it. "Well, if it gets no worse than that, I can manage to stand it," thought Cinderlad.

One day at a time! Live in the now! These two concepts are important keys to managing our current situation. Until we master them, a simple hunger pain may set off a fear of "never having enough" that can escalate into an eating binge. A moment of being alone and quiet may trigger a fear of abandonment that leads us to a "quick fix." An initial attraction to another person may quickly blossom into a fantasy of "happily ever after" that plunges us into despair if it fails to materialize.

When we learn how to focus on the present moment, our negative feelings lose their power over us. When we set aside both our past fears and future fantasies and live in the now, we can accept our feelings without letting them control us. With the help of program members and friends, we can withstand whatever trials come our way.

If I am hit by emotional upheaval today, I will ask myself if I feel safe. If the answer is "No," I will seek the help I need to weather the storm.

In a little time the creaking began again, and the earth quaked so that all the hay flew about the boy. "Oh! If it gets no worse than that I can manage to stand it," thought Cinderlad. But then came a third rumbling, and a third earthquake, so violent that the boy thought the walls and roof had fallen down, but when that was over everything suddenly grew as still as death around him.

When we are able to put aside the negative thoughts and fantasies that kept us locked in passive roles and attitudes, we are ready to experiment with different behaviors. It is exhilarating to discover our new capabilities, but it can be frightening too. When we change, those around us may begin to react to us differently. It can take some time to establish a comfortable balance in our relationships. We are sometimes shaken by strong emotions before we find the serenity we are seeking.

Each new experience changes us to some degree, and may cause temporary discomfort. Although we believe we are ready to leave abusive situations where the walls and roofs are rumbling and falling down around us, we may still fear being alone and abandoned. Learning to handle conflicting feelings is an essential part of recovery. The ability to live serenely in a world that is constantly changing is a benefit we gain from the program.

I don't have to run from fear today. I am learning the difference between self-destructive situations and those that initiate and support healthy change.

Everything was quiet, and everything stayed quiet, and when he had lain still a short time he heard something that sounded as if a horse were standing chewing just outside the barn door. He stole away to the door, which was ajar, to see what was there, and a horse was standing eating. It was so big, and fat, and fine a horse that Cinderlad had never seen one like it before, and a saddle and bridle lay upon it, and a complete suit of armor for a knight, and everything was of copper, and so bright that it shone again.

*I*f we can be still for a short time, the quiet gives us an opportunity to reflect on what is happening around us. When our emotional turmoil subsides and we look around, our unclouded eyes give us a sharper view of the world and allow us to see opportunities for growth. Thanks to our program, we can reach out to trusted sponsors and friends for validation and encouragement.

Unleashing our own physical, intellectual, sexual and spiritual power can cause great emotional upheaval. Although we may experience initial discomfort, these inner drives are rich sources of creative action and renewal when we channel their energy in constructive directions. Taking time to improve our conscious contact with our Higher Power by working Step Eleven is a vital part of this process.

I will not be afraid to venture into quiet places today. Hidden treasure may lie where I least often look.

"Ha, ha! it is thou who eatest up our hay then," thought the boy; "but I will stop that." So he made haste, and took out his steel for striking fire, and threw it over the horse and it became so tame that the boy could do what he liked with it. So he mounted it and rode away to a place which no one knew of but himself, and there he tied it up.

*T*he aspects of our lives that we examine in Steps Four and Five identify the hidden enemies that prevent us from gathering our harvest of joy. Each unproductive attitude and behavior we release in Steps Six and Seven is another barrier removed from the path to constructive action. The amends process in Steps Eight and Nine increases our ability to act decisively instead of spending hours, days or even weeks in endless ambivalence or violent resistance.

Life is not simply a matter of finding right and wrong answers; it is a question of determining what opportunities will be overlooked and which ones will be pursued. Like Cinderlad, we can use the simple tools the program provides to transform our feelings and desires into creative sources of energy and action. The Twelve Steps redirect our approach to life and introduce us to a process of discovering and developing our own potential.

By applying the Steps to my life, I can increase my ability to respond rapidly and confidently to new opportunities when they arise.

When he went home again his brothers laughed and asked how he had got on. "You didn't lie long in the barn, if even you have been so far as the field!" said they. "I lay in the barn till the sun rose, but I saw nothing and heard nothing, not I," said the boy. "God knows what there was to make you two so frightened." "Well, we shall soon see whether you have watched the meadow or not," answered the brothers, but when they got there the grass was all standing just as long and as thick as it had been the night before.

*T*here is a difference between the genuine laughter we share over our human failings and the snicker that ridiculing others generates. Making fun of those around us is a tempting way to make ourselves feel better and shield us from reality. Actually, it does neither. When we become more comfortable with ourselves and our behaviors, we no longer have to put others down to make ourselves feel better.

In recovery we learn that we don't need to justify our actions. How we tend our fields is our business— not someone else's. We simply step away from people we don't trust and let the facts speak for themselves. Likewise, we find it's not our job to offer unsolicited solutions to other people's problems. They will find inspiration and encouragement when they see that we've found a way to solve our own.

Unless I owe an amend, I don't have to explain myself to anyone. My actions will speak for themselves.

The next St. John's eve it was the same thing again: neither of the two brothers dared to go to the outlying field to watch the crop, but Cinderlad went, and everything happened exactly the same as on the previous St. John's Eve; but all three earthquakes were much, very much more violent than they had been the year before.

*O*ur lives are not always evenly balanced. Periods of calm are often followed by violent upheavals that cause us to lose sight of the total picture. Through faith in our Higher Power and trust in the program, we learn to weather the storms. Talking with those who have supported and nurtured our progress reminds us that we have survived worse turbulence.

As we change and grow, our new behaviors may evoke fear and uncertainty in us. Rather than letting our feelings limit us, we can examine them with the help of others as part of working Step Six. When we become entirely ready to let go of old behavior patterns, we open the way for constructive thinking that initiates and supports productive risk-taking.

Is fear standing in the way of something I want to do today? I will rely on the Steps as tools to move through fear with confidence.

Then everything became still as death again, and the boy heard something chewing outside the barn door, so he stole as softly as he could to the door, which was slightly ajar, and again there was a horse standing close by the wall of the house, eating and chewing, and it was far larger and fatter than the first horse, and it had a saddle on its back, and a bridle was on it too, and a full suit of armour for a knight, all of bright silver, and as beautiful as anyone could wish to see.

Many of our worst fears occur because we don't think we can handle the natural upheaval that change brings to our lives. Trying to control our panic only adds to our difficulties. The answer lies in learning to let go of our anxiety and give ourselves time to assess the situation. We don't have to act on our emotions immediately. Like Cinderlad, we can wait for the stillness after the storm and then calmly survey the scene.

When we become willing to explore our feelings with people we trust, we often find that we possess hidden reserves of energy. Getting in touch with our own spiritual center during times of prayer and meditation makes us less likely to be swept off balance. As a result, our rewards are greater than we had hoped they could be.

*I will take advantage of the quiet after the
storm to look closely at my feelings.
I have a powerful source of
energy within me.*

"Ho, ho!" thought the boy, "Is it thou who eatest up our hay in the night? but I will put a stop to that." So he took out his steel for striking fire, and threw it over the horse's mane, and the beast stood there as quiet as a lamb. Then the boy rode this horse, too, away to the place where he kept the other, and then went home again.

*I*f we patiently wait for the storms in our lives to pass, we can review the aftermath from a better perspective. In a peaceful state of mind, we often discover other options and solutions to our problems. When we are no longer being driven blindly by unseen internal forces, we have a better chance of selecting an appropriate action and confidently carrying it out.

Cinderlad used an ordinary tool of his trade to tame the horse that was to become his secret strength. The Twelve Steps are just as powerful and serve as our secret force. Using the program to safely release our suppressed rage can free us of old resentments and lead us toward healing. Frustration then becomes a friend instead of an enemy, motivating us to take constructive action.

If I find myself in the middle of emotional upheavel today, I will stop, look and listen. When I take time to ask for direction, my Higher Power provides it.

"I suppose you will tell us that you have watched well again," said the brothers. "Well, so I have," said Cinderlad. So they went there again, and there the grass was, but that did not make them any kinder to Cinderlad.

Signs that we are growing and changing may instill fear and resentment in people close to us. They may react to these feelings by treating us unkindly. Even though we may realize this behavior has more to do with them than it does with us, their disapproval can still cause uncomfortable feelings. We may place greater demands upon ourselves and expect to maintain even higher standards of performance, hoping this will encourage people to treat us fairly.

By associating with program members who think highly of themselves, we diminish our chances of being the target of someone else's envy. We can look to our emotionally healthy friends for help and understanding, knowing that they are truly interested in our progress and not in their own personal gain.

An important element in recovery is learning to take pride in our accomplishments. Instead of envying others, we can be kind to ourselves and recognize that through a commitment to recovery our own grass is growing taller.

I will not allow the attitudes or opinions of others to inhibit my growth. I am in recovery and the facts speak for themselves.

When the third St. John's night came neither of the two elder brothers dared to lie in the outlying barn to watch the grass, for they had been so heartily frightened the night they had slept there that they could not get over it, but Cinderlad dared to go, and everything happened just the same as on the two former nights. There were three earthquakes, each worse than the other, and the last flung the boy from one wall of the barn to the other, but then everything suddenly became still as death.

*A*ll living things go through seasons of growth and periods of rest. At times when nothing seems to be happening, we keep the fires burning as best we can. Then suddenly another challenge presents itself and we are given an opportunity to decide whether to meet it or run away.

Fear may overwhelm us each time we think about trying something new and risking an encounter with the unknown. Reciting Step Three and turning our will and our lives over to the care of our Higher Power gives us the courage to move forward. Through sharing at meetings, we have heard what can be accomplished when we turn our will and our lives over to the care of our Higher Power.

Today I can choose to go forward or stay where I am. I will not allow fear to prevent me from facing and meeting life's challenges.

When he had lain quietly a short time, he heard something chewing outside the barn door; then he once more stole to the door, which was slightly ajar, and behold, a horse was standing just outside it, which was much larger and fatter than the two others he had caught.

*P*articipation in the fullness of life means accepting changing moods and seasons, times of turbulence and calm, as well as moments of lightness and darkness. Through our program of recovery, we find a way to keep our balance amidst the varying circumstances in our lives.

Asking for guidance before we pursue an uncertain course of action helps us center ourselves and redirect our energy. Like Cinderlad, we can maintain a positive attitude by being patient and having faith in ourselves and in the outcome. Even fear and anger can produce good results. Fear is useful when it prevents us from exposing ourselves to harmful situations. Anger, when it is used constructively, can provide the energy we need to make positive changes in our lives.

Taking a daily inventory in Step Ten helps us put our instincts and emotions to good use. Rather than internalizing fear and anger, we admit our feelings and take prompt corrective action where necessary. Using Step Eleven and praying for knowledge of God's will for us is also a helpful tool in converting our negative feelings into positive forces for change.

When I feel driven by forces beyond my control, I can use my conscious contact with my Higher Power to redirect my negative energy.

"Ho, ho! It is thou, then, who art eating up our hay this time," thought the boy, "but I will put a stop to that." So he pulled out his steel for striking fire, and threw it over the horse, and it stood as still as if it had been nailed to the field, and the boy could do just what he liked with it. Then he mounted it and rode away to the place where he had the two others, and then he went home again.

*C*inderlad gained insight into what was occurring in the fields because he was willing to be patient and observe what was happening around him. When we pause to take a fresh look at ourselves, we also gain new insight into our lives and the lives of others. Taking action based upon this knowledge is an important part of our recovery. Unless moments of understanding are followed by times of decision, precious opportunities for growth may be lost.

Successful living requires continual self-assessment and confidence in our ability to respond to whatever challenges we encounter. Each time a new opportunity presents itself, we have a chance to grow. When we look carefully at what has come our way and take action by using the tools we have available, our capacity for positive growth is enhanced. Challenges strengthen us and add greatly to our storehouse of wisdom and experience.

I will continue to use the Steps to help me respond to new challenges.

Then he went home again. The two brothers mocked him, and told him that they could see that he must have watched the grass very carefully that night, for he looked just as if he were walking in his sleep; but Cinderlad did not trouble himself about that, but just bade them go to the field and see. They did go, and the grass was standing, looking as fine and as thick as ever.

*I*nstead of reacting defensively when people like Cinderlad's brothers laugh at us, we can focus on finding our own direction. Fulfillment does not depend on changing other people's perceptions of us; it depends on being able to initiate positive change for ourselves and giving other people the freedom to take responsibility for themselves.

Steps Eight and Nine help us build a foundation for the establishment of healthy boundaries. Through these Steps we can clear away the wreckage of our past by listing the harm we have inflicted on others and making restitution where possible. This frees us from the guilt we carry as a result of our past behavior. We gradually learn to take full responsibility for our part in events and let others assume responsibility for theirs. We cannot change other people, but we can limit how they affect us.

I will follow my inner direction today and not worry about what others may think or say.

The King of the country in which Cinderlad's father dwelt had a daughter whom he would give to no one who could not ride up to the top of the high hill of glass, slippery as ice. Upon the very top of this the King's daughter was to sit, and the man who could ride up and take three golden apples should marry her, and have half the kingdom.

*M*any of us have dreams of acquiring the prize that awaits us at the top of the hill. We may even fantasize about ways in which we can magically obtain the reward. Recovery allows us to deal honestly with our secret aspirations and helps us identify parts of our personalities that have been hidden away. This awareness brings us closer to reaching the reward at the top of the hill—recovering our wholeness and having the life we desire.

Taking inventory in Step Four helps us uncover the missing pieces of ourselves that need to be developed and strengthened. Sharing what we discover with a person we trust in Step Five is a significant milestone on the road to wholeness. The things that frighten us most can sometimes be transformed into our greatest assets when we look at them closely and approach them honestly.

The hills I've been afraid to climb are not as steep as they once appeared to be. I will risk bringing my dreams out into the open and making them a reality.

J
U
L
Y

20

When the day appointed by the King had come, everyone who could walk was there to see who won the King's daughter. Cinderlad's two brothers were there too, but they would not hear of letting him go with them, for he was so dirty and black with sleeping and grubbing among the ashes that they said everyone would laugh at them if they were seen in the company of such an oaf. "Well, then, I will go all alone by myself," said Cinderlad.

*H*ow nice it would feel to be like Cinderlad—free of shame and fully accepting of who we are! When we come to terms with our negative self-image and the limits it places on our ability to function, we no longer need to hide in the ashes. When we realize how many of our present actions are determined by decisions we made in childhood, we begin to interpret our behavior differently. We establish new values and become less vulnerable to unprovoked attack.

When we heal the shame that caused us to have a poor opinion of ourselves, we no longer have to shy away from others to protect ourselves from possible rejection. Our self-esteem improves as we become more confident in ourselves and our abilities.

If I feel threatened by what others say, I will ask myself why it bothers me. I no longer need to be ashamed of who I am.

When the two brothers got to the glass hill, all the princes and knights were trying to ride up it, but it was all in vain, for no sooner did the horses set foot upon the hill than down they slipped. Suddenly a knight came riding up on so fine a horse that no one had ever seen the like of it before. The other knights all called out to him that he might just as well spare himself the trouble of trying to ride up the hill, but he did not heed them, and went up as if it were nothing at all.

*N*o matter how nobly we set out to conquer the obstacles in our path, our efforts sometimes come to naught. Things do not fall into place the way we thought they would, and we give up. Like the princes and the knights, we simply convince ourselves that whatever it was, it was not worth the trouble.

We can stop this negative attitude by attending twelve-step meetings regularly. We see from the experiences of others that we don't always achieve instant success. We become more confident that we can succeed if we are willing to be patient and keep trying. By working the Steps and interacting with fellow members, we build new resources and increase our ability to meet life's challenges.

I will develop a new set of aspirations and be aware of the inner resources I need to make my dreams a reality.

Thus he rode for a long way—it may have been a third of the way up—but when he had got so far he turned his horse round and rode down again. The Princess thought she had never seen so handsome a knight, and while he was riding up she was sitting thinking: "Oh! how I hope he may be able to come to the top!" And when she saw that he was turning back she threw one of the golden apples down after him, and it rolled into his shoe. But when he had come down from off the hill he rode away so fast that no one knew what had become of him.

*O*ften we do not reach the top of the hill on the first attempt. Even though we have identified our goals and are working hard toward achieving them, we must set aside time for rest. It is not reasonable to expect that we can make the changes required and restore our strength overnight. Sometimes we have to turn aside short of our goal in order to gather more of the energy we need to reach the top.

Meanwhile, we are inspired when we see examples of how the Steps work in the lives of others. No one can push us up from the bottom or pull us to the top. But they can throw us golden apples to remind us that the goal is within our reach. When we receive such encouragement, we are renewed and inspired by the knowledge that we are invited to keep trying.

I do not have to take on more than I can handle today. I can set limits on how far I climb.

At night Cinderlad's brothers came home again and had a long story to tell about the knight riding up the glass hill. "Oh! I should have liked to see him too," said Cinderlad, who was as usual sitting by the chimney among the cinders. "You indeed!" said the brothers, "you look as if you were fit to be among such great lords, nasty beast that you are to sit there!"

*T*he judgments we make of others often reflect negative aspects of our own character that we haven't accepted or forgiven. Sometimes our assessments conveniently cover up the fact that changes are needed in our lives. When we condemn others, as Cinderlad's brothers did, we expose our own shabbiness and inadequacies.

Blaming other people for past assaults on our self-esteem is not healing and retards our progress. Healing begins when we change our self-image. As we learn to respect ourselves, we find that we no longer have to depend on respect from others. When we find ways and reasons to love ourselves, begging those around us for love is no longer attractive or necessary. When we take responsibility for our own self-esteem, our need for approval from other people diminishes dramatically.

Today I will cherish the worthy child within me and look for things to praise instead of criticize.

Next day the brothers were for setting out again, and this time too Cinderlad begged them to let him go with them and see who rode; but no, they said he was not fit to do that, for he was much too ugly and dirty. "Well then, I will go all alone by myself," said Cinderlad.

*I*t is frightening to think of returning to old behaviors that isolated us from others. Convinced no one could ever care about us, we may have locked ourselves away with television sets, food, cigarettes, alcohol or drugs for company. We may have distracted ourselves with spending sprees or promiscuous sex, wanting to make a connection while protecting our true selves with invisible armor. Some of us became involved in endless activity by taking care of people and things to escape our inner loneliness.

Part of recovery is learning to act independently, to sometimes go all alone by ourselves without feeling lonely and rejected. Working the Steps brings us back to where we started—to face our aloneness. But there is an important difference. In recovery, we learn to accept and value our separateness while maintaining our connection with others. We find a Higher Power that allows us to undertake our individual journeys and follow the course of our own destinies. We discover the true nature of our world, where loving oneself generates the capacity to love others. Our sense of belonging and relatedness grow in proportion to our ability to maintain our separate identity.

I am learning to be comfortable alone. It helps me to value myself as well as others.

All the princes and knights began to ride again, and not one of them could get even so far as a yard up the hill. Next came a knight riding on a steed that was much, much finer than that which the knight in copper armour had ridden. The other knights called to him, but the knight rode straight away to the glass hill. And when he had ridden two-thirds of the way up he turned his horse round, and rode down again. When the Princess saw him turning she threw the second apple after him, and it rolled into his shoe. As soon as he got down the glass hill he rode away so fast that no one could see what had become of him.

*T*he journey to recovery can't be made in one day. It must be taken one step at a time. Even the smaller successes we achieve sometimes exhaust our available resources. When our travel becomes too arduous, we can fall back, claim our partial victories and return later with a fresh horse.

When we attend meetings and work the Steps, our journey becomes easier. Instead of getting two-thirds of the way up the hill, we find that we can reach the top if we keep persisting.

Prayer and meditation are critical elements in this process. They are necessary to the full restoration of our strength and serenity. Conscious contact with our Higher Power helps us to develop the patience and loyalty that learning to love ourselves requires.

*I will rejoice in the victories of today
instead of worrying about the
tasks that lie ahead of me.*

At night the two brothers went home as they had done the night before and told how things had gone, and how everyone had ridden, but no one had been able to get up the hill. "But last of all," they said, "came one in silver armour, and oh, but he could ride! "Oh, how I should have liked to see him too!" said Cinderlad. "Oh, indeed! he was a little brighter than the ashes that you sit grubbing among, you dirty creature!" said the brothers.

*H*ow often do we sit on the sidelines of a game we are drawn to but don't feel competent to play? We watch admiringly as others, more brightly armored than we, face the challenges and succeed beyond our fondest dreams. Resigning ourselves to failure sometimes leads to the development of hidden resentments that provoke us to distance ourselves from others. This may add to our problems and prevent us from discovering alternative behaviors that they might have shared with us.

Life takes on a new dimension when we stop worrying about what others think of us and begin to seek the guidance of our Higher Power. The ashes we sit in gradually become the silver armor we use in the successful fight to find and restore our true selves. Soon we have victories to celebrate and many new ways to appreciate the blessings that come to us as part of our recovery.

*I will resist the temptation to resign myself
to failure today and be grateful for the
signs of my recovery, no matter
how small they may be.*

On the third day everything went just as on the former days. Cinderlad wanted to go with them to look at the riding, but the two brothers would not have him in their company, and when they got to the glass hill there was no one who could ride even so far as a yard up it. At last, after a long time, came a knight in golden armour. He rode straight away to the glass hill, and galloped up it as if it were no hill at all. As soon as he had ridden to the top, he took the third golden apple from the lap of the Princess, and then turned his horse about and vanished from their sight.

*I*n recovery, we run our own race and climb the hill at our own pace. The Princess at the top of the hill is a reminder of the power within us that reaches out to help us and is waiting to be claimed. The golden apples represent our spiritual awakening as we discover our true potential. They give us the incentive to accept new challenges and move onward and upward.

If we continue to use the Twelve Steps as part of our lives, we are not likely to fail in our efforts to develop our potential. By working the Steps one day at a time, we slowly exchange fear for trust and engage our whole being in the pursuit of realistic goals. As we grow and change, we develop the ability to love ourselves and begin to enjoy peace, serenity and joy.

> *I will use the power and energy avail-*
> *able to me today, remembering*
> *that recovery comes one*
> *day at a time.*

When the two brothers came home again at night, they had much to tell of how the riding had gone that day, and at last they told about the knight in the golden armour too. "Oh, how I should have liked to see him too!" said Cinderlad. "Well, he shone nearly as brightly as the coal heaps that thou art always raking amongst, dirty creature that thou art!" said the brothers.

*I*n recovery, we are never required to reveal anything about our lives that we don't want to divulge. "Carrying the message" does not mean we must expose vulnerable parts of ourselves to people whom we haven't learned to trust. It merely suggests that we share whatever we choose as part of our commitment to recovery. We may even keep our successes secret for awhile, enjoying the positive energy they generate and taking time to become familiar with the changes they represent.

Understanding that other people may criticize us for what they fear most in themselves lessens the hurt of rejection. Secure in the knowledge that we are doing what is right for us, our newfound confidence shines as brightly as if we were wearing golden armor. Part of our growth is knowing that we are not obligated to renovate anyone else's life. Our commitment in Step Twelve is to share what we can of our story—reserving the freedom to speak or be silent without being judged.

It is my choice to reveal only those parts of me that I am willing to share. I am learning when to speak and when to remain silent.

Next day all the knights and princes were to appear before the King and the Princess in order that he who had the golden apple might produce it. They all went in turn, first princes, and then knights, but none of them had a golden apple. "But somebody must have it," said the King, "for with our own eyes we all saw a man ride up and take it." So he commanded that everyone in the kingdom should come to the palace, and see if he could show the apple. So Cinderlad was forced to go to the King's palace.

*E*ach of us possess the golden apples that symbolize our restoration to wholeness. Others make their own journeys and find their personal identity, and we are free to do the same. The joy of having a spiritual awakening is personal and belongs to us alone—no one can share it with us.

We must look beyond external facades to find truth and meaning in our lives. Those who appear to be more powerful than we are don't necessarily have answers that will work for us. We must be willing to examine our behaviors and break down the wall of denial that has prevented us from facing ourselves honestly. No one else can do it for us. Others can act as coaches, companions or guides along the way, but the solutions—the golden apples—lie within us. We are the only ones who can claim them and put them to work in our lives.

*I will renew my commitment to the Steps
and reach for the golden apples that
signify my spiritual awakening.*

"Hast thou the golden apple?" asked the King. "Yes," said Cinderlad, and he took all the three apples out of his pocket, and with that threw off his sooty rags and appeared there before him in his bright golden armour, which gleamed as he stood.

When we realize that we are worthy and can appear without shame before the King in whatever we are wearing, we have no further need for disguises. We can discard our masks and reveal our true colors. When we unconditionally accept both the light and darkness within us, we are free to choose which we present to the world.

We begin our journey to recovery by accepting our powerlessness and becoming willing to try a new way of life. We look fearlessly at our attitudes and behaviors, and begin to strive for change in our lives and relationships. When we turn to our Higher Power for guidance and direction in fulfilling our potential, we reach out for the golden apples that are there for us. We become grateful for the inner diversity that gives fullness and richness to our lives.

I am free of shame and am ready to accept the diverse parts of me—the good and bad, the strong and weak, the seen and unseen.

"Thou shalt have my daughter, and half of my kingdom, and thou hast well earned both!" said the King. So there was a wedding, and Cinderlad got the King's daughter. Everyone made merry at the wedding, and if they have not left off their merry-making they must be at it still.

*R*ediscovering the joy of spontaneous celebration may be the greatest gift the program offers us. There is a warmth and sense of community in shared laughter that is special and unique among program members. We are fortunate when we find people we can laugh with in spite of our pain and conflict.

Finding that we can laugh at ourselves and see humor in even our most serious problems is part of the recovery process. We can also learn to forgive ourselves and others for the hurts we suffered on the way to adulthood.

We cannot be free and spontaneous if we have not given ourselves and others the freedom to make mistakes. Nor is there anything to be gained by fostering old resentments. Refusing to release our anger and confusion will only deepen our wounds—it won't heal them. When we finally let go of the past we are free to fully experience the present. Then we can look to each day with gratitude for the discovery of our capacity to love.

I will take the steps necessary to experience joy and laughter in my life. Today I will find humor in a serious matter.

East of the Sun

here once was a poor husbandman who had a very large family. One evening, a white bear rapped on the window-pane of their cottage. He offered to make the man rich in exchange for his youngest daughter.

The girl went with the bear and they journeyed to a castle. Each night a man came and lay beside her. She never saw him, for he always arrived after dark and went away before daylight. The white bear gave the girl everything she asked for, but she became lonely. He agreed that she might visit her family if she would promise not to talk to her mother alone. Her mother persuaded her to talk about the mysterious man who visited her at night and gave her daughter a candle to illuminate his face while he slept.

When she lit the candle, she discovered a beautiful prince in her bed. Drops of tallow fell onto his shirt and awakened him. He confessed that his stepmother had bewitched him so that he became a white bear by day. Because the girl had interrupted the spell, he had to return to his stepmother's castle, which lay east of the sun and west of the moon. There he was to marry a troll princess with a nose three ells long.

The girl was determined to follow him. During her journey, she asked directions from three aged women who each gave her gifts. She was then carried to her destination on the backs of the four winds. She traded her gifts to the prince's long-nosed fiancee for three nights in his room. He was given a sleeping potion and did not awaken on the first two nights. He avoided it on the third night and was reunited with his beloved. He said he would refuse to marry anyone who could not remove the tallow from his shirt. When all of the trolls failed, the girl was given a chance to try. When the shirt came clean, the spell was broken and the stepmother, the long-nosed princess and all the trolls burst. The prince released the captives in the castle and returned to his own with the girl who had freed him.

Once upon a time there was a poor husbandman who had many children and little to give them in the way either of food or clothing. They were all sitting together by the fireside when suddenly someone rapped three times against the window-pane. The man went out to see what could be the matter, and when he got out there stood a great big white bear. "Good-evening to you," said the White Bear. "Will you give me your youngest daughter? If you will, you shall be as rich as you are now poor."

*W*e all experience moments when the white bear knocks on our window, jolting us out of our normal routine and prompting us to look closely at our lives. This often happens when our emotional resources have been exhausted and the brave front we present to the world can no longer hide our feelings of insecurity. When we reach this point, we are ready to take Step One—realizing our powerlessness and our inability to manage our own lives.

Few of us pay much attention to the first knock on our window. We must hear it more than once before we are able to respond. If the message we hear is one of hope, we may decide to accept what is offered. If we do not, we may choose to remain where we are, desperately trying to hold on to the little security we have left.

I believe in the power of the Twelve Steps to enrich my life. Today I will renew my commitment to continue my journey.

Truly the man had no objection to be rich, but he thought to himself: "I must first ask my daughter about this," so he went in and told them that there was a great white bear outside who had promised to make them all rich if he might have the youngest daughter. She said no, and would not hear of it; so the man went out again, and settled with the White Bear that he should come again next Thursday evening, and get her answer.

*B*ecoming accustomed to the idea that change can have a positive effect on our lives takes time. We may believe that change of any kind usually causes things to get worse instead of better. The idea that a "power greater than ourselves can restore us to sanity," as Step Two suggests, may be as foreign to us as a white bear appearing at the window offering to make us rich and prosperous.

Few of us make a commitment to recovery the first time it is offered to us. We may have to sit in many meetings and listen to people talk about their experiences before we believe that positive change might also be possible for us. Listening to others describe their relationship with a Higher Power helps us to develop an awareness of our own. Our willingness to listen to and accept other people's ideas is part of the process of discovering what works best for us.

As I strengthen my partnership with my Higher Power, it becomes easier to consider making changes in my life.

Then the man persuaded her, and talked so much to her about the wealth that they would have, and what a good thing it would be for herself, that at last she made up her mind to go, and washed and mended all her rags, made herself as smart as she could, and held herself in readiness to set out. Little enough had she to take away with her.

*F*ortunately we don't have to be rich, intelligent or successful to begin our journey through the Twelve Steps. We are not required to make ourselves as smart as we can or hold ourselves in readiness to set out. All we have to do is decide to trust the process and begin to work the Steps one day at a time.

A twelve-step program gives us a chance to examine the resources we have available to us, no matter how meager or inadequate they may seem to be. In the process we wash and mend all our rags so that we can set out again with renewed courage. We find that our talents are not as depleted as we thought, and that successful living may be only a matter of doing the best we can with the resources available to us.

I have what I need to embark on my journey.
I am only required to do the best I can
with the resources I have.

Next Thursday evening the White Bear came to fetch her. She seated herself on his back with her bundle, and thus they departed. When they had gone a great part of the way, the White Bear said: "Are you afraid?" "No, that I am not," said she. "Keep tight hold of my fur, and then there is no danger," said he.

*O*ur journey through the Steps is not always without peril. We must tighten our hold on reality and hold fast to the promise of a new life. Sometimes the trail seems too long and we become unsure of the destination. Although it might seem that we have lost control of our lives, we are actually closer to being in control than ever before.

Few of us enter the program with strong faith in ourselves. We may even doubt our ability to find a way out of our poverty and despair. Transforming our weakened hopes into confidence in a successful outcome takes honesty, open-mindedness and unfailing trust in our Higher Power. Honestly admitting our fears to other people can help us to overcome them. Being open-minded about our lives helps us to develop new attitudes and adopt new ways of looking at the world around us. Trusting in our Higher Power enables us to experiment with new behaviors that lead to improved lives and relationships.

Am I being as honest and open-minded as I can be today? I can use the tools of the program to strengthen my determination.

And thus she rode far, far away, until they came to a great mountain. Then the White Bear knocked on it, and a door opened, and they went into a castle where there were many brilliantly lighted rooms which shone with gold and silver, likewise a large hall in which there was a well-spread table. The White Bear gave her a silver bell, and told her that when she needed anything she had but to ring this bell, and what she wanted would appear.

*W*e sometimes experience a keen sense of euphoria when we first come into the program. If we are accustomed to isolating ourselves, it may feel like we have entered a castle with brilliantly lighted rooms when we find a supportive group of people who understand us. In many instances we don't have to say or do anything because they can sense how lonely or discouraged we feel.

When we attend meetings and experience a feeling of truly belonging, we can relax and enjoy it. It helps us to become more comfortable with ourselves. As we progress, we come to believe that we are worthy of unconditional love, even though we are not perfect. When we can accept ourselves just as we are, we stop trying so desperately to gain the approval of others.

The Steps are like silver bells. Learning to ring them by putting them to work in my life is the key to achieving my heart's desires.

So after she had eaten, and night was drawing near, she thought she would like to go to bed. She rang the bell and found herself in a chamber where a bed stood ready made for her. When she had put out the light a man came and lay down beside her, and behold it was the White Bear, who cast off the form of a beast during the night. She never saw him, however, for he always went away before daylight appeared.

When we enter the program, most of us are only vaguely aware of the beast slumbering inside us. By striving to be perfect and win the approval of others, we have suppressed the rage and resentment we feel at our inability to be ourselves.

One of our tasks in recovery is to uncover and release the anger buried deep within us. Many of us show an angry face to the world almost everywhere we go. An important task in recovery is to uncover the gentler side of ourselves and accept the risk of exposing the soft vulnerability under our violent facade.

When we find safe places to express our feelings without harming others, we begin to understand and integrate all aspects of our personalities. In Step Four we have an opportunity to examine our behavior and see the areas in our lives where we are experiencing difficulties. We find that we don't have to be afraid of our instincts. They can be a source of satisfaction and reward when our lives are brought into balance.

I can use the inventory in Step Four to explore suppressed parts of myself and learn to accept all aspects of my personality.

So all went well and happily for a time, but then she began to be very sad for all day long she had to go about alone. Then the White Bear asked what she wanted, and she told him that in her parents' house there were all her brothers and sisters, and it was because she could not go to them that she was so sorrowful.

*W*e become very lonely when we cannot see our families or others who are close to us. When we communicate only in the darkness through sex or some other form of unspoken communication, our relationships are incomplete. If we are afraid to openly express our thoughts, feelings and desires, we begin to feel cut off from others, no matter how deep the bond between us may appear to be.

It is difficult for us to communicate clearly and openly, we may begin to depend on other people to sense our needs rather than continue our struggle to express them directly. Participation in meetings and sharing our Fifth Step with another person helps us become more comfortable with free and open discussion. Being honest about our experiences and allowing others to see both our laughter and our tears takes away our loneliness and isolation.

*I am willing to be seen in the daylight
today and expose my true feelings
to other program members.*

"There might be a cure for that," said the White Bear, "if you would but promise me never to talk with your mother alone, but only when the others are there too; for she will take hold of your hand," he said, "and will want to lead you into a room to talk with you alone; but that you must by no means do, or you will bring great misery on both of us."

*F*or many of us, secrecy is a confusing topic. Keeping secrets is a sign of loyalty, an unspoken pledge that we can be trusted to keep other people's confidences. Sharing secrets can be a useful way to define various levels of intimacy and closeness. To some extent, we base our trust of others on how well they appear to keep our private matters to themselves.

Keeping certain secrets can lead to big trouble. When we hide our problems, we prevent them from being exposed so that a solution can be found. We may do ourselves a disservice by remaining silent in order to maintain the status quo. This is especially true if keeping them makes us uncomfortable or causes harm to ourselves or others. It is critical to our recovery that we find someone we can be open with about all aspects of our lives.

Have I found someone I can trust with my deepest secrets? By sharing what I usually hide, I take another step toward freedom.

So one Sunday the White Bear came and said that they could now set out to see her father and mother. At last they came to a large white farmhouse. "Your parents dwell here now," said the White Bear, "but do not forget what I said to you, or you will do much harm both to yourself and me." The White Bear turned round and went back again.

Sometimes we try very hard to maintain our relationships, even if we are unhappy, by keeping our problems a secret from the very people who could help us. We may think we are protecting ourselves, but this form of dishonesty usually sabotages our relationships. We may try to keep things on an even keel by ignoring our needs and making the best of bad situations. If our fear of loss or abandonment is strong, we may not be able to risk losing what we have by confronting our situation honestly.

We can use Step Eight to review our present relationships and determine whether or not harm is being done to anyone involved. Making amends in Step Nine sometimes clears up the difficulties by allowing us to see where adjustments in our behavior can improve the quality of our relationships.

*I will use Steps Eight and Nine to evaluate
my relationships and make amends
when necessary.*

There were such rejoicings when she went in. But in the afternoon, after they had dined at mid-day, all happened just as the White Bear had said. Her mother wanted to talk with her alone in her own chamber. But she remembered what the White Bear had said, and would on no account go. "What we have to say can be said at any time," she answered. But somehow or other her mother at last persuaded her, and she was forced to tell the whole story.

*M*any of us have problems setting and maintaining personal boundaries. We haven't learned that we have a right to keep some things to ourselves even when someone is pressuring us for an answer. Sometimes we even allow others to persuade us to reveal the whole story, regardless of the consequences. For some of us, the problem takes a different form. Our loyalty to our families or partners is so great that we are willing to harm ourselves by hiding the truth.

This hurts us in two ways. We limit the possibility of finding solutions to our problems, and we deepen our sense of shame and confusion. Exposing our feelings and talking honestly about our problems to others help us release our shame. It is important to realize that we are free to keep silent until we are ready. Learning what to tell, when to tell and who to tell is a sign that we are progressing in our recovery.

I have a choice to speak or to remain silent.
I will not allow shame and fear to
influence my decisions.

So she told how every night a man came and lay down beside her when the lights were all put out, and how she never saw him, because he always went away before it grew light in the morning, and how she continually went about in sadness, thinking how happy she would be if she could but see him, and how all day long she had to go about alone, and it was so dull and solitary.

*F*eeling alone and sad during the day and happy and fulfilled at night can be an unbearable burden. A separation between our conscious and unconscious behaviors or a difference between what we do openly and secretly can cause feelings of distress. Whatever the reason behind our conflicting feelings and actions, we cannot be comfortable with ourselves until we bring all aspects of our lives into closer alignment.

Admitting our discomfort and recognizing our unhappiness is not an easy thing to do. We may feel ashamed at our inability to deal effectively with the situation and be afraid to talk about it. We may be frightened that others will reject us if we are honest and reveal the truth about ourselves. We can thank our Higher Power each time we have the courage to release another part of our story. When we tell it to someone else, we break its hold over us.

*I will tell another part of my story today,
trusting that my Higher Power
will be there to guide me.*

"Oh!" cried the mother, in horror, "you are very likely sleeping with a troll! But I will teach you a way to see him. You shall have a bit of one of my candles, which you can take away with you hidden in your breast. Look at him with that when he is asleep, but take care not to let any tallow drop upon him."

*T*he thought of shedding light on our lives and relationships is often frightening. We can never be certain what we will find. We may discover that we are involved in a relationship that meets our material needs but leaves us feeling lonely. What if the person we are sleeping with turns out to be a troll? Are we ready to decide whether or not to remain in the relationship?

Our twelve-step program provides the tools we need to examine our behavior and learn to make healthy choices in our lives. Step Four begins the process of self-examination, where we make an inventory of ourselves and have an opportunity to honestly assess our attitudes and behaviors. By the time we reach Step Nine and are making amends, we have a better understanding of what we want for ourselves and what we must do in order to obtain it.

By taking my inventory and making amends, I can shine light on another aspect of my life today.

So when she had reached home and lit her candle she saw him, and he was the handsomest prince that eyes had ever beheld. It seemed to her that she must die if she did not kiss him that very moment. So she did kiss him, but while she was doing it she let three drops of tallow fall upon his shirt, and he awoke.

*W*henever we are desperate to possess someone or something, it may feel like we have fallen under a spell. We become so infatuated by some person or object that we lose our ability to be rational. When we experience alternating moments of joy and grief, and are carried away by an emotional landslide, we may think we are in love. Instead, this can be a sign that we are not comfortable with ourselves and are looking to outside sources for fulfillment.

When we light our candles and look closely at what we are doing, we often realize that we are being driven by a desire to merge with something or someone more powerful than we are. This is a signal to stop and ask our Higher Power for help. Step One reminds us how unmanageable our lives can become when we turn to other people or things in an effort to feel comfortable with ourselves.

If I become obsessed with someone or something,
I will ask for help in examining my needs.

"What have you done?" said he; "I have a stepmother who has bewitched me so that I am a white bear by day and a man by night; but now all is at an end between you and me, and I must leave you, and go to her. She lives in a castle which lies east of the sun and west of the moon, and there too is a princess with a nose which is three ells long, and she now is the one whom I must marry."

*E*vil mothers or stepmothers are often responsible for many of the problems that fairy tale heroes and heroines encounter. This doesn't mean that mothers are bad, but they can affect us negatively if we become too dependent on their protection. If we do not learn to stand on our own two feet, our ability to make a serious commitment to someone else can be impaired.

The tendency to be overly dependent on others often causes stress and can lead us into addictive and compulsive behaviors. If we invest too much of our time and energy in other people, we may feel empty or unfulfilled and seek escape through mood-altering activities and substances. Attending meetings and discussing our problems helps us avoid repeating these self-destructive behaviors. We draw strength and hope from seeing how others have learned to meet their need for security in healthier ways.

I will continue to be aware of my tendency to be dependent on other people and things. When I need help, I can attend a meeting or call a friend.

She wept and lamented, but all in vain, for go he must. Then she asked him if she could not go with him. But no, that could not be. "Can you tell me the way then, and I will seek you—that I may surely be allowed to do!" "Yes, you may do that," said he, "but there is no way thither. It lies east of the sun and west of the moon, and never would you find your way there."

Most of us know the tears and sadness that come when a loved one leaves and we cannot follow. We are forced to accept that life holds no guarantees that someone or something will always be there for us. As we learn to take better care of ourselves, we stop denying our losses and search for other ways to satisfy our needs.

Giving up sources of security and pleasure, however harmful they may be, takes courage and determination. It helps to remember that we have a Higher Power who can help us turn our disappointments into victories. Things may seem as hopeless to us as finding a castle east of the sun and west of the moon, but that is exactly where the Steps can lead us. Working the Steps gives us a chance to recover our ability to generate warmth and life like the sun, and reflect the light to others like the moon. This is part of the spiritual awakening that restores our connection to other people.

I will renew my commitment to recovery today and look forward to positive changes in my life.

When she awoke in the morning, she was lying in the midst of a dark, thick wood. By her side lay the self-same bundle of rags which she had brought with her from her own home. When she had wept till she was weary, she set out on her way. At last she came to an aged woman playing with a golden apple. The girl asked her if she knew the way to the Prince who lived in the castle which lay east of the sun and west of the moon. "How do you happen to know about him?" enquired the old woman. "maybe you are she who ought to have had him?" "Yes, indeed, I am," she said.

Many of us have suffered so many losses that we are weary from all the tears we have shed. We feel like we are right back where we started—with the self-same bundle of rags which we brought with us from home. Step Two, coming to believe that a power greater than ourselves can restore us to sanity, gives us the hope that we can attain a spiritual awakening if we continue our journey through the Steps.

Maintaining a commitment to recovery requires strength and hope. If we become discouraged, we can attend meetings and talk with others who are willing to help us. When we are steadfast in our commitment to the goal of self-restoration, we gradually find the joy, freedom, peace and serenity that are available to all of us.

I will mourn my losses and not revert to my old style of living. I am on the road to recovery.

"So it is you then?" said the old woman; "I know nothing about him but that he dwells in a castle which is east of the sun and west of the moon. You will be a long time in getting to it, but you shall have the loan of my horse, and then you can ride on it to an old woman who is a neighbour of mine: perhaps she can tell you about him. When you have got there you must just strike the horse beneath the left ear and bid it go home again; but you may take the golden apple with you."

Recovery is a slow journey that we travel one day at a time. Along the way we receive certain gifts—bits of knowledge or inner wisdom that help us make positive changes in our lives. Through reliance on our Higher Power, we are given the energy and direction we need to get from one stage of our journey to the next. We return that energy by sharing our experience, strength and hope with other people we meet along the way.

The unconditional love and support of fellow members is the golden apple we receive from participating in a twelve-step program. Knowing we are loved and supported gives us the courage to continue on the journey, certain that we will find the secret to loving others along the way.

The gifts I receive from attending meetings and sharing with others are signs that I am loved and respected.

So the girl seated herself on the horse, and at last she came to an aged woman with a gold carding-comb. The girl asked her if she knew the way to the castle, but she said what the first old woman had said. "You shall have the loan of my horse and you can ride to an old woman, and when you have got to her you may just strike the horse beneath the left ear and bid it go home again." Then she gave her the gold carding-comb, for it might be of use to her, she said.

*C*arding combs are used to separate fibers so that they can be spun into thread. The Twelve Steps are a similar tool that we can use to comb through our behaviors and attitudes to determine which ones are helpful and which are not. We begin this work with an inventory in Step Four, which we share with another person in Step Five. We start to correct our ineffective behaviors in Step Six when we become "entirely ready" to let go of the things that are impeding our progress.

This part of our journey involves making a realistic appraisal of our needs and desires. Listening to others talk about their drives and aspirations helps us identify our own. When we discover that old behaviors have served little purpose in our lives, we can begin to find more effective ways of attaining our goals.

I will make an honest effort to become "entirely ready" to let go of old behaviors and make way for new ones that meet my needs more effectively.

So the girl seated herself on the horse, and after a very long time she came to a great mountain, where an aged woman was spinning at a golden spinning-wheel. Of this woman, too, she enquired if she knew the way to the Prince. This old crone knew the way no better than the others. "But you may have the loan of my horse, and I think you had better ride to the East Wind, and ask him: perhaps he will blow you thither." Then she gave her the golden spinning-wheel.

*T*he Twelve Steps teach us another aspect of love—the ability to nurture and take care of ourselves. Learning to meet our needs while remaining sensitive to the needs of others may challenge us if we have a tendency to take care of them and ignore ourselves. A safe way to begin is by listening carefully to other people when they share their feelings and experiences and become willing to honestly share our own without trying to change them.

In recovery, we learn the advantages of taking a cooperative approach to life. Sharing our experience, strength and hope at meetings can be mutually beneficial. It helps us to grow and allows us to encourage others without feeling a need to take responsibility for their lives. Telling our stories helps us to utilize the Twelve Steps—our golden spinning-wheel—to spin the raw materials of our past into strong and beautiful threads for use today.

I can take advantage of the Steps and spin new threads to weave into the fabric of my life.

The girl had to ride for a long and wearisome time, but then she asked the East Wind if he could tell her the way to the Prince. "I do not know the way, but if you like, I will go with you to my brother the West Wind: he may know that." So she seated herself on his back, and they did go swiftly!

*W*inds from the east where the sun rises signal new beginnings and hope for the future. They can be a source of renewal in the midst of a long and wearisome time by bringing a breath of fresh air to our tired spirits.

We encounter many East Winds in the program—people whose smiles and encouragement help and support us. They can renew our hope and help us conquer our fear of change. While they may not be willing or able to carry us to our final destination, they can help us by pointing us in the right direction.

There are many opportunities for new beginnings in the program that can be exciting, but they may evoke fear in us. Fortunately, we have access to a Higher Power who will carry us through the fearful times and support us in the exciting times. We cannot see the end of our journey, but we can trust that we will be led safely each step of the way.

I am encouraged by the hope of new beginnings, and am learning to rely on my Higher Power to guide me through times of change.

When they got there, the East Wind went in and said he would like to hear if the West Wind knew whereabouts the castle was. "No," said the West Wind; "but if you like I will go with you to the South Wind, and perhaps he can tell you what you want to know. You may seat yourself on my back, and then I will carry you to him." So she did this, and journeyed to the South Wind, neither was she very long on the way.

*E*ach new beginning brings something to an end. Endings are a necessary part of the cycle of life and growth. If we are to be creative and discover new ideas, we must learn to let go of old ones gracefully. Winds from the west where the sun sets signal endings and help to remind us of the power of the Steps to carry us through times of loss.

Learning to deal successfully with beginnings and endings is a significant milestone for those of us who are uncomfortable with change. Our fear of change may have kept many of us locked in relationships and behaviors that were damaging to us and to others. When we ask our Higher Power to remove our short-comings in Step Seven, we indicate our willingness to let go of old attitudes and behavior patterns so that new ones have an opportunity to develop.

When I am able to deal with change gracefully,
I have occasion to celebrate.

When they got there, the West Wind asked the South Wind if he could tell her the way to the castle. "Well," said he, "I have never blown so far as that. If you like, I will go with you to my brother the North Wind; he is the oldest and strongest of all of us. You may sit upon my back, and then I will carry you there." So she seated herself on his back, and they were not long on the way.

*W*inds from the south are warm and tropical, reminding us that our journeys do not consist solely of struggle and hard work. We are meant to enjoy the process of recovery and the many occasions when we feel warm and contented. We are learning to live one day at a time without trying to cram more into a day than we can easily and satisfactorily accomplish.

Many of us have forgotten how to relax and let the wind carry us through the flow of our lives. It helps to stop in the middle of a busy day and take a few minutes to unwind. We can close our eyes and imagine ourselves on the ocean, in a peaceful forest or being carried along softly on the back of the South Wind. We don't have to travel alone, carrying the burdens of the world on our shoulders. We can ask for the help we need in getting to our destination.

If I relax and go with the flow today, I will be able to enjoy the process of recovery.

When they came near the North Wind's dwelling, they felt cold gusts a long while before they got there. "What do you want?" he roared from afar, and they froze as they heard. Said the South Wind: "It is I, and this is she who should have had the Prince. And now she wishes to ask you if you can tell her the way." "Yes," said the North Wind. "I know where it is. I once blew an aspen leaf there, but I was so tired that for many days afterwards I was not able to blow at all. If you are not afraid to go with me, I will take you on my back."

*O*ur recovery journeys are not always peaceful. At times we encounter a cold North Wind whose icy gusts disturb our pleasant progress. We may be especially prone to the North Wind's influence when we begin preparing our amends list in Step Eight. Examining the effect our actions and behaviors have had on the lives of others can stir up emotional storms within us. We are often prone to judge ourselves harshly and take on guilt that isn't rightfully ours.

It's important to consider getting outside help when we prepare our amends list. Talking to a sponsor, friend or counselor can help provide an objective view of our part in past events and relationships. The purpose of Step Eight is not to find reasons to punish ourselves, but to free us from the unpleasant consequences of our former actions.

> *When I encounter a cold North Wind and judge myself harshly, I will seek help from a trusted confidant.*

And away they went, high up through the air. They tore on and on, and the North Wind grew tired. He sank and sank until at last he went so low that the crests of the waves dashed against the heels of the poor girl he was carrying. But they were not very far from land, and there was just enough strength left in the North Wind to enable him to throw her onto the shore, immediately under the windows of a castle which lay east of the sun and west of the moon.

*T*he last leg of a long journey is often the hardest. The end is in sight, the direction is clear, but the goal may seem far from our reach. We wonder if we will have enough energy to keep going and reach our goal, or if the effort required to finish will be worth it.

A daily renewal of our commitment to recovery gives us the burst of energy we need to get us through these critical times. It helps to remember how far we've already come and what we have accomplished in getting to this point. We've passed through intense emotional storms and survived depression when the sea threatened to drown us. We've taken one step at a time, one day at a time. We've drawn on inner resources we didn't know we had. We've had encouragement from people like ourselves who want us to reach our destination.

I will trust my strong commitment to the program,
knowing that I have everything I need
to reach the shore.

Next morning she sat down beneath the walls of the castle to play with the golden apple, and the first person she saw was the maiden with the long nose, who was to have the Prince. "How much do you want for that gold apple of yours?" said she. "If I may go to the Prince who is here, and be with him tonight, you shall have it." said the girl. So the Princess got the golden apple, but when the girl went to the Prince's apartment that night he was asleep. The poor girl called to him, and shook him, and between while she wept; but she could not wake him.

*T*he golden apples of unconditional love that we receive from other people in the program are critical to our recovery. They help us learn to love ourselves and recover our self-worth. Gradually, we can begin to love others in the same way by using our golden apples to encourage them in their quest for wholeness.

As part of working Step Twelve, we can offer our love to others not yet involved in the program, realizing that they may not be ready to receive it. They may still be under the spell of the maiden with the long nose—caught in their own dreams and illusions. We can set an example and encourage them to look at themselves honestly, but we cannot force them to do so. We can be grateful for our progress and continue to work the Steps that allow us to maintain it.

> *I can carry the message to others, as Step Twelve suggests, and use my golden apples to encourage them.*

In the daytime she sat down once more beneath the windows of the castle, and began to card with her golden carding-comb. The Princess asked her what she wanted for it, and she replied that it was not for sale, but that if she could get leave to go to the Prince, and be with him during the night, she should have it. But when she went up to the Prince's room he was again asleep, and, let her shake him, or weep as she would, he still slept on, and she could not put any life in him.

*T*he Twelve Steps—our carding-comb—can be used to tear apart the fibers of our lives. We explore our strengths and weaknesses and prepare ourselves for the spiritual awakening we are hoping for. The self-knowledge and self-acceptance we gain from sifting through our lives also helps us know and accept other people. We benefit greatly when we carry the message to others.

The self-understanding we develop through the program helps us reach out to others in a gentle and non-threatening way. We avoid grief and disappointment when we remember that no matter how much we may want to help, others may not be receptive to us, just as we were perhaps unresponsive to helpful attention at one time. The pain may be too severe, or the fear of the unknown too great for them to risk leaving their present security.

I can carry the message of my spiritual awakening to others, but I cannot force them to open their eyes.

When day had quite come, the girl seated herself under the castle windows, to spin with her golden spinning-wheel, and the Princess with the long nose wanted to have that also. The girl said if she could get leave to go to the Prince and be with him during the night, she should have it. There were some people who had been carried off and they had heard how a woman had wept and called on him two nights running, and they told the Prince of this. So that evening, when the Princess came once more with her sleeping-drink, he pretended to drink, but threw it away behind him.

*W*e spin many threads in the course of our recovery. We use some old ones and add some new ones and begin to weave different patterns into our lives. The more willing we are to experiment with new techniques, the more successful we will be at creating healthy new behaviors for ourselves.

In the process of developing new patterns of behavior, we draw others into our lives, but we cannot control their decision to confront reality or to ignore it. We do not always know what would give them the incentive to throw away their sleeping-drink. Often it has little or nothing to do with us, no matter how closely our lives are interwoven. It is important for us to remember that we are responsible only for our own recovery. We can offer help to others, but we cannot force them to take it.

*When I came into the program, I exchanged
my "sleeping-drink" for a chance to
become happy, joyous and free.*

So, when the girl went into the Prince's room this time he was awake, and she had to tell him how she had come there. "You have come just in time," said the Prince, "for I should have been married to-morrow; but I will not have the long-nosed Princess, and you alone can save me. I will say that I want to see what my bride can do, and bid her wash the shirt which has the three drops of tallow on it. This she will consent to do, for she does not know that it is you who let them fall on it."

*T*he right combination of our willingness to share our story and the receptiveness of someone else to hear it, can be a major turning point in our lives. Our decision to turn away from the long-nosed Princess and look at what we want signals the end of a long enchantment and the beginning of a new journey. The story of how we did that can be an inspiration to us as we tell it, and to others as they listen.

Being willing to look at our behaviors and relationships honestly requires a sincere commitment to change. It takes courage to face the possibility of loss and upheaval. We can call on the wisdom and experience of other program members to help us evaluate our situations. When we trust our Higher Power to guide our actions and decisions, it becomes easier to maintain our commitment by being honest with ourselves and others.

The Steps offer a solution to my problems. I can pass any test life gives me by using the principles of the program.

The next day the Prince said, "I must see what my bride can do. I have a fine shirt which I want to wear as my wedding shirt, but three drops of tallow have got upon it, and I have vowed to marry no one but the woman who is able to do it." The Princess with the long nose began to wash, but the more she washed and rubbed, the larger the spots grew.

We can't expect to fix problems that are not our responsibility. We may be very good at washing shirts, but we only compound the problem when we try to do someone else's laundry. It is healthier for us to stop trying to fix things and allow the responsibility to fall where it belongs. If we don't, we may become angry and frustrated with ourselves, the other people involved and the problem we're trying to solve. We then become victims instead of the successful rescuers we set out to be.

Working the Steps helps us resolve the anger and resentment that sometimes accompany our unsuccessful attempts to save others. When we stop denying reality and realize that we're making matters worse, we can stop thinking of ourselves as problem-solvers who can clean up any mess that comes our way.

I will take responsibility for myself and allow others to be responsible for themselves.

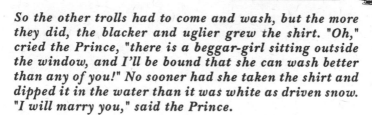

So the other trolls had to come and wash, but the more they did, the blacker and uglier grew the shirt. "Oh," cried the Prince, "there is a beggar-girl sitting outside the window, and I'll be bound that she can wash better than any of you!" No sooner had she taken the shirt and dipped it in the water than it was white as driven snow. "I will marry you," said the Prince.

*U*ntil we experience the joy and freedom of being able to relate openly to others, we may think we have to cover up all our imperfections in order to be accepted. If we try to do so by creating an illusion that doesn't match who we are, we may find ourselves in the position of having to add one lie to another just to maintain our facade. When we try to white-wash our shirts by covering up who we are, we only become less attractive.

Our shirts truly come clean when we learn to be honest about who we are and what we want. We won't ever be perfect, but we learn that openness is attractive. Learning to show others who we are helps us allow them the freedom to be themselves.

*I will "come clean" today, remembering that
honesty fosters healthy relationships.*

Then the old troll-hag flew into such a rage that she burst, and the Princess with the long nose and all the little trolls must have burst too, for they have never been heard of since. The Prince and his bride set free all the folk who were imprisoned there, and took away with them all the gold and silver that they could carry, and moved far away from the castle which lay east of the sun and west of the moon.

*P*ersistent attempts to control what we can't control or make things happen that aren't meant to be can cause us to feel angry and resentful. Like the old troll-hag, we may become so enraged that we feel as though we are going to burst.

The Serenity Prayer helps us release the controlling side of our personality. Learning to accept the things we cannot change and finding the courage to change the things we can results in greater peace of mind. The key is developing the wisdom to know the difference.

As we progress in recovery, we develop personal resources that make us less dependent on others for our well-being. We discover the benefits of collaborating in mutual endeavors without expecting others to take care of us or trying to take care of them. We return to a healthier existence with more than enough treasure to make our way through life.

I am willing to leave my illusions behind me and live with the richness that reality makes available to me.

Prince Hyacinth

PRINCE HYACINTH

There once was a prince who was placed under a spell before he was born by an angry enchanter who said to his father: "You shall have a son, who will never be happy until he finds out his nose is too long." The king laughed, thinking that anyone could recognize a long nose when he saw one. He died without informing his wife about what has transpired.

The queen was horrified when she saw her infant son's gigantic nose, but was placated when her ladies-in-waiting told her it was not as large as it looked. Members of the royal court told dreadful stories about people with short noses, and Prince Hyacinth became convinced that his nose was a mark of fine distinction.

The prince grew up and fell in love with the portrait of a little princess who had a small, saucy nose. One of his courtiers conjectured that small noses were appropriate for women but not suitable for men.

The princess agreed to marry Prince Hyacinth, but the enchanter whirled her away. The prince searched for her, trusting his horse to find the way. During his journey, he met an ancient woman who was actually a good fairy who wished to free the prince from his curse.

She retrieved the princess from the enchanter, locked her in a crystal palace and placed it in the prince's path. He could not break through the walls, but the princess was able to extend her hand for him to kiss. No matter how hard he tried, his long nose always prevented him from kissing her. When he exclaimed that his nose must be too long, the crystal prison shattered instantly, and the prince was united with his beloved.

"You shall have a son, who will never be happy until he finds out his nose is too long." Though the King was horribly afraid of the enchanter, he could not help laughing at this threat. *"If my son has such a long nose as that, he must always see it or feel it; at least if he is not blind or without hands!"*

*N*one of us wants to confront our flaws—our long noses—if we can avoid it. They make us feel different, and that hurts. It's sometimes easier to deny the pain by closing our eyes, folding our hands and assuming a passive attitude. This way, we hope to protect ourselves from rejection and disappointment.

Failure to acknowledge our weak points blinds us to our strong points as well. Although we can be grateful to denial for helping us survive until we found the program, we can view its passing without regret. When we uncover our true nature and fully accept and acknowledge who we are, we can begin to experience peace within ourselves.

Our Step Four inventory gives us an opportunity to look at all aspects of ourselves and realize what determines many of our actions. When we understand and accept our behavior, we can begin to identify some of our actual needs and take the first step in finding successful ways to satisfy them.

I am becoming aware of who I am. I will no longer allow my distorted perceptions to stand in the way of my happiness.

The Prince had large blue eyes and a sweet little mouth, but his nose covered half his face. The Queen was inconsolable when she saw this great nose, but her ladies assured her it was not really as large as it looked. The Queen was pleased with what they told her, and when she looked again, his nose certainly did not seem to her quite so large.

As part of our denial, we learn many ways of distorting reality to smooth and manage our lives. Like the Queen's ladies, we convince ourselves and others that things are not as they seem. Many of our problems arise from the false notion that we can control the world and generate the changes we want in order to get our needs met. When this stops working for us, we are ready for Step One—admitting that we are powerless and that our lives are unmanageable— that we cannot control ourselves or other people.

Learning to be honest with ourselves and others requires a serious commitment on our part. It takes practice to know when to be open and when to hold back. Fortunately we don't have to figure it out alone. We have a Higher Power to give us inner direction and a twelve-step program that helps us develop new ways of responding to others who also want to cultivate trustworthy relationships.

I will be honest even if it would be easier to lie. I will watch out for situations where I am tempted to deny my feelings and take care of someone else.

The Prince was brought up with great care; and, as soon as he could speak, they told him all sorts of dreadful stories about people who had short noses. No one was allowed to come near him whose nose did not more or less resemble his own, and the courtiers, to get in favour with the Queen, took to pulling their babies' noses several times a day to make them grow long.

Many of us grew up with people who had good intentions and attempted to change us to meet their ideal of success. They hoped their efforts would help us manage life more easily than they did. Instead, their constant pushing and pulling convinced us that we would never be right, no matter what was done.

At first glance, a twelve-step program seems to offer more of the same. We're asked to make some changes in our behavior, admit the true condition of our lives and then be willing to trust in a power greater than ourselves. We work the Steps to foster our individual development and allow all of our features to assume their natural shape. The freedom to grow physically, emotionally and spiritually, according to our own inner guidelines, is one of the rewards of recovery.

I am learning to respect my individuality and trust my inner direction.

His room was hung with pictures, all of people with very large noses; and the Prince grew up so convinced that a long nose was a great beauty, that he would not on any account have had his own a single inch shorter."

*I*t's difficult to get a true picture of ourselves if everyone around us is afraid to be honest with us. If we are exposed to people who go to great lengths to deceive us, like the Prince was, we may resist believing the truth. Out of pride or a need to avoid shame, we sometimes justify attitudes or behaviors that sabotage our own best interests. Believing that rich people are never happy may quiet our envy, but it may also cover up our fear of success. Congratulating ourselves for not being loud and obnoxious may temporarily boost our self-esteem, but it can also prevent us from dealing with the shyness that hinders our spontaneity.

When we stop justifying our behavior and recognize our defects of character, we are prepared for Step Six and are "entirely ready" to have our Higher Power remove them. Identifying our shortcomings and turning them over to our Higher Power takes our focus off the negative aspects of our behavior. We can then see life's challenges in a more realistic light and develop a positive attitude that allows us to meet them constructively and creatively.

I will stop justifying my character defects so that I can be entirely ready to have them removed.

When the Queen thought it was time that he should be married, she commanded that the portraits of several princesses be brought for him to see. The Dear Little Princess, whom he thought quite charming, had a little saucy nose, which was a cause of great embarrassment to the courtiers, who had got into such a habit of laughing at little noses that they sometimes found themselves laughing at hers before they had time to think.

*L*ife is difficult when we give others the power to establish our values for us and determine whether our noses are too long or too short. We sacrifice our identities and deny our feelings when we respond to others the way we think they want us to instead of being honest with them. Trying to keep up with their changing tastes and priorities adds to the already unmanageable burden of thoughts, feelings and attitudes that we are trying desperately to manipulate.

Learning to react to people and situations honestly takes time, faith and practice. When we become comfortable with our own values and responses, our self-esteem increases. We can laugh spontaneously at what we find funny without worrying about what others think. We can make decisions based on what we want and like. This helps us get in touch with who we are and makes us less dependent on others for happiness and approval.

I will stop laughing at things I don't really find funny. I will take steps to recover my own values along with my sense of humor.

284

Two were banished for their disrespect in laughing at her little nose. The others learnt to think twice before they spoke, and one even went so far as to tell the Prince that, though no man could be worth anything unless he had a long nose, still, a woman's beauty was a different thing. The Prince made him a splendid present as a reward for this good news.

*O*ur progress is impeded when we behave as the courtiers did and tell others what they want to hear instead of what we feel. There may be splendid payoffs in the beginning, but we usually wake up at some point to find we have given ourselves away. By focusing on pleasing others rather than reacting honestly, our spontaneous inner child is banished and our identity is lost.

If we tend to lose our individuality in relationships with other people, we may approach Step Three with some suspicion. The idea of turning our will and our lives over to the care of anyone or anything else may frighten us. As we become comfortable with this Step, we find that there is a vast difference between adjusting our values to accommodate another person and turning to a Higher Power for inner direction.

I am learning to respect myself and my values. I do not need approval from others to feel good about myself.

The Prince sent ambassadors to ask the Dear Little Princess in marriage. The King, her father, gave his consent. The Prince was just advancing to kiss her hand when the enchanter appeared as suddenly as a flash of lightning, and, snatching up the Little Princess, whirled her away out of their sight!

We are all familiar with the experience of seeing change occur as quickly as a lightning flash. We know how it feels to have our dreams snatched out of sight by forces we can neither understand nor control. We each have our own ways of coping with sudden change. Some of us stop planning for the future, believing it is easier to want nothing than to face another disappointment. Or, we sometimes retreat to fantasy worlds or engage in compulsive behaviors, trying to control everything and everybody in our lives.

Being in a twelve-step program and working the Steps protects us from the painful consequences of unexpected change. Knowing that we have what we require to meet any challenge that comes our way helps us relax and adapt to variations in our lives. Believing that we are part of a larger picture makes it possible for us to move forward into the unknown with courage. The ability to take action in spite of an uncertain future is the secret strength that can turn our seeming defeats into victories.

I can accept disappointment as an opportunity for change, knowing that my Higher Power never closes one door without opening another.

The Prince was left quite inconsolable, and declared that nothing should induce him to go back to his kingdom until he had found her again, and refusing to allow any of his courtiers to follow him, he mounted his horse and rode sadly away, letting the animal choose his own path.

Many of us have tried to find happiness by using relationships, compulsive behaviors or addictive substances to ease our way through life's losses and disappointments. In the process we often lose touch with our true selves. Like the Prince who rode sadly away to find his Princess, we enter the program in desperation, looking for a way to recover broken connections with ourselves and others. Finding peace and serenity requires solitude, soul-searching and a willingness to let go of attitudes and behaviors that support our denial. It means surrendering to a Higher Power who, like the Prince's horse, will help us find our way.

Some of us are fearful of undertaking such a difficult journey. It helps to remember that we recover slowly—one day at a time. When we stumble and fall, we can get up and go on. Whatever our age or past experience, growth and change are viable options if we are open to new possibilities and are willing to seek out situations that promote and sustain healthy development.

My Higher Power is with me on my journey through the Steps. I will not insist on finding my way alone, but will gratefully accept guidance.

As the night fell, the Prince caught sight of a light, which seemed to shine from a cavern. He rode up to it, and saw a little old woman. She put on her spectacles to look at Prince Hyacinth, but it was quite a long time before she could fix them securely because her nose was so very short. The Prince and the Fairy (for that was who she was) had no sooner looked at one another than they went into fits of laughter and cried at the same moment, "Oh, what a funny nose!"

*G*etting past our external appearances and recognizing what we have in common with others seems impossible at times. We have difficulty believing that people with short noses can understand or sympathize with those who have long noses. We may say to ourselves, "He was born rich. How could he ever understand the shame of living in this neighborhood?" "She is so pretty. How could she know how it feels to have an imperfection like mine?"

Attending meetings gives us an opportunity to meet people who have experienced many of the same fears that we face today. Sharing our story with others helps us to uncover the shame that causes us to laugh at someone else to protect ourselves from being hurt. Listening to others helps us accept ourselves so that we don't have to push them away in order to feel safe.

I will look beyond external appearances today. Help and compassion are available where I least expect to find them.

"Really, madam," said the Prince, *"I wish you would leave off mentioning my nose. It cannot matter to you what it is like. I am quite satisfied with it, and have no wish to have it shorter. One must take what is given one."*

*H*ow many times have we said, "I can't do anything about it—I must take what is given to me." "There's no use complaining about it—that's just the way it is!" "There's no reason to think about it—I'll never have anything I want anyway!" Statements like these usually mean we're having trouble accepting certain aspects of our lives. We want them to be different, but we don't know how to change them.

We can initiate positive changes by first admitting that we are powerless over other people and circumstances. When we choose to alter our views, we react differently to people and events, and the world around us changes. We begin to associate with others who have the same positive attitude toward life and are responsible for their own behavior.

Although we cannot control the growth and development of those around us, we can acquire the serenity to accept the things we cannot change without feeling resentful. We can find the courage to change the things we can without demanding control over the outcome. This frees us from feelings of helplessness and allows us to appreciate whatever opportunities for joy are available to us at the moment.

*Today I will look for reactions that block
my ability to change and ask for the
willingness to let them go.*

"Plague take the old lady! How she does go on about my nose!" said the Prince to himself. "How stupid people are not to see their own faults! that comes of being a princess: she has been spoilt by flatterers. For my part I never will be taken in by them. I know my own defects, I hope!"

*I*t's often easier to see the faults of others than it is to see our own. It's difficult to acknowledge that what disturbs us most about other people often reflects our concerns about ourselves. We may criticize someone for being too outgoing, but be secretly envious that she attracts more attention than we do. We may judge someone harshly for being so self-centered, while hiding our resentment that he seems to get his way most of the time and we don't.

Despite the discomfort they cause us, these aggravations can put us in touch with our true feelings. Careful examination of our reactions to other people can help us discover who we are and what we want to be like. When we acknowledge our own motives and make the necessary changes in our approach to life, other people's opinions and behaviors cease to bother us. Knowing and accepting ourselves frees us from being controlled by others and takes away our need to dominate or manipulate them.

By examining my reactions to others, I can learn about myself and make changes that will be healthy for me.

The Prince grew so impatient at the Fairy's continual remarks about his nose that he rode hastily away. But wherever he came he thought the people mad, for they all talked of his nose, and yet he could not bring himself to admit that it was too long, he had been so used all his life to hear it called handsome.

*M*any of us have spent a good part of our lives thinking people were mad when they told us things we didn't want to hear. We may have formed impressions of ourselves at an early age based on our perception of what others thought about us. If we don't stop to examine their validity, these false messages may continue to influence us throughout our lives. It may be that the negative voices we hear today reflect more of how we see ourselves than how others see us.

Getting accurate feedback about the effect we have on others can help us form healthier relationships. Sharing our inventory with another person in Step Five is an opportunity to be open and honest about ourselves. If we are willing to listen to their perceptions of us and are ready to stop running, we can begin to experience the benefits of honest communication.

I will explore whether or not self-destructive behaviors are interfering with my ability to meet my needs. I will look closely at my blind spots.

The old Fairy, who wished to make him happy, at last hit upon a plan. She shut the Dear Little Princess up in a palace of crystal, and put this palace down where the Prince could not fail to find it. His joy at seeing the Princess again was extreme, and he set to work with all his might to try to break her prison; but in spite of all his efforts he failed utterly.

We come to the program separated from our innocent and precious child. Like the Prince, we know the frustration of being unable to break the crystal palace and reach the person within. Our tendency to deny our needs and feelings can break our connection with our deepest selves and prevent us from knowing who we are and what we want from life.

Many of our past efforts to discover our true selves ended in disappointment. It takes humility to admit that we are still looking for ways to achieve a satisfying life—that we are tired of failing in our attempts to break through our prisons. We need courage to reach out to others and a willingness to try again. We can use the Steps to further release the inner strengths that have the power to make us whole.

I have faith in the power of the Steps to restore me. I will look to my Higher Power for help in releasing my inner strength today.

In despair he thought at least that he would try to get near enough to speak to the Princess, who, on her part, stretched out her hand that he might kiss it; but turn which way he might, his long nose always prevented it. For the first time he realized how long it really was, and exclaimed: "Well, it must be admitted that my nose is too long!" In an instant the crystal prison flew into a thousand splinters.

*H*onestly acknowledging the condition of our lives—admitting that our noses are too long—is an important step toward healing and wholeness. Breaking through denial frees us from illusion and isolation and paves the way for a spiritual awakening—a new awareness of our supportive relationships with others and the world around us. Our self-imposed crystal prisons shatter when we recognize the obstacles that hinder us, admit that our old ways of coping aren't working and reach out for new approaches to life's challenges.

Our journey begins with Step One. We admit that we are powerless and that our lives are unmanageable. Step Two reminds us that a power greater than ourselves can restore us to wholeness. These two Steps help us recognize that we have a right to happiness, joy and freedom. The remaining Steps help us remove the barriers that stand in the way of our success.

I will work the Steps daily, knowing they hold the key to peace and serenity in my life.

"Much good it was for me to talk to you about your nose!" *said the Fairy. "You would never have found out how* *extraordinary it was if it hadn't hindered you from* *doing what you wanted to."*

It is easy to see other people's noses, but we can't accurately see our own without a mirror. Even then, we don't always see a true image because the view that is reflected is distorted by our feelings about it. The same is true of our self-defeating behaviors; we see faults in others before we recognize them in ourselves.

Most of us don't recognize our defects until they prevent us from getting what we want. When we become willing to acknowledge the obstacles that stand in the way of our happiness, we find that our difficulties are not unique. Discovering that others have struggled with imperfections like ours and turned them into assets gives us renewed hope.

When we are finally free to be ourselves, new opportunities for self-expression become available to us. As we develop new skills and become more useful to ourselves and others, we find new meaning and purpose in our lives. We recover the joy of healthy connection with others through a pattern of mutual respect and relatedness that benefits all involved.

When I look in the mirror today,
I will be proud of the image
I see. I am worthy and
deserving of love.

Hansel and Grettel

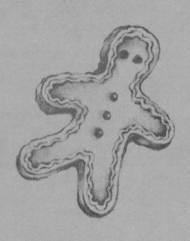

nce upon a time, during a great famine, a poor woodcutter and his wife could no longer support their children, and decided to send them away. The father was reluctant to part with Hansel and Grettel, but finally agreed that they be abandoned in the forest. Hansel prepared for this event by collecting white pebbles from the garden and using them to mark the path when his parents led him and his sister into the forest. That evening, the pebbles reflected the light of the moon, and the children were able to find their way home.

Not long after, the famine struck once more and the children were again faced with the same problem. Because the front door was locked, Hansel could not collect any pebbles. He used crumbs from the bread he had been given to mark the path home. They were eaten by birds and the children could not find the way.

As they wandered, they discovered a little cottage made of bread, sugar and cakes. When they began to nibble from the roof, a witch enticed them inside with promises of splendid meals and comfortable beds. When Hansel and Grettel entered the cottage, they fell under her power. The witch locked Hansel in a cage and forced Grettel to prepare food to fatten up her brother so he would become a tasty meal.

One day, the witch told Grettel to crawl into the oven to see if it was hot enough to bake bread. Sensing that the woman intended to bake her, Grettel pretended that she didn't know how. When the witch moved toward the oven to show her how, Grettel pushed her inside and slammed the door. The children took the precious jewels and pearls that filled every corner of the house and escaped.

When they returned home, they discovered that their stepmother had died so they shared the jewels they had collected with their father. They were no longer poor.

Once upon a time there dwelt on the outskirts of a forest a poor woodcutter with his wife and two children. When there was great famine in the land, he couldn't even provide them with daily bread. One night he sighed and said to his wife: "What's to become of us? how are we to support our children, now that we have nothing more for ourselves?" "I'll tell you what, husband, early tomorrow morning we'll take the children out into the thickest part of the wood. They won't be able to find their way home, and we shall be rid of them."

*I*n most fantasy families, parents provide their children with abundant riches—healthy meals, a fine education, lots of rest and recreation, and plenty of love and affection. When the children leave home, they are full of self-esteem and energy, and are equipped with many of the skills needed to meet life's challenges.

In real life, not all parents are blessed with the ability to be good role models for their children. They work with the tools that they developed while growing up, and they are not always able to meet our needs.

Working the Steps with the support of other program members helps us develop the skills we need to journey through the thickest part of the wood. As we become more confident in our abilities, we let go of our anger and resentment over what was not done for us by our parents. By improving our conscious contact with our Higher Power, as Step Eleven suggests, we can minimize our fears and know that we are being guided safely and wisely through life.

I am grateful for my growing competence. I am acquiring the skills necessary to find my way through the forest of life.

The children, too, had not been able to sleep for hunger, and had heard what their step-mother had said to their father. And when the old people had fallen asleep Hansel got up and stole out. The moon was shining clearly, and the white pebbles which lay in front of the house glittered like bits of silver. Hansel bent down and filled his pocket with as many of them as he could cram in. At daybreak, they all set out together on the way to the forest, and Hansel dropped the white pebbles out of his pocket on to the path.

Many of us are surprised to find that our seemingly independent and resourceful actions actually hide deep feelings of need and dependence. Dropping pebbles to lead us back to the fantasized security of our past is not the answer. The secret is to become our own loving parent and learn to nurture ourselves.

Participation in a fellowship committed to self-revelation helps us achieve this goal by offering us support and encouragement. Learning to accept and understand our own neediness is the first step in becoming ready to release it. In twelve-step meetings we can discuss our fears and find understanding and support from others.

The Twelve Steps are not pebbles that lead us back to our childhood homes. They are suggested actions that help us to identify our neediness and release the ties that support our dependency on others.

Today I will move forward with my life, looking back only to clear the wreckage of my past.

At last it was pitch-dark. Grettel began to cry, and said: "How are we ever to get out of the wood?" But Hansel comforted her. And when the full moon had risen he took his sister by the hand and followed the pebbles, which shone like new threepenny bits, and showed them the path. They walked all through the night, and at daybreak reached their father's house again.

Some of us left home bewildered and afraid of the dark like Grettel; others strode off bravely like Hansel, our confidence bolstered by the fact that we knew a secret way back. We may have left home and then returned, living with our parents long after our childhood friends had moved away.

Our dependency on other people is not always apparent to us. We may limit contact with our families, thinking that we have become self-sufficient, but then look to others to take care of us. Or we may devote our energies to meeting the needs of others so they will not abandon or reject us.

We can use Step Four to examine our current resources and recognize areas where we still depend on caretaker figures. When we are honest and thorough in our inventory, we find that our resources are not as meager as we thought they were. Identifying and focusing on our strengths helps us develop our potential and gives us the confidence we need to lead independent lives.

I will use my ingenuity to move forward instead of backward today. I am willing to look at the past, but I do not intend to dwell on it.

Not long afterwards there was again great dearth in the land, and the children heard their mother address their father in bed one night: "Everything is eaten up once more; we have only half a loaf in the house. The children must be got rid of; we'll lead them deeper into the wood this time, so they won't be able to find their way out again. There is no other way of saving ourselves."

Most of us know what it's like to be lost in the woods, feeling alone and abandoned, convinced that there is no way of saving ourselves. Through sharing with others in twelve-step meetings, we gain insight into ways that deal more effectively with our feelings. Part of our journey involves meeting people who can help us recognize and work through our fear of abandonment.

Relying on support from other people who are comfortable with their lives encourages us to proceed. It becomes easier to create a healthy environment for our inner child when we can admit our fear of being left alone and ask for help from our Higher Power to overcome it.

Being honest with myself and others helps me to stay out of the deep woods. I can call a sponsor or close friend to help me work the Steps.

But the children were awake, and heard the conversation. When the old people were asleep Hansel got up, and wanted to go out and pick up pebbles again, but the woman had barred the door. At early dawn the woman came and made the children get up. They received their bit of bread. On the way to the wood Hansel crumbled it in his pocket, and every few minutes he stood still and dropped a crumb on the ground. When the moon appeared, they found no crumbs, for the thousands of birds that fly about the woods and fields had picked them up.

Sometimes we must alter our plans and adapt to situations over which we have no control. This can be a sign that we haven't found the right solution yet, or that there are alternatives still to be considered. We sometimes waste energy engaging in futile attempts to prevent the inevitable, rather than accepting it and making adjustments as needed.

Reciting the Serenity Prayer can help us to decide when to scatter our stored energy and when to conserve it. We ask for the serenity to accept the things we cannot change—the ways other people treat us—and the courage to change the things we can—the attitudes and outlooks that keep us locked in unhealthy behaviors and situations. Finally, we ask for the wisdom to know the difference.

I am finding relief from my paralysis. I will use the Serenity Prayer if I feel frusrated.

On the third morning after they had left their father's house they set about their wandering again, but only got deeper and deeper into the wood, and now they felt that if help did not come to them soon they must perish.

*I*t is frightening to think that we are going deeper and deeper into the wood, and may never find our way out. When we stop looking frantically for ways to escape, we begin to discern that the solution lies within us. In the process of developing secure identities, we must look for a source of power within ourselves instead of trying to find our way back to former caretakers.

Some of us married early to get away from home and avoid facing the world alone. We thought we had found someone who would give us the love and security we wanted so desperately. How disappointing to find instead, another lost child like ourselves, who was just as bewildered as we were—if not more so.

We cannot place responsibility for our well-being in the hands of others and expect to lead happy lives. True freedom comes from entering the dark forest despite our fear and confusion, trusting in our Higher Power to guide our journey and using the Steps to find our way home.

I will make conscious contact with my Higher Power and my inner child today. The Steps will lead me in the right direction.

At midday they came to a little house; and when they came quite near they saw that the cottage was made of bread and roofed with cakes, while the window was made of transparent sugar. Hansel stretched up his hand and broke off a little bit of the roof to see what it was like, and Grettel went to the casement and began to nibble at it. Thereupon a shrill voice called out from the room inside: "Nibble, nibble, little mouse, Who's nibbling my house?" The children answered: "Tis Heaven's own child, the tempest wild," and went on eating.

*W*hen we're desperate, the thought of a quick fix often brings overwhelming relief. We get so excited by the promise of another high that we don't stop to look at the possible consequences. We often give into our inner cravings as Hansel and Grettel did, and then feel ashamed for indulging ourselves.

We forget that we can fill our inner emptiness only temporarily with chocolate shakes, new jobs, casual sex, shopping sprees or big wins. When we feel empty again, the void is often bigger than before. Lasting satisfaction comes when we find more substantial ways to meet our emotional and spiritual needs. Thanks to our program, we don't have to do this alone. We have found others who are traveling the same road to give us direction and support.

If I develop a craving for something unhealthy today, I can go to a meeting. This allows me to move past temptation.

Suddenly the door opened, and an ancient dame leaning on a staff hobbled out. Hansel and Grettel were so terrified that they let the food they had in their hands fall. But the old woman shook her head and said: "Oh, ho! you dear children, who led you here? Just come in and stay with me, no ill shall befall you."

*I*t's easy to be deceived by offers of aid if we are hungry, angry, lonely or tired, especially when we're told that no ill will befall us. Afraid we can't make it on our own and desperate for help and comfort, we often ignore the danger signals that accompany dependent behavior. We are seduced by internal messages that say, "This is what you need right now. Go ahead and enjoy it."

As our self-defeating behavior increases, we may find ourselves in more desperate situations, frustrated by weight we can't lose, relationships we can't count on or bills we can't pay. We become trapped in vicious cycles where one pacifier only leads to the need for a better one.

Breaking this cycle of behavior is not easy. It means letting go of unrealistic expectations and old ways of obtaining quick relief for our pain. When we put an end to our search for an easier, softer way, we are ready to take the action required to channel our behavior in a more positive and trustworthy direction.

I will remember that what I do today is likely to affect how I feel tomorrow.

The old woman appeared to be friendly, but she was really an old witch who had waylaid the children, and had built the bread house in order to lure them in. When anyone came into her power she killed, cooked, and ate him, and held a regular feast-day for the occasion. Early in the morning, she seized Hansel with her bony hand and carried him into a stable, and barred the door on him. Then she went to Grettel, and cried: "Get up, you lazy-bones, fetch water and cook for your brother. When he's fat I'll eat him up."

When we allow our dependencies to control our lives, we lose our freedom and limit our ability to think for ourselves. We become prime candidates for being taken hostage like Hansel or put into service like Grettel. We are driven to meet the needs of other people because we believe we can't survive without them. When we give others this power over us, they waste our energy, feed on our strength and try to take over our lives in exchange for promises of security and care.

Life becomes much easier when we find ways to nurture and protect ourselves. Relinquishing our dependence on others does not mean we cannot have close relationships. On the contrary, we can relate to people more intimately when we stop giving them the power to control our lives.

Today I will avoid situations that promise quick relief. I can find more effective ways to nurture my inner child.

Every morning the old woman hobbled out to the stable and cried: "Hansel, put out your finger, that I may feel if you are getting fat." But Hansel stretched out a bone, and the old dame, whose eyes were dim, couldn't see it, and thinking always it was Hansel's finger, wondered why he fattened so slowly. When four weeks passed and Hansel still remained thin, she lost patience and determined to wait no longer. "Hi! Grettel, be quick and get some water. Hansel may be fat or thin, I'm going to kill him to-morrow and cook him."

*B*y the time we get to a twelve-step program we usually have accumulated a large collection of survival tools. Otherwise, we would not have made it this far. Many of us narrowly escaped being eaten alive on several occasions and may have surrendered our self-esteem in the process.

When we are ready for Step Five and can admit our part in things, we begin to see the extent to which our dependency limits us. This awareness helps us become willing in Step Six to give up behaviors that work against us in favor of more beneficial ones. We can then stop employing our wits and creativity to escape the clutches of the witches who seek to devour us and begin putting our energies to more positive use.

I am aware of attitudes and expectations that make me a candidate for other people's traps. As I begin to live more fully, I will overcome my dependency on others.

In the morning Grettel had to hang up the kettle full of water, and light the fire. The old dame pushed Grettel out to the oven. "Creep in," said the witch, "and see if it's properly heated," She meant to close the oven and let the girl bake. But Grettel perceived her intentions, and spoke: "I don't know how I'm to do it; how do I get in?" "You silly goose!" said the hag, "the opening is big enough; see, I could get in myself;" and she poked her head into the oven. Then Grettel gave her a shove that sent her right in, shut the iron door, and drew the bolt.

*W*e usually come into the program in the midst of situations that threaten us emotionally, physically and spiritually. Our problems may have become so intense that we feel we have no place else to turn. Relationships we thought would rescue us may now overwhelm us; compulsive habits that distracted us may have become boring; ways of looking at the world that protected us from disappointment now cause us intense pain.

Working the Steps helps us to strengthen the inner messages that guide us to make changes in our self-defeating behavior. We become more aware of our capabilities as Grettel did when she developed a plan to save herself from the witch. Developing faith in our Higher Power enables us to respond quickly to these messages when we are required to do so.

Today I will ask my Higher Power for help in relinquishing behaviors and relationships that are destructive to me or to my inner child.

Grettel flew straight to Hansel, opened the stable-door, and cried: "Hansel, we are free; the old witch is dead." Then Hansel sprang like a bird out of a cage when the door is opened. How they rejoiced, and fell on each other's necks, and jumped for joy, and kissed one another!

*W*hat a wonderful thing to put our old fears to rest and be free of the terrors of the past! Replacing the critical tapes in our heads with new supportive messages and overcoming our inability to feel or express love gives us a sense of peace that we may never have known or even imagined. By escaping the restrictions our search for security placed on us, we begin to experience the benefits that working the Twelve Steps can provide in our lives.

It is a joyous occasion when our cage doors are opened and we rejoice in our newfound freedom. We may still get into tight spots, but in a twelve-step program we develop the means to remove ourselves from situations that are unhealthy for us. We can use Steps Four and Five to identify and expose the traps which we tend to fall into most readily. Steps Six and Seven are a means to remove whatever behavior leads us into these waiting traps.

Today I will make an effort to attend a meeting and share my experience, strength and hope to help others escape from their cages.

And as they had no longer any cause for fear, they went into the old hag's house, and there they found, in every corner of the room, boxes with pearls and precious stones. "These are even better than pebbles," said Hansel, and crammed his pockets full of them; and Grettel said: "I too will bring something home;" and she filled her apron full. "But now," said Hansel, "let's go and get well away from the witches' wood."

When we are confined in cages of neediness and entangle ourselves in compulsive activity, it is hard to imagine that we were once free spirits and could ever be free again. It is even more difficult to conceive of the treasures that are hidden away under our dependent attitudes and behaviors. Like Hansel and Grettel, we collect many jewels when we defeat the witches that block our independent development.

When we discover that we can make our way through life without being overly dependent on other people, we can enter into true partnerships with our Higher Power, our families, our friends and colleagues. We no longer need to depend entirely on them to support us or give us identity. Knowing we can choose to remove ourselves from situations that stifle our growth and development gives us the courage to become involved in intimate relationships without being afraid of losing our identity.

The program offers me many jewels. When I explore the Twelve Steps in depth, I uncover more treasures.

When they had wandered about for some hours they came to a big lake. "We can't get over," said Hansel; "I see no bridge of any sort or kind." "Yes, and there's no ferry-boat either," answered Grettel; "but look, there swims a white duck; if I ask her she'll help us over." The duck swam towards them, and Hansel got on her back and bade his little sister sit beside him. "No," answered Grettel, "we should be too heavy a load for the duck: she shall carry us across separately."

Sometimes we approach large obstacles and don't have the strength or energy to face them alone. We fail to realize that we're not expected to handle everything in life without assistance. When we learn to ask for help, we often receive it from the most unlikely sources. People we think will have the least capacity to understand our problems sometimes surprise us and offer solutions from their own experiences that seem tailor-made for us.

We do not have to travel through the forest without companions, but at some point in our journey, there will be lakes that we must cross alone. The discovery that help is always available from our Higher Power, no matter how far away from friends and family we may be, is part of the spiritual awakening we experience as a result of working the Steps. Trusting in our Higher Power gives us the freedom to enjoy periods of solitude as well as companionship, and to be self-reliant as well as closely related to others.

Today I will take advantage of the Steps to deal with whatever obstacles block my path. I welcome guidance from my Higher Power in every situation.

The good bird did this, and when they were landed the wood became more familiar to them, and they saw their father's house in the distance. Then they set off to run, and bounding into the room fell on their father's neck. Grettel shook out her apron so that the pearls and precious stones rolled about the room, and Hansel threw down handfuls out of his pocket. Thus all their troubles were ended, and they all lived happily ever afterwards.

*C*hoosing to embark on our journey through the woods and breaking the cycle of our self-defeating behavior can lead to happy endings. We do not need or expect others to abandon their pursuits to feed and nurture us. We no longer look for someone who will provide for us and protect us from harm. The circumstances which kept us from leading independent lives are being eliminated and replaced by newly developed abilities to nurture and protect ourselves.

Some of us know the joy of being able to share our experience, strength and hope with family members and close friends who we once thought had rejected us. Those of us who have been unable to mend our broken relationships can find comfort in the realization that we can share excess treasure to share with other people who are willing to accept our gifts of friendship and love.

*I will be responsible for my own actions
and allow others the dignity of
taking care of themselves.*

The Fir-Tree

THE FIR-TREE

nce upon a time there lived a little fir-tree. He had everything he needed to live happily in the forest— sunlight, fresh air and many companions—but he hated feeling small and powerless. He spent most of his time thinking about what life would be like when he grew up—about the glories that would be his when someone finally recognized his magnificence.

During the winter, woodcutters chopped down some of the smaller trees. The fir-tree learned from the sparrows that these would be beautifully decorated and placed in warm houses in the town. "Am I destined to the same brilliant career?" he wondered. One December, he was the first to be chosen and chopped down. He was surprised by the sadness he felt at leaving his home, but he was soon too caught up in the busy activities around him to think about his loss. He was carried into a beautiful room and decorated with sugarplums, apples, nuts, candles and a gold star. "Tonight it will be lighted!" the children exclaimed. "If it were only evening!" thought the fir.

When the tapers were lit, a crowd of children rushed into the room to plunder the tree for gifts. After they left, he thought, "Tomorrow I shall be decked out again with candles, toys, and glittering ornaments." However, the next day he was dragged to the lumber room and thrown into a dark corner.

When the winter passed, the servants dragged the tree outside into the daylight. When he realized how withered and yellow his branches were, he wished he had been left lying in the dark corner of the lumber room. He remembered his fresh youth in the wood and the merry Christmas Eve. "Too late! Too late!" thought the tired old tree. "If only I had enjoyed myself whilst I could!"

THE FIR-TREE

There was once a pretty little fir-tree in a wood. It was in a capital position, for it could get sun, and there was enough air, and all around grew many tall companions, both pines and firs. The little fir-tree's greatest desire was to grow up. It did not heed the warm sun and the fresh air, or notice the little peasant children who ran about chattering when they came out to gather wild strawberries. They would sit down by the little fir-tree and say, "What a pretty little one this is!" The tree did not like that at all.

Being young can have its disadvantages. We may feel smothered by those around us or think that we are too small to matter. When all of our attention is focused on growing up, we never learn to enjoy ourselves right where we are. Instead, we spend our time and energy trying to be bigger or better and fail to notice or appreciate the precious gifts—the sun and the fresh air—that surround us.

Many of us carry this pattern of thinking about what is coming next into our adult lives. We may accept that we won't grow any taller, yet we forge ahead in other areas and try to be someone we're not. We set one unrealistic goal after another in our search for prestige, hoping that our accomplishments will make us look and feel good. Recovery teaches us to slow down and enjoy the moment. Success has little value if we can't stop to enjoy its rewards.

I will ask my Higher Power for help in letting go of the need to be something that I'm not.

"Oh! if I were only a great tree like the others!" sighed the little fir-tree, "then I could stretch out my branches far and wide and look out into the great world! The birds would build their nests in my branches, and when the wind blew I would bow to it politely just like the others!" It took no pleasure in the sunshine, nor in the birds, nor in the rose-coloured clouds that sailed over it at dawn and at sunset.

*C*onstantly comparing ourselves to others and looking forward to a time when everything will be perfect can cause us frustration and undermine our serenity. Expectations are productive when they give us the impetus we need to set goals for ourselves and then strive to achieve them. If we become so involved with our dreams that we lose sight of our present blessings, we soon become empty inside. We lose our ability to move forward, our goals become meaningless fantasies and we see no value in the sunshine, birds and other pleasures in our lives.

Recovery allows us to be present in the moment and appreciate what we have and who we are today. As our self-acceptance and appreciation of our current surroundings grow, we begin to recogize the many opportunities for happiness that arise each day. We need only let go and trust in the guidance of our Higher Power, knowing that when we are slowed down it is for a reason.

I will remain in the present moment today
and be grateful for the gifts of life.

Then the winter came, and the snow lay white and sparkling all around, and a hare would come and spring right over the little fir-tree, which annoyed it very much. But when two more winters had passed the fir-tree was so tall that the hare had to run around it. "Ah, to grow and grow, and become great and old! That is the only pleasure in life," thought the tree.

*I*f we were raised in an emotionally unavailable family, our feelings of helplessness and shame can be very painful. Many of us carry these memories into our adult lives, causing us to feel small and unimportant, even when we have grown up. We continue to fantasize about a time when we will become big and powerful so that people will not be able to take advantage of us.

When a hare springs right over us and makes us aware of our perceived inadequacies, we may try to control our feelings by repressing them. If we are ashamed and embarassed, we may try to hide from our true feelings. We do this at great risk to ourselves, for these emotions continue to smolder inside us. Our pain lessens when we find a safe place to uncover our feelings and recognize them for what they are—mere reflections of past helplessness rather than present incompetence.

I will not allow feelings of shame and inadequacy to interfere with the joy I feel today.

In the autumn the woodcutters used to come and hew some of the tallest trees. The young fir-tree would shiver as the magnificent trees fell crashing to the ground, their branches hewn off, and the great trunks left bare, so that they were unrecognisable. In spring, when the swallows and storks came, the fir-tree asked them, "Do you know where they were taken?" The stork nodded his head saying, "I met many new ships as I flew from Egypt; there were splendid masts on the ships. They had the scent of fir-trees." "Oh, if I were only big enough to sail away over the sea too!," said the tree.

Childhood shame often produces grandiosity in adulthood. The more insecure and shameful we feel, the harder we try to be accepted. We sometimes sacrifice our identity without considering the possible consequences. We say to ourselves, "What does it matter if I have to submit to the indignity of having my branches hewn off and my great trunks left bare? Surely it's worth it to become a symbol of strength and pride!"

We may spend time dreaming about the day that someone will single us out for a position of honor. We are fortunate when we discover that we don't have to be taller, older or more experienced in order to lead a happy life. It is then that we can change our outlook and focus on the opportunities for self-fulfillment that surround us.

Today I will relax and enjoy the person I am. If I can accept myself, others will accept me.

"What sort of thing is the sea? What does it look like?".
"Oh, it would take much too long to tell you all that,"
said the stork, and off he went.

*I*t is distressing when we are told that it would take
too much time to answer our questions. It is normal
to react with hurt and anger to people who ridicule,
belittle or never have enough time for us. If we accept
their views without questioning them, we may not
develop the self-esteem we need to be able to keep
asking until we find the answers. If we stifle our
feelings of pain and anger instead of releasing them,
we may experience periods of depression or uncon-
trollable rage.

A twelve-step program of recovery helps us develop
a sense of self-worth and feelings of belonging. In
meetings, we find people who will listen without being
judgmental or laughing at us. As we become more
confident in our ability to interact with others we can
begin to participate more fully in the wider world. Our
self-acceptance grows, and we find we are less influenced by other people's moods and reactions.

> *As my self-esteem increases, I am less*
> *affected by people who ridicule*
> *me or don't have time for me.*

"Rejoice in your youth," said the sunbeams. "Rejoice in the sweet growing time, in the young life within you." And the wind kissed it and the dew wept tears over it, but the fir-tree did not understand.

*W*hen we ignore our feelings and perceptions, we stunt our development and miss the opportunity to rejoice in the sweet growing times and in the young life within us. If we lose our sense of oneness with the world around us, an important source of meaning and purpose disappears, leaving us empty inside. It is difficult to make real contact with nature or other people if we are repressing our feelings and are unable to respond to all that life has to offer.

Part of the recovery process is learning to understand the strength of the Twelve Steps. When we come to believe in a power greater than ourselves as Step Two suggests, we acknowledge and accept that we are part of a living world in which we can make a vital contribution. The miracle of working the Steps is possible for us once we entrust ourselves—mind, body and spirit—to the care of our Higher Power. The strength we gain from this partnership enables us to achieve peace and serenity even as the wind of life whirls around us.

I will rejoice in the beauty of the world around me, content to know that each stage of life offers its own rewards.

THE FIR-TREE

Towards Christmas-time quite little trees were cut down, some not as big as the young fir-tree, or just the same age, and now it had no peace or rest for longing to be away. These little trees, which were chosen for their beauty, kept all their branches; they were put in carts and drawn out of the wood by horses. "Whither are those going?" asked the fir-tree; "they are no bigger than I, and one there was much smaller even! Why do they keep their branches? Where are they taken to?"

Many of us are resentful when life doesn't seem to treat us fairly. Like the fir tree, we question why we are not chosen for our beauty, size or goodness. We don't realize that what we want might not be beneficial to us. The fact that others receive more attention than we do makes us angry and inhibits our ability to have a healthier view of life.

Coming to terms with reality means accepting the fact that life isn't always fair and that we can't expect to always get what we want. Comparing ourselves to other people limits our ability to be all we can be and causes us endless frustration. When we stop worrying about the rewards that others receive and focus on finding our own direction, we are free to fulfill our potential. We become grateful for the many gifts we have received and learn to appreciate what we have.

I am grateful for the blessings in my life and realize that I can harm myself if I put unnecessary focus on what others have.

"We know! We know!" twittered the sparrows. "Down there in the city we have peeped in at the windows and seen them planted in the middle of the warm room and adorned with the most beautiful things—golden apples, sweetmeats, toys and hundreds of candles." "Am I destined to the same brilliant career?" wondered the fir-tree excitedly. "That is better than sailing over the sea!"

*W*hen we feel discontent and discouraged, it is tempting to lose ourselves in grandiose dreams of magically achieving the recognition we think we deserve. We are especially vulnerable to promises of instant success and tantalizing images of golden apples, sweetmeats and toys. We may spend many years in a world full of empty promises, dreaming about what might have been if only we were bigger, better or more beautiful.

As we become aware of who we are and how we fit into the world around us, our self-image improves. As we find more opportunities for self-fulfillment, the unattainable fantasies we once dreamed about become less attractive to us, while the realistic goals we establish become more attainable. Our skills for living improve, and we recognize that liking who we are and where we are is enough to satisfy us.

Regaining a sense of purpose in my life is part of my commitment to recovery. I have stopped dreaming about future recognition to escape feeling unimportant.

"I am sick with longing. If it were only Christmas! If I were only in the cart! If I were only in the warm room with all the splendour and magnificence!"

*T*here is nothing wrong with dreaming and speculating about what our lives could be like under different circumstances. The ability to imagine ourselves in different places and situations helps us to set goals and prepare for the difficulties that we might experience in achieving them. However, if we spend our time dreaming, we often feel cheated. If low self-esteem prevents us from believing we will ever be successful, it will be difficult to achieve our goals.

Each time we sigh, "If only!", we turn aside from our Higher Power and lose the chance to be fully alive. As we become more aware of the present and are increasingly able to appreciate the experiences each day offers, the trust we place in our Higher Power grows. When we let go of our obsession with the future, we find that happiness is within our reach. We recognize that life offers joy and peace to all of us.

I will give up the instant gratification that fantasy offers. Opportunities for true satisfaction are found only in the present.

"And then? Then comes something better, something still more beautiful, else why should they dress us up? There must be something greater, something grander to come— but what? Oh, I am pining away! I really don't know what's the matter with me!"

*L*iving in anticipation of the future may appear to offer emotional gratification, but it is not a healthy thing to do. Fantasizing about exciting outcomes may provide an immediate lift, but the aftermath can be devastating. Waking up from a daydream to find our world in the same turmoil as we left it can pull us down even further than where we started. When we imagine perfect scenarios instead of working toward realistic goals, we risk eventual disappointment. If we waste the present moment dreaming about a flawless future, our hold on reality slips and we turn aside from the chance to live life to the fullest.

Enjoying what we have now without imagining how much better the future will be does not come naturally. It requires trust and patience, and a firm belief that our Higher Power is in charge. Learning to focus our awareness on the present takes practice and the willingness to accept our current limitations as well as new opportunities.

Are unrealistic expectations shutting me off from life? I will not sacrifice the present by fantasizing about the future.

"Rejoice in us," said the air and sunshine, "rejoice in your fresh youth in the free air!" But it took no notice, and just grew and grew.

*I*t is hard to rejoice in the free air when we feel trapped by forces beyond our control. At times like these, we can ask the question, "Whose trap am I in today?" We may be hearing old messages from the past that are still echoing in our ears. These tapes prevent us from enjoying the freedom to exercise present options, and render us incapable of finding pleasure in today.

We have choices regarding what we want to do. We can choose to continue listening to voices from the past or switch to a more positive channel. We can attempt to force our growth, or we can relax and enjoy life as it gradually unfolds. We can struggle stubbornly to achieve unattainable goals, or risk branching out in what might prove to be a more realistic direction. Being attentive to others helps us become aware of the true extent of our self-absorbing fantasies. In meetings, listening to other people with a respectful, open mind strengthens our connection with them. As we share our experiences, we become more aware of healthier behaviors that can empower our active participation in life.

I am experiencing joy in the present. Living in the past or future causes me pain and confusion.

At Christmas-time it was the first to be cut down. The tree fell to the ground with a groan; it felt bruised and faint. It could not think of happiness, it was sad at leaving its home. It knew, too, that it would never see again its dear old companions. Altogether the parting was not pleasant.

When we live in a fantasy world, the intrusion of reality can be a dreadful blow to us. When we center our lives in dreams of the future, any rude awakening to reality leaves us with nothing but regret for lost opportunities. Living in the present and making the most of our opportunities gives us a chance to build memories that sustain us in difficult times.

Living only for tomorrow is a tool for survival and a hard habit to break. It prevents us from ever having to make an honest assessment of ourselves and our lives. Sharing our personal inventory in Step Five helps us to uncover the thoughts and behaviors that prevent us from enjoying life in the present. We then can see how we tried to protect ourselves from reality by living in the future. This process marks the beginning of a new relationship with life that enables us to participate fully in the present.

I will set aside all thoughts of what might have been, could have been or should have been. Accepting the past frees me to welcome life on healthier terms.

When the tree came to itself again a man was saying, "This is a splendid one, we shall only want this." Then came two footmen in livery and carried the fir-tree into a large and beautiful room. The young ladies and the servants decked it out. On its branches they hung little nets full of sugarplums, gilt apples and nuts, and over a hundred tapers were fastened among the branches. Right up at the top was fixed a gold tinsel star. "To-night," they all said, "to-night it will be lighted!" "Ah!" thought the tree, "if it were only evening!"

Many of us are programmed at an early age to continually strive for greater and greater achievement. If we continue this pattern into our adult lives, we are likely to find that even when our dreams are coming true and others are proud of us, we still sacrifice the present by concentrating our sights on the future. Like the fir tree, even when we have received the ultimate tinsel star, we worry about when we will be lighted.

Discovering our true identity helps to break this cycle. When we set aside our shame and accept ourselves the way we are, we can give up waiting to be chosen. We can let go of our need for gold stars and begin developing relationships based on equality, reciprocity, love and trust.

If I relax and enjoy who and what I am, I won't need or want other people's decorations.

What will happen next?" thought the tree. "I wonder whether the trees will come from the wood to see me, or if the sparrows will fly against the window panes? Am I to stand here decked out thus through winter and summer?" The fir-tree had real bark-ache from sheer longing, and bark-ache in trees is just as bad as head-ache in human beings.

*F*ew of us can escape speculating about how a relationship or job will work out, wondering what will happen when our tapers are lit. Our minds seem to move in a hundred different directions whenever we face the prospect of something new. Unfortunately, many of our questions go unanswered. The fear and anticipation generated by thinking about them is sometimes so paralyzing that we may never find the answers. Many of us feel safer staying where we are rather than risking the pain of making wrong choices.

Until we give ourselves permission to make mistakes, change our minds or try again when we fail, we remain in the awkward position of wondering whatever will become of us and aching like the fir tree. Participating in a twelve-step program helps us to find our own direction through faith and trust in a power greater than ourselves.

I will choose where I want to go today and what I want to do. Conscious contact with my Higher Power keeps me on course.

Now the tapers were lighted. What a glitter! What splendour! The tree quivered in all its branches so much, that one of the candles caught the green, and singed it. "Take care!" cried the young ladies, and they extinguished it. Now the tree did not even dare to quiver. It was really terrible! It was so afraid of losing any of its ornaments, and it was quite bewildered by all the radiance.

*W*e are sometimes content to let others decorate us, thinking that they have better taste than we do. We deny our own preferences in order to be liked and admired, but eventually the burden becomes too heavy for us. When we realize how badly we hurt inside, we are ready to change our behavior.

Fortunately we're not stuck in one place like the fir tree, or we wouldn't have found our program of recovery. By attending meetings and working the Steps, we can shed the choices made for us by others and replace them with our own. Through involvement in the program, we can be ourselves and be even more loved and appreciated than we were before. The secret is to stop trying to be what others expect us to be and begin to be who we really are.

*I trust that other people will like me even
if I shed some of my decorations and
let them know the real me.*

And then the doors were opened, and a crowd of children rushed in. The children stood quite silent, but only for a moment, and then they shouted again, and danced round the tree, and snatched off one present after another. Then the children were given permission to plunder the tree. They rushed at it so that all its boughs creaked; if it had not been fastened by the gold star at the top to the ceiling, it would have been overthrown.

*E*vents do not always happen the way we expect they will. Dealing with unforseen occurrences is especially difficult when we have given up our personal power and put the responsibility for our happy endings in the hands of someone else. Even after we have begun to assume responsibility for our own lives, we sometimes find ourselves in the midst of unexpected turmoil and upheaval. Like the star attached to the ceiling that helped the fir tree stand firm on its own, our Higher Power keeps us from being overthrown.

When we surrender ourselves to the care of our Higher Power in Step Three, we can begin changing the things we can and coming to terms with the things we cannot change. Anger and fear no longer dominate our lives when we learn to accept and manage both the joy and the pain that are part of daily living.

With the help of my Higher Power, I can survive in the midst of turmoil.

O
C
T
O
B
E
R

17

"A story! a story!" cried the children, and dragged a little stout man to the tree; he sat down beneath it, saying, "Here we are in the greenwood, and the tree will be delighted to listen!" But I am only going to tell one story. Shall it be Henny Penny or Humpty Dumpty who fell downstairs, and yet gained great honour and married a princess?" There was a perfect babel of voices! Only the fir-tree kept silent, and thought: "Am I not to be in it? Am I to have nothing to do with it?"

It's difficult to live on the fringes of life, wondering if we'll ever be able to make a significant contribution. But we cannot share in life's drama until we give up the behaviors that separate us from others. Low self-esteem can lead us to strive to be the center of attention, and low self-worth often causes us to accept being used to enhance someone else's celebration.

Becoming full participants in life requires us to reach beyond ourselves and learn to give as well as receive. We are fully capable of having intimate relationships when we can grant others our undivided attention, interest and concern without losing sight of who we are and what we want. When we acquire these skills, we begin to attract other people who also know how to lead, follow and walk hand-in-hand.

I know there is a time for giving and a time for receiving. Being willing to do both makes me fully alive.

"Humpty Dumpty fell downstairs and yet married a princess! yes, that is the way of the world!" thought the tree, and was sure it must be true, because such a nice man had told the story. "Well, who knows? Perhaps I shall fall downstairs and marry a princess." And it rejoiced to think that next day it would be decked out again with candles, toys, glittering ornaments, and fruits. "To-morrow I shall quiver again with excitement. I shall enjoy to the full all of my splendour." And the tree stood silent and lost in thought all through the night.

Many of us spend time regretting the past and imagining perfect futures. This diversion delays us from taking action to correct the errors which are almost certain to prevent us from reaching our goals. Covering our present pain with fantasy is a poor substitute for the joy that can come from working toward making our rational plans come to fruition.

Learning to accept responsibility for our wrongs and forgive those who have harmed us helps us to repair the damage we have caused. When we make amends in Step Nine, we relieve ourselves of the guilt that we carry and initiate the healing process. As we develop healthy relationships and become comfortable with others, we begin to be inspired by stories about fir trees and princesses instead of using them as a means of escape.

I will not fantasize about new situations to give myself another chance at happiness. I can stop worrying about outcomes and enjoy the present moment.

Next morning the servants came in. "Now the dressing up will begin again," thought the tree. But they dragged it out of the room, and up the stairs to the lumber-room, and put it in a dark corner, where no ray of light could penetrate. "What does this mean?" thought the tree. "What am I to do here? What is there for me to hear?"

 M ost of us know how it feels to be abandoned and have our dreams evaporate into thin air, or plummet from a state of cheerful anticipation into dark despair. We may repeat this pattern throughout our lives, being happy one moment, then falling with no warning into deep sorrow. If we have experienced long-term depression, it may be difficult to remember a period when we knew anything other than desolation or grief. Perhaps we have lost faith altogether and given in to hopelessness.

Talking with fellow program members helps us to emerge from the dark corners of sorrow and depression where many of us have hidden for so long. Although being alone in the dark is scary, it can be even more frightening to move into the light. Sharing our fears and concerns with others who have successfully made the journey is helpful, and they can often give us insight on what we can do to make our trip easier. Maintaining conscious contact with our Higher Power can give us peace and serenity even in the midst of chaos and confusion.

My chances of finding and maintaining my serenity improve when I share my thoughts with those who understand my fears.

And it leant against the wall, and thought and thought. And there was time enough for that, for days and nights went by, and no one came. "Now it is winter out-doors," thought the fir-tree. "The ground is hard and covered with snow, they can't plant me yet, and that is why I am staying here under cover till the spring comes. How thoughtful they are!"

*A*llowing our well-being to depend on the good intentions of others can result in painful dilemmas. When we act helpless, we spare ourselves the anxiety of making poor decisions but relinquish the privilege of making our own choices. It is hard to feel secure when our happiness is dependent on the actions of other people. When we see others act in ways that are injurious to our best interests, we may do our best to rationalize their behavior, fantasize a happy ending and hope for the best.

It is lonely being trapped in dark attics where we are completely dependent on others. We escape by taking responsibility for our own lives. By following our inner direction, we become free to participate in partnerships with others and take an active part in the world.

Today I will examine my dependence on others and take responsibility for my needs and desires.

"*Only I wish it were not so terribly dark and lonely here; not even a little hare! It was so nice out in the wood, when the snow lay all around, and the hare leapt past me; yes, even when he leapt over me: but I didn't like it then. It's so dreadfully lonely up here.*"

When our lives don't go as planned, we look back longingly at the past. We idealize our childhood and wish we could return to a time when life was simple and satisfying. Some of us look back like the fir tree did and feel sad about the opportunities we missed when we focused on the future instead of accepting and enjoying the present.

When we become comfortable with the present, we don't need to occupy ourselves with thoughts of the past. We develop the skills to communicate with other people and respect our own needs as well as the needs of others. We learn to listen attentively and express our feelings openly at the appropriate time. Sharing our experiences in order to help other people is a sign that Step Twelve is working in our lives. When we carry the message to others and practice the principles of the Steps in all our affairs, we benefit greatly and inspire those around us.

Today I will share the experience of my recovery as part of my commitment to carry the message to others.

"Squeak, squeak!" said a little mouse, stealing out, followed by a second. They sniffed at the fir-tree, and then crept between its boughs. "Where do you come from?" asked the mice, "and what do you know?" Have you been in the storeroom, where cheeses lie on the shelves, and hams hang from the ceiling, where one dances on tallow candles, and where one goes in thin and comes out fat?" "I know nothing about that," said the tree. "But I know the wood, where the sun shines, and the birds sing." And then it told them all about its young days.

*R*ecovery requires that we tell our story. This helps us to understand and accept who we are and acknowledge who we are becoming. Some of us know about storerooms where cheeses lie on the shelves and some of us are familiar with the deep woods where the sun shines and the birds sing. We learn that, while our experiences are unique, we share many common feelings and attitudes with others.

Listening to the stories of others who are in recovery broadens our understanding of why we are the way we are. Telling our story helps us to accept our past struggles and cast aside our shame. By connecting with our past, gratitude toward our Higher Power grows, and we begin to appreciate the progress we are making by working the Steps. Our respect for our present strengths increases as we come to understand the experiences which helped us to become strong.

I have found a place where I can safely tell my story, communicate openly with others and deepen my relationships.

The little mice had never heard anything like that before, and they listened with all their ears, and said "Oh, how much you have seen! How lucky you have been!" "I?" said the fir-tree, and then it thought over what it had told them. "Yes, on the whole those were very happy times."

*O*ne of the benefits of taking the Fifth Step is to see events in our lives reflected from another person's perspective. As the result of their recovery, others are often able to pinpoint patterns in our relationships or behavior that we can't see. Through their insight we are encouraged to recognize and appreciate facets of our past that we may have overlooked. Satisfying experiences, constructive lessons or certain strengths can remain hidden until they are revealed to us through the eyes of another.

Recalling pleasurable experiences often involves reliving some of the pain from the past. A key to being happy in the present is to stop running from painful events and begin to examine and exorcise them. No matter how difficult our previous experiences have been, we have survived them. As we discover the gifts of the past and unwrap them in the light of our new life, we may come to realize that, on the whole, they were very happy times.

*Today I will reflect on my past and be
grateful for how much I have seen
and how lucky I have been.*

*But then it went on to tell them about Christmas Eve,
when it had been adorned with sweetmeats and tapers.
"How lucky you have been, you old fir-tree!" "I'm not at
all old," said the tree. "I only came from the wood this
winter. I am a little backward, perhaps, in my growth."*

Reviewing our lives in a constructive manner can
protect us from repeating old patterns of ineffective
behavior. We often find that while our outer circumstances have changed, we still face the same old
problems. The habits of a new friend might remind us
of a former spouse and the conflicts in that relationship. Difficulty in a new job might be similar to
problems we had with a former employer. We may
have come a long way, but like the fir tree, we seem to
be backward in our growth.

When we examine our histories thoroughly and
honestly in Step Four, we are likely to uncover recur-
ring patterns of behavior that hindered our development. As we progress in recovery, we can identify and
examine all the various issues and concerns that rise
to the surface. We cannot find everything the first
time around, no matter how conscientious we are.
Taking a daily inventory in Step Ten gives us an
opportunity to take advantage of these memories as
they occur and make changes or amends as needed.

*I am learning to use the lessons of my past to
help make quality choices in the present.*

"How beautifully you tell stories!" said the little mice. And next evening they came with four others, who wanted to hear the tree's story, and it told still more, for it remembered everything so clearly and thought: "Those were happy times! But they may come again. Humpty Dumpty fell downstairs, and yet he married a princess; perhaps I shall also marry a princess!" And then it thought of a pretty little birch-tree that grew out in the wood, and seemed to the fir-tree a real princess, and a very beautiful one too.

*T*he stories we tell ourselves can have a strong influence on our lives. It's encouraging to imagine that we can fall downstairs and still marry a princess—that we can hit bottom and still succeed. Life is a process of stopping and starting—of trying and succeeding, trying and failing and trying once more.

Daydreams are generally harmless, but we must be careful not to let fantasies interfere with our present opportunities. If we get too involved with our dreams of glory like the fir tree did, we might miss the prince or the princess who has been beside us all the time. Blending our plans and hopes for the future with our present reality helps to ensure that life will not pass us by while we are in the midst of a fantasy.

I will learn to appreciate present opportunities. What I choose today will have an impact on my future.

"Who is Humpty Dumpty?" asked the little mice. And then the tree told the whole story; it could remember every single word, and the little mice were ready to leap onto the topmost branch out of sheer joy! Next night many more mice came, and on Sunday even two rats; but they did not care about the story, and that troubled the little mice, for now they thought less of it too.

*L*ike the mice who were vulnerable to the opinions of the rats, we are susceptible to the opinions of others to some degree. Some of us become social chameleons and take on a new identity with each new friend. Others are determined to have differing viewpoints just to prove we're not influenced by those around us. Either of these self-defeating behaviors can prevent us from displaying our true feelings. Our need to constantly take into account the judgments of others can restrict our ability to explore and enjoy the things we might otherwise respond to instinctively.

Improving our conscious contact with our Higher Power in Step Eleven takes our focus off external influences. By praying for knowledge of our Higher Power's will for us, we become better able to resist the influence of others and understand more clearly our own values and preferences.

> *I am capable of choosing what
> is important to me.*

"Is that the only story you know?" asked the rats. "The only one," answered the tree. "That's a very poor story. Don't you know one about bacon or tallow candles? a storeroom story?" "No," said the tree. "Then we are much obliged to you," said the rats, and they went back to their friends. At last the little mice went off also, and the tree said, sighing: "Really it was very pleasant when the lively little mice sat round and listened whilst I told them stories. Now that's over too. But I will think of the time when I shall be brought out again, to keep up my spirits." But when did it happen?

Some of us are dreamers; we enjoy stories of orphans who marry royalty. Others are realists; we want to hear about material substances such as bacon and tallow candles. We express our needs and opinions differently, but we all are searching in some way for solutions to feelings of being powerless.

Thankfully, we are more fortunate than the fir tree—we don't have to wait to be brought out again. In a twelve-step program, we meet people who share their feelings openly and don't criticize the stories of others. We learn to share our experience, strength and hope, knowing that there will be an interested friend who will listen. Fellow program members know the discomfort of being ignored and are willing to offer us an attentive ear. They've learned that shared experiences help everyone take constructive action.

I am grateful for a program where I can find strength and hope in shared experience.

It was one morning when they came to tidy up the lumber-room; the boxes were set aside, and the tree brought out; they threw it really rather roughly on the floor, but a servant dragged it off at once downstairs, where there was daylight once more. "Now life begins again!" thought the tree. It felt the fresh air, the first rays of the sun, and there it was out in the yard! Everything passed so quickly; the tree quite forgot to notice itself, there was so much to look at all around.

*W*holehearted involvement in life often frees us from our self-centeredness. When we connect with our surroundings, we forget our preoccupation with ourselves. The inhibitions and self-consciousness that keep our free spirits locked in dark winter attics disappear, blown away by the fresh breezes of being ourselves. Warmed by the first rays of spontaneous joy, we begin to reconnect with life and its many blessings.

In this state of peace we experience the wonder of being alive. We have new friends, a Higher Power and a program that provides us with roadways to recovery. We lose our preoccupation with past losses and future expectations. We are involved in the sights and sounds of everyday life and are no longer preoccupied with distant times. Being fully immersed in the present moment is a priceless part of the spiritual awakening that a twelve-step program provides.

Today I will enjoy a breath of fresh air and experience the light of the new day.

"Now I shall live," thought the tree joyfully, stretching out its branches wide; but, alas! they were all withered and yellow; and it was lying in a corner among weeds and nettles. And the tree looked at all the splendour and freshness of the flowers in the garden, and then looked at itself, and wished that it had been left lying in the dark corner of the lumber-room; it thought of its fresh youth in the wood, of the merry Christmas Eve, and of the little mice who had listened so happily to the story. "Too late! Too late!" thought the old tree. "If only I had enjoyed myself whilst I could."

*H*ow lucky we are to have a chance to live in the now! The process of recovery revitalizes us so that we are full of life again, no matter how yellow and dead we thought we had become. The Twelve Steps give us a way to transform the past into a meaningful and significant part of the present.

There is no need to suffer like the fir tree did, sighing, "Too late! Too late!" if we use the Steps each day. Remembering that recovery is achieved one day at a time, we can trust that happiness is within our grasp. The journey is sometimes painful, difficult and full of sudden stops and starts, but there is new joy and fulfillment to be discovered along the way.

*I will enjoy my life today, knowing that it
is never too late to find happiness.*

And a servant came and cut the tree into small pieces, there was quite a bundle of them; they flickered brightly under the great copper in the brew-house; the tree sighed deeply, and each sigh was like a pistol-shot. But for each report, which was really a sigh, the tree was thinking of a summer's day in the wood, or of a winter's night out there, when the stars were shining; it thought of Christmas Eve, and of Humpty Dumpty, which was the only story it had heard, or could tell, and then the tree had burnt away.

*I*f we have learned to live one day at a time, to savor each moment to the fullest, we have no reason to think about where our stories will end. We will have learned the secret of happiness and be able to treasure the gifts that each day brings. The alternative is to race through life, mercilessly pushing ourselves from one goal to the next. When our time is up, we are left to wonder where it has all gone and where we were while it was happening.

Living each moment to the fullest does not guarantee that we will be ready to say goodbye when the time comes. However, it does help us not to feel cheated as the fir tree did, because it never took time to live.

I am aware of the vitality in and around me. Rather than isolate myself from life, I will partake of the happiness that is available to me.

The children played on in the garden, and the youngest had the golden star on his breast, which the tree had worn on the happiest evening of its life; and now that was past—and the tree had passed away—and the story too, all ended and done with. And that's the way with all stories!

*L*ike the fir tree, we may have turned our backs on many of life's opportunities and ended up with regrets. There are a host of reasons why we behaved this way, many of which are rooted in fear of the unknown. For many of us, feelings such as pride, self-consciousness, unworthiness and insecurity limited our ability to engage in life.

Unlike the tree, we still have opportunities for change and growth. We can choose to improve our lives or decide to stay where we are. Recovery offers us a chance to learn new behaviors and find better ways to relate to our feelings. Through working the Steps, we can be awakened to full participation in life. We can take what we need from the fir tree's legacy—a tale of lost life—and leave the rest behind us. After all, it is the fir tree's story and it need not be ours.

I choose to enjoy the sun, wind and rain today. Life calls me to embrace the fullness of the present moment.

Beauty and the Beast

BEAUTY AND THE BEAST

ne day a wealthy merchant lost every ship he had upon the sea and was forced to retire with his twelve children to a small house in a desolate place. His sons and daughters despaired at the idea of leading such a life. Only Beauty, the youngest, adjusted to the change. Later, the man heard that one of his ships had been found. When he left to reclaim it, all of his children asked him to bring back expensive gifts, except for Beauty, who requested only a rose.

The merchant arrived at the port to find that his former partners had already divided up his property. He left for home empty-handed. On his way, he came upon a deserted castle and decided to stay the night. The next morning, he remembered Beauty's request and picked a rose from the garden for her. A frightful beast appeared and said in a terrible voice, "Who told you that you might gather my roses?" The man was concerned for his life, but the beast offered to spare him in exchange for one of his daughters.

The merchant returned home and told his children the sad story of his journey. Beauty offered to go to the beast, since she felt she had caused her father's misfortunes. When she arrived at the castle the beast was very kind to her and eventually she forgot her fears. Every evening he asked her to marry him, but she refused. While sleeping, she often dreamt of a handsome prince, who said, "Only try to find me out, no matter how I may be disguised." Although amply entertained, she longed to visit her family. The beast agreed on the condition that she return in three months or he would die. At home Beauty became bored and thought of the castle. One night she dreamt that the beast was dying, so she returned to him.

When she arrived, he was near death. She realized how much she loved him and agreed to marry him. With this, the enchantment was broken. The beast was restored to his natural form, that of the prince of whom she had been dreaming.

Once upon a time, in a very far-off country, there lived a merchant who was enormously rich. As he had, however, six sons and six daughters, he found that his money was not too much to let them have everything they fancied. But one day a most unexpected misfortune befell them, and from great wealth they fell into the direst poverty.

*M*any of us have experienced sudden financial reversal at some point in our lives. Some of us may react by becoming too cautious and saving everything we can for the rainy day we are certain will return. Other times we may respond by denying our financial situation and spending everything we earn as soon as we receive it or incurring debts without thinking about how they will be repaid.

Although our finances can be adversely affected by circumstances beyond our control, we may blame ourselves for not being able to provide for ourselves or our families as well as we think we should. The decision to turn our will and our lives over to our Higher Power in Step Three gives us courage to face reality. As we progress in recovery we understand some of the behaviors that prevent us from putting our financial affairs in order. Talking to others who also have difficulties with money helps to relieve our fear of failure and find solutions to our problems.

*Money can be a source of pleasure or pain.
Today I will look at the behaviors that
reinforce my insecurity and ask for
help in removing them.*

All that was left was a little house in a desolate place, and to this he was forced to retreat with his children. The daughters at first hoped that their friends, who had been so numerous while they were rich, would insist on their staying in their houses. But they soon found that they were left alone, and that their former friends even attributed their misfortunes to their own extravagance, and showed no intention of offering them any help.

*W*hen friends don't act as we hope they will, we may feel abandoned. We resent them for not being able to solve our problems and interpret their inability to do so as a sign that they don't care.

We may compound our sense of loss with intense self-blame and punishment. Through our recovery program, we can begin taking positive action to change our circumstances.

Today we have access to a group of people who know what it's like to experience setbacks and defeat. They encourage us in times of crisis by suggesting useful tools we can use or skills we can develop to get back on our feet. Their experience, strength and hope is a vital resource in our recovery.

*I will stop blaming myself and others for
my misfortunes and begin seeking
solutions to my problems.*

The girls regretted losing the luxuries of their former life; only the youngest, who was called Beauty, tried to be cheerful. She set to work to make the best of things and to try to persuade her sisters to join her in dancing and singing. They would do nothing of the sort, and they declared that this miserable life was all she was fit for.

*I*n recovery, we discover that our attitude toward life has a major influence on determining how comfortable we are. If we are cheerful, like Beauty, and make the best of things, it will be easier to accept our situation. Being grateful for the gifts we have protects us from the dissatisfaction that fuels compulsive behavior. It relieves us of the insecurity that often paralyzes us or pushes us to work too hard or worry too much. When we are grateful for what we have, we can relax and enjoy it instead of grieving for things we have lost or never achieved.

Knowing that we are making the best of our present circumstances improves our self-esteem. This knowledge gives us the energy to find new solutions to our problems. Making whatever changes are possible and learning to recognize and accept the things we cannot change helps us to increase our present happiness.

I am grateful for what I have today. I am willing to strive for higher goals, but will not be critical of myself if I don't achieve them overnight.

After two years their father received the news that one of his lost ships had come safely into port with a rich cargo. The sons and daughters loaded their father with commissions for jewels and dresses. Only Beauty did not ask for anything. Her father said, "And what shall I bring for you, Beauty?" "The only thing I wish for is to see you come home safely," she answered. Her father told her to choose something. "I beg that you will bring me a rose," she said. "I have not seen one since we came here, and I love them so much "

*I*f our fathers were attentive to our needs, emotionally and spiritually, we can probably identify with Beauty's desire for her father to return with a rose as a symbol of his love for her. If we grew up with emotionally unavailable or unresponsive parents, the idea of a gesture symbolizing that love may have little meaning for us.

Sharing with others who understand our need for love and nurture helps us to develop healthy ways of reparenting ourselves. Believing that we can be restored to sanity, as Step Two suggests, gives us the hope that we can recover our self-worth. Listening to the experiences of others in the program gives us the courage to take the action necessary to restore our self-esteem.

*I am worthy and deserving of love. I
will reach out to others today.*

So the merchant set out but only to find that his former companions had divided between them the goods which the ship had brought; he found himself as poor as when he started. He was obliged to leave the town in the most terrible weather. Falling snow had covered up every path. At length he made out some sort of track, and though at the beginning it was so rough and slippery that he fell down more than once, it presently became easier, and led him into an avenue of trees which ended in a splendid castle.

*V*ery early in our recovery we come to realize that our efforts to manage our lives or the lives of others are futile. We begin to understand that there are a myriad of things that are beyond our control, including some of the actions of our friends. Gradually, we learn to distinguish the difference between what we can and cannot change. We begin to realize that trying to make the impossible happen is a terrible waste of our energy.

When we learn to accept things the way they are, our confidence in our ability to handle whatever comes our way improves. We may not find splendid castles in the midst of terrible snowstorms, but through our work on Step Three, we find that our Higher Power will guide us out of despair and confusion. We also learn that the support of other program members is only a phone call away.

I can call a friend or attend a meeting if doubt or confusion enter my life today.

It seemed to the merchant very strange that no snow had fallen in the avenue. When he reached the first court of the castle he saw before him several splendidly furnished rooms. He stopped in a room where a clear fire was burning, and very soon fell into a sweet sleep. When his extreme hunger wakened him after several hours he was still alone; but a little table, upon which was a good dinner, had been drawn up close to him, and he lost no time in beginning his meal.

*A*lthough we may not be aware of it, many of us go through life expecting to live in magnificent castles with splendidly furnished rooms. We think that our families, partners and friends should be aware of our needs and preferences instinctively. We become angry when they don't please us or give us what we want without our having to ask.

Step Four gives us an opportunity to look honestly at our expectations so that we can assess their effect on our lives. Unreasonable expectations interfere with our serenity and place a strain on our relationships. Realistic requests sometimes go unmet because we have failed to make them clear. Attending meetings and sharing our thoughts with others helps us to separate our unrealistic expectations from those that are valid.

I will be open about what I want from others today.
I cannot expect them to read my mind.

He began to wonder what he should do, and to amuse himself by pretending that all the treasures he saw were his own. Then he went down into the garden, and though it was winter everywhere else, here the sun shone, and the birds sang. The merchant said to himself: "All this must be meant for me. I will go this minute and bring my children to share all these delights."

*P*laying "Let's Pretend" can be fun unless it interferes with our ability to deal with reality. Emulating someone we admire can be a constructive pastime if it is useful to us in attaining our goal. Pretending that someone else's possessions are ours and acting as though they were is inappropriate and unhealthy.

Many of us play this game without being aware of it. We may establish a relationship with someone we feel is better looking than we are in an effort to enhance our own self-image. If we are quiet and reserved, we may choose friends who are active and outgoing. Then we participate only in things they suggest without ever developing interests of our own.

As we work through the Twelve Steps, we begin to recognize aspects of our personalities that we may have previously ignored. As we become more familiar with who we are, our need to have others make up for our deficiencies diminishes. We regain what was lost when we began trying to live our lives through the activities of others.

I can trust the Steps to help me become the person I really want to be.

He turned down the path which led to the stable. This path had roses on each side of it. They reminded him of his promise to Beauty, and he stopped and had just gathered one to take to her when he was startled by a strange noise behind him. Turning round, he saw a frightful Beast, which seemed to be very angry and said, in a terrible voice, "Who told you that you might gather my roses?"

*I*f we do not know how to ask directly for what we want, we may try to meet our needs in devious ways. Some of us learn to manipulate others by playing on their sympathies or feelings of guilt. We may convince ourselves that the suffering we endured entitles us to have certain things, even if it means taking them without permission. We forget that we put ourselves under obligation to someone else when we gather roses that we haven't planted.

When those behaviors stop working for us, we become willing to look at the attitudes and feelings that encourage them. Becoming ready to let them go and find more effective ways of meeting our needs is the purpose of Steps Six and Seven. Successful completion of these Steps allows us to make true amends in Step Nine by changing our behavior in ways that allow us to plant our own rose garden.

> *Am I looking to others to do things I could*
> *be doing for myself? I will plant the*
> *seeds of change today.*

The merchant dropped the fatal rose and cried: "Pardon me, noble sir. I could not imagine that you would be offended by my taking this rose." He began to tell the Beast all his misfortunes, not forgetting to mention Beauty's request. "I thought that I might at least take Beauty her rose," he said. "I beg you to forgive me, for you see I meant no harm."

Some of us have trouble controlling our impulses. When we see something we want, we may go after it without considering the consequences. We may think if we don't act quickly we may not get another chance, or that our need is too great to worry about what will happen later. We might assume, like Beauty's father, that the effects of our actions will be so slight that we won't have to be concerned with them. We may believe that other people, who seem to have much more than we do, won't miss what little we try to take from them.

Continuing to take a personal inventory in Step Ten and promptly admitting our wrongs helps us monitor our impulsive decisions. When we correct our mistakes daily, we begin to think ahead and ask ourselves if what we are about to do is worth making whatever amend may be required. Taking time each day to assess the effectiveness of our current choices saves us from pain and discomfort.

*I will stop and consider the possible conse-
quences before I take action today.*

The Beast said: "I will forgive you if you will give me one of your daughters." The merchant accepted this proposal, though he did not really think any of his daughters would come. After a hasty breakfast, he mounted his horse, and he was still wrapped in gloomy thoughts when it stopped before the door of the cottage. He hid the truth, saying sadly to Beauty as he gave her the rose: "Here is what you asked me to bring you; you little know what it has cost."

*M*any of us have difficulty determining the limits of our obligations and responsibilities. We sometimes do things for others because we think we have to, not because we want to. We may sacrifice more than we realize by surrendering our own desires in exchange for approval, or trying to make ourselves indispensable so others will not abandon us.

When we continually make sacrifices at the expense of our own well-being, it may be a sign that we are still feeling needy. If we are committed to recovery and are willing to risk making changes, we can work toward removing the neediness that underlies many of our self-defeating behaviors. Then we can experience the joy of making decisions that support relationships based on love instead of obligation

I am becoming aware of my own needs and how they influence my interaction with others.

But this excited their curiosity so greatly that presently he told them his adventures. The girls were very angry with Beauty, and said it was all her fault, and that if she had asked for something sensible this would never had happened. Poor Beauty said to them: "I have indeed caused this misfortune. Who could have guessed that to ask for a rose would cause so much misery? I will go back with my father to keep his promise."

We sometimes find ourselves in a situation like Beauty, faced with unpleasant outcomes that are far different from what we imagined. Others may blame us for what is happening and seem to be more concerned with how they might be affected than how we will survive. Assigning blame to others, taking it upon ourselves or making excuses because our intentions were innocent does not remove the problem. In the end we must decide if anything can be done to correct it, and whether or not we are willing to take whatever action is required.

If we are uncertain about what to do, we can choose to discuss the problem with a friend or sponsor. In the course of preparing our list of amends in Step Eight, many of us find we have a tendency to blame ourselves unnecessarily for things that happened in the past. Discussing these situations with others helps us look objectively at what we can do to correct our mistakes.

*I can call on a sponsor or friend for help
in making up my list of amends.*

They mounted together the horse which had brought him back. It seemed to fly rather than gallop; indeed, she would have enjoyed the journey if she had not feared what might happen to her at the end of it. When they had dismounted her father led her to the little room he had been in before, where they found a splendid fire burning, and the table spread with a delicious supper.

*M*any of us can understand the fear that kept Beauty from enjoying her journey. We sometimes miss the pleasure of travel by worrying about what might be waiting for us at our destination. As we work our way through the Steps, we begin to see how fear can contaminate our happiness. We slowly gain faith that our Higher Power is leading us in the right direction and will help us to face any situation we might encounter.

In recovery, we learn to take action in spite of our fears. When our efforts result in unexpected consequences, we learn that we can choose to accept them or take steps to correct them. Each action we take teaches us something new and ultimately reduces our level of anxiety. Learning that we can make decisions, act on them and later alter our course as required, enhances our confidence and self-esteem.

If I am letting anxiety prevent me from
moving forward, I will ask for help
in assessing my fears.

They had hardly finished their meal when the noise of the Beast's footsteps was heard approaching, and Beauty clung to her father in terror. "Have you come willingly?" asked the Beast. "Will you be content to stay here when your father goes away?" Beauty answered bravely that she was quite prepared to stay.

*W*e are often unwilling to move into areas that are unfamiliar to us. Rather than being as courageous as Beauty was, we may be overcome with fear and choose to retreat. Because this relieves our anxiety, we can fall into the habit of trying to solve our problems by avoiding them. When we do this, we continue to be ruled by fear and frustrated by our lack of progress.

Remembering that we only have to take one step at a time helps prevent fear from overpowering us. When panic strikes, we can ask ourselves, "Can I handle what's before me right now?" If we are honestly working the Steps and relying on our Higher Power for direction, we feel comfortable in answering "Yes." Using Step Eleven to maintain our conscious contact with our Higher Power gives us the courage to move ahead, leaving our fear and indecision behind.

Working the Twelve Steps and maintaining conscious contact with my Higher Power helps me to keep moving forward on my journey.

Beauty felt sure that her father was leaving her for ever, so she was very sad when a bell rang sharply and warned them that the time was come for them to part. The merchant was forced to bid Beauty a hasty farewell; and as soon as he was mounted he went off at such a pace that she lost sight of him in an instant. Then Beauty began to cry, and wandered sadly back to her own room.

*W*hen we face major losses it helps to remember that endings can be a signal of new beginnings. If we have faith that life has good things in store for us, we can learn to move forward and let go of the past.

This does not mean that we shouldn't mourn when we feel sad. If we react like Beauty and express our sorrow by crying, we will find it easier to accept our loss. When someone we love is no longer involved in our lives, it may feel like we are giving up a part of ourselves. We begin to be comforted when we discover that the love and hope they gave us continues to influence our lives.

Sometimes we begin to idealize people we lose, adjusting our memories with visions of how we would have liked them to be. This may prevent us from forming new relationships because no one else measures up to this idealized image. Talking about our loss with others helps us retain a realistic picture of the past so that it doesn't intrude upon our present opportunities for happiness.

*I can mourn my losses and still
have faith in the future.*

She lay down and instantly fell asleep. And then she dreamed that a young prince, handsomer than anyone she had ever seen, and with a voice that went straight to her heart, came and said to her, "Ah, Beauty! you are not so unfortunate as you suppose. Here you will be rewarded for all you have suffered elsewhere. Only try to find me out, no matter how I may be disguised. Be as true-hearted as you are beautiful, and we shall have nothing left to wish for."

When we lose a relationship that is important to us, or face some other major life change, we may feel like we have lost our identity. Life may seem empty and lacking in purpose. We may worry that nothing will ever be meaningful to us again.

Finding the Prince—getting in touch with the desires of our heart and making a decision to follow them—can be painful and frustrating, especially if we have always looked to others to tell us what is best for us. Taking a fearless inventory of ourselves, as Step Four suggests, gives us a chance to look at what we want and how we have tried to obtain it in the past.

Talking to others about our efforts in Step Five helps us discover ineffective behaviors that may stop us from achieving our dreams. Life takes on new meaning when we get in touch with our innermost dreams and feelings and remain true to them.

Today I will take another step toward fulfilling my own dreams.

Beauty found her dreams so interesting that she was in no hurry to awake, but presently the clock roused her by calling her name softly twelve times. So she got up and began to explore some of the many rooms of the palace. The first she entered was lined with mirrors, and Beauty saw herself reflected on every side, and thought she had never seen such a charming room.

Most of us enter the program with beaten and tattered self-images. We resist starting our Step Four inventory, fearing it will only reflect our defects like a room lined with mirrors. We discover that this Step also involves identifying our assets because we are asked to look at ourselves as honestly as we can. Our goal in recovery is to identify strengths upon which we can build, as well as attitudes and behaviors that interfere with our lives. When this is accomplished we can capitalize on our strengths and replace our ineffective behaviors with those that better suit our needs.

When we share openly with others in meetings, we begin to see ourselves from new perspectives. Our self-doubt slowly fades and our confidence increases. Having the courage to explore our personalities opens the doors to many mirrored rooms that reflect positive new images. Step Four can be an exciting adventure if we can work through our fear and detach from our self-criticism.

As I begin to like myself more, I am pleased with what I see in the mirror.

Then she passed through into a room which contained every musical instrument under the sun, and here she amused herself for a long while in trying some of them, and singing until she was tired. The next room was a library, and she saw everything she had ever wanted to read, as well as everything she had read, and it seemed to her that a whole lifetime would not be enough even to read the names of the books, there were so many.

*O*ur view of the world and our ability to appreciate it broadens when we are in recovery. We find that working the Steps gives us the courage to explore new options and experiment with new behaviors. Like Beauty, who amused herself with all the musical instruments, we devote ourselves to new activities or reacquaint ourselves with old ones. We become free to learn to ski, play the guitar or dance when we can stop worrying about falling, playing a wrong note or stepping on our partner's toes.

Becoming less self-conscious and concerned with proving ourselves to others restores our natural curiosity about the world around us. We develop a sincere interest in other people's thoughts and experiences when we lose the self-centered fear that keeps our attention focused on ourselves. We recover the wonder we felt as a child when we are able to see the world through new eyes.

I will pattern myself after Beauty and be open to the wonder in the world around me.

Presently she heard the Beast coming. The Beast was not nearly so terrible as she had supposed at first. When he got up to leave her, he said in his gruff voice: "Do you love me, Beauty? Will you marry me?" "Oh! What shall I say?" cried Beauty, for she was afraid to make the Beast angry by refusing. "Say 'yes' or 'no' without fear," he replied. "Oh! no, Beast," said Beauty hastily. "Since you will not, good-night, Beauty," he said. And she answered: "Good-night, Beast," very glad to find that her refusal had not provoked him.

Many of us don't know how to say "no" because we are afraid of making someone angry when we refuse their request. Our need for approval and fear of abandonment causes us to say "yes" to things we really do not want to do.

Fear of causing other people pain may have kept us in relationships that we wanted to end. It may even have prevented us from trying to get close to people. Because we were so afraid of rejection ourselves, we may have been overly sensitive to the possibility of hurting other people's feelings.

When we realize we have the right to say "yes" or "no," we discover that expressing our preferences can be exciting. It frees us from feelings of depression and powerlessness and gives us an opportunity to do the things that we enjoy. Getting in touch with our Higher Power helps us know what we want to say; working with others in the program helps us practice saying it.

I am finding the freedom to make my own choices and not be afraid.

The next morning she decided to amuse herself in the garden, for the sun shone, and all the fountains were playing; but she was astonished to find that every place was familiar to her, and presently she came to the brook where she had first met the Prince in her dream, and that made her think more than ever that he must be kept a prisoner by the Beast.

*T*aking opportunities to relax and find out what makes us happy can bring us untold joy. Recovering our ability to laugh and entertain ourselves lets us relive moments when we were young and carefree. When we get in touch with these childlike feelings, we sometimes have a sense, like Beauty, that we are in a familiar place. It may seem like a valuable part of us that was being held prisoner can finally be set free.

Deciding to develop a relationship with our lost inner child can be frightening. What if we discover a beast waiting to devour us because we ignored it for so long? Can we really hope to find a prince—a royal child—waiting to be liberated? Recovery shows us that we can realize our full potential by remaining true to ourselves and following our inner dreams.

*I will follow my dream today and work toward
developing a loving relationship
with my inner child.*

When she was tired she went back to the palace, and found a new room full of materials for every kind of work—ribbons to make into bows, and silks to work into flowers. Then there was an aviary full of rare birds, which were so tame that they flew to Beauty as soon as they saw her, and perched upon her shoulders and her head. "Pretty little creatures," she said, "How I wish that your cage was nearer to my room." Opening a door, she found to her delight that it led into her own room, though she had thought it was quite the other side of the palace.

*T*he program gives us new materials with which to construct useful lives. When we recover our own sense of purpose, the anxious and resentful thoughts that used to race endlessly through our heads slow down and stop. Eventually they become tame and friendly like the rare birds that perched upon Beauty's shoulders and head.

Coming to believe that we are interesting and worthwhile people is a sign that Step Two is working in our lives and that we are being restored to sanity. Letting thoughts of hope and cheerfulness into our lives and taking time to hear the birds sing gives us a new sense of contentment. This helps us become willing to participate in additional activities which increase our sense of usefulness and purpose. Like Beauty, we have found a room full of materials for every kind of work.

Today I will make room in my head for positive thoughts and look for signs of hope.

There was one room which was empty, except that under each of the windows stood a very comfortable chair; and the first time she had looked out of the window it had seemed to her that a black curtain prevented her from seeing anything outside. The second time she went into the room, she sat down in one of the chairs, when instantly a curtain was rolled aside, and a most amusing pantomime was acted before her; there were dances, and coloured lights, and music, and Beauty was in ecstacies.

*W*e may have entered the program hoping it would make us a little less lonely, yet never dreaming we might find lights and music. Our view of the world changes as we begin to work the Steps and remove the negative attitudes that obscure our view.

When we are tired enough, we stop pretending that we have no problems—that we're not lonely or that we have things under control when we don't. Our curtain of denial rolls aside when we take Step One and admit our powerlessness and the unmanageability of our lives. When we attend meetings, we observe other members and open our eyes, ears and hearts to their suffering and joy. We may not yet be able to see the magic in our own lives, but we can see it at work in the lives of others and feel encouraged by their experiences.

I will look for opportunities to add music to my life today. I am opening my eyes, ears and heart to new experiences.

After that she tried the other seven windows in turn, and there was some new and surprising entertainment to be seen from each of them, so that Beauty never could feel lonely any more. Every evening after supper the Beast came to see her, and always before saying goodnight asked her in his terrible voice: "Beauty, will you marry me?" And it seemed to Beauty, now she understood him better, that when she said: "No, Beast," he went away quite sad.

*U*nderstanding, accepting and appreciating our own history, and allowing ourselves to enjoy other people's stories takes away much of our loneliness. When we are interested and receptive to what we hear each time we attend a meeting, our negativity and fear begin to disappear. Finding people we can relate to takes our attention off ourselves and fosters our self-acceptance.

We learn that we can listen without feeling obligated to find solutions to other people's problems. When we can say "no" to someone and acknowledge their legitimate feelings of disappointment without feeling obligated to say "yes," we take another step toward freedom. The quality of our lives improves when we can share our feelings with others and encourage them to share their feelings with us.

I can respect other people's feelings without having to say "yes" to things I don't want to do.

But her happy dreams of the handsome young Prince soon made her forget the poor Beast, and the only thing that at all disturbed her was to be constantly told to distrust appearances, to let her heart guide her, and not her eyes. At last, happy as she was, Beauty began to long for the sight of her father and her brothers and sisters.

Staying busy relieves our loneliness, but it does not take away our deep longing for relationships with others. We all have a need to be with people to whom we can relate in ways that are comfortable, fulfilling and rewarding.

Sometimes we overlook opportunities to have these kinds of relationships. If we are overly influenced by external appearances or first impressions, we may not give other people a fair chance. Comparing our idealized memories of past relationships to our current situation may impede our efforts to get close to others. Longing to return to the way things used to be may prevent us from moving ahead with our lives.

Attending meetings gives us an opportunity to see beyond external appearances and helps us establish new connections with the present. Telling our stories and working on our inventories take us back to the past, but do not leave us there. When we reclaim the old threads of our lives, we can weave them into the fabric of our present.

I will look beyond external appearances today and risk seeing people in new ways.

Upon hearing this the Beast seemed sadly distressed. "Ah! Beauty, is it because you hate me that you want to escape?" "No, dear Beast," answered Beauty softly. "I do not hate you, but I long to see my father again. Only let me go for two months, and I promise to come back to you." The Beast replied: "Remember your promise, for if you do not come in good time you will find your faithful Beast dead. Fear nothing, sleep peacefully, and before long you shall see your father once more."

*I*f we stay away from things that are important to us for long periods of time, they may begin to fade and die. When old dreams and aspirations surface during the process of recovery, we sometimes have the feeling that we have revived them just in time—that they were in danger of being lost forever had we continued to ignore them. The same is true of relationships. If we fail to nurture them, they also may fade away.

Despite our growth and change in the program, we may feel like Beauty and long to return to old ways of life. When we take Step Three and begin to trust our Higher Power, we develop an inner security that makes us less likely to act on these feelings. When we move away from childish fantasies of unlimited protection and authority, we become ready to develop relationships based on equality and mutual support.

I will assess my priorities today so that I can continue to maintain contact with the things most important to me.

She went to bed, but could hardly sleep for joy. Then a strange sound woke her. She suddenly heard her father's voice, and rushed out and greeted him joyfully. But though they were rich now and had plenty of acquaintances, Beauty found that nothing amused her very much; and she often thought of the palace, especially as at home she never once dreamed of her dear Prince, and she felt quite sad without him.

When we are feeling lonely or insecure, we may try to revive our old ways of life. Often we find that things have changed, that certain people, places or behaviors no longer satisfy us. This can be a clear sign that it is time for us to move ahead and find new interests or develop new relationships. We can be grateful for the feelings of dissatisfaction which press us forward and motivate us to make positive changes in our lives.

By following the Steps, we find the strength we need to make our own way in the world. Recovery offers us a chance to develop faith in a Higher Power that will inspire us throughout our lives.

Feeling uncomfortable may be a sign that I am in the wrong place. I will have the courage to move forward today.

Then her sisters seemed to have got quite used to being without her, and even found her rather in the way, but her father and brothers begged her to stay, and seemed so grieved at the thought of her departure that she had not the courage to say good-bye to them. Every day when she got up she meant to say it at night, and when night came she put it off again, until at last she had a dismal dream which helped her to make up her mind.

Many of us struggle with questions of obligation and loyalty in our relationships. Some of us become so tied to parents or siblings that we are unable to leave home when we should. We may procrastinate and put off saying goodbye, like Beauty, because we think we will cause others pain. Or, we might tear ourselves away with over-inflated feelings of independence, only to find later that we have not really broken the emotional ties.

Fortunately, like Beauty, we have gotten in touch with our dream and are leaving old behaviors behind in order to follow it. Each of us travels a unique path on the road to recovery. Working the Steps frees us from feelings of guilt and unnecessary obligation and provides the courage we need to find our own way.

I will pay close attention to my dreams today. They help me to see things that I could be doing to improve the quality of my life.

She thought she was wandering in a lonely path in the palace gardens, when she heard groans which seemed to come from some bushes hiding the entrance of a cave. She found the Beast stretched out upon his side, apparently dying. Beauty was so terrified by this dream that she said good-bye to her father and all her brothers and sisters, and she said firmly: "I wish to go back to my palace and see my Beast again."

*B*y working the Steps and attending meetings, we learn to respect our thoughts and feelings. We can take the opinions and desires of other people into account, but they can no longer bribe us or intimidate us into doing things their way. If they request our assistance, and we are ready and able to help them, we can choose to do so.

Our presence may be wanted or needed in many places, but it is our responsibility to decide where we want to be and with whom we want to spend our time. When we learn to establish priorities, we can avoid spreading ourselves too thin and begin to enjoy all aspects of our lives. Making decisions that satisfy and nurture us is one of the joys of recovery.

*Today I will honor and respect my own
thoughts and feelings.*

She fell asleep, and woke up to hear the clock saying, "Beauty, Beauty," which told her that she was in the palace. But when no Beast appeared she was really frightened, so she ran down into the garden to search for him. There was the cave, and in it lay the Beast. "Oh! He is dead; and it is all my fault," said Beauty, crying bitterly. Looking at him again, she fancied he still breathed, and fetching some water from the fountain, she sprinkled it over his face, and to her great delight he began to revive.

Recovery is a process that involves reviving tired lives and renewing old relationships. The Twelve Steps and the encouragement we receive from other program members slowly awaken us, and we begin to see ourselves in a new light.

We may find that self-defeating behaviors have interfered with our ability to establish healthy relationships. We do not have to blame ourselves, like Beauty did, but can free ourselves from the past when we assess the damage and do our best to make restitution for our part in the situation.

The amends we make in Step Nine may not repair all of our relationships. There are parts of the past we may have to relinquish by accepting the fact that we have done all we can, but it is not in our power to restore them. The lessons we learn by making our amends give us new insights that improve our ability to form new relationships and improve our present interaction with others.

I am repairing the damage of my past one day at a time.

"Oh! Beast, how you frightened me!" she cried. "I never knew how much I loved you until just now," "Can you really love such an ugly creature as I am?" said the Beast faintly. "Go back now and rest, I shall see you again by-and-by." Beauty went back to the palace, where supper was awaiting her; and afterwards the Beast came in as usual. When the time came for him to go, and he asked, as he had so often asked before, "Beauty, will you marry me?" She answered softly, "Yes, dear Beast."

*L*earning to accept imperfection and look beyond it to the essential beauty and wonder of life is part of the spiritual awakening in Step Twelve. We all have weaknesses and inadequacies that frighten us. We may try to hide our anger and helplessness from others, thinking these feelings make us unlovable. Learning to express ourselves without harming others or expecting them to take responsibility for us increases our self-acceptance and makes it easier for them to approach us.

Self-renewal comes after we establish an honest, open relationship with ourselves. When we can accept ourselves as we are and let go of our futile efforts to be perfect, we can begin to accept others the way they are. Letting go of unrealistic expectations and demands that others be perfect frees them to show us who they really are in ways that are intimate and affirming.

I will look for the beauty in those around me today without demanding perfection from myself or them.

As she spoke a blaze of light sprang up and in letters all made of fire-flies, was written: "Long live the Prince and his Bride." Turning to ask the Beast what it could all mean, Beauty found that he had disappeared, and in his place stood her long-loved Prince! Then two ladies entered the room. "How can I ever thank you enough, charming girl, for having restored my dear son to his natural form?" one cried. The marriage was celebrated the very next day, and Beauty and the Prince lived happily ever after.

*W*hen we learn to take responsibility for our actions and forgive ourselves for the mistakes of the past, we are able to forgive others for their errors also. Knowing and accepting all aspects of ourselves—our strengths and our weaknesses, our intuition and our logic, our successes and our failures—joins the Beauty and the Beast in all of us. When we accept our imperfections and recover our self-worth, we pave the way for healthy, loving lives and positive relationships with others.

We are restored to our natural form when we let go of the thought that we are somehow defective, that we are not good enough to love or be loved. When we reach the spiritual awakening in Step Twelve, we can let go of self-rejection and become free to both give and receive.

*As I discover more about myself, I am
learning to love and be loved.*

The Fisherman
and His Wife

nce upon a time, a fisherman pulled a large flounder from the shining sea. "Let me go," said the fish. "I am an enchanted prince." The fisherman put him back in the water and returned home empty-handed to his wife. When he told her that he had caught an enchanted prince, she demanded that he return to the sea, call the flounder and ask for a cottage to replace their humble hut.

The fisherman was not happy with this idea, but he agreed to go. When he got there the sea had turned green and yellow. He called to the fish and told him that his wife would like a cottage. "Go home," said the flounder. "She has it." The man returned to find a beautiful cottage. "Here we shall remain and live very happily," he thought, but his wife became discontent with the cottage and asked her husband to request a castle from the flounder. "It's not right," the fisherman thought, but he went. The sea had turned dull and thick, but the flounder replied as before: "Go home; she is standing before the door."

The next morning the wife decided she would be king, and after that, emperor and pope. The husband thought there could be nothing else to wish for, but his wife's wishing powers were boundless. The next morning, she was watching the sun rise, and thought, "I must be a god." By the time the man reached the sea, a storm was raging so fiercely he could scarcely stand. "What does she want now?" asked the flounder. "Alas, she wants to be a god." "Go home, then; she is sitting again in the hut," the enchanted fish replied, and there they remain.

There was once a fisherman and his wife who lived in a little hut close to the sea, and the fisherman used to go down every day to fish; and he would fish and fish. So he used to sit with his rod and gaze into the shining water; and he would gaze and gaze. Now, once the line was pulled deep under the water, and when he hauled it up he hauled a large flounder with it. The flounder said to him, "Listen, fisherman. I pray you to let me go; I am not a real flounder, I am an enchanted Prince. Put me back into the water and let me swim away."

We never know what we'll find when we go on a fishing expedition. The mystery is part of the fun of casting a line into the sea. Will we find a tasty supper, an old shoe or an enchanted flounder beneath the shining waters?

When we learn to relax and allow creative ideas and aspirations to break through the surface, we experience a similar kind of excitement. Ideas that seem outrageous to us at first glance sometimes appear in the course of our Step Eleven meditation. We may stifle them by thinking, "That's the most ridiculous thing I've ever heard of! Forget it! It will never work!" It might be better to put them back in the water and let them swim around until we see how to make constructive use of them. Our creative ideas can be a source of powerful and rewarding action if we have the courage to follow them.

Am I letting my old negative thought patterns push aside creative solutions to my problems? I will be open to ideas that come from within today.

"Well," said the man, "you need not make so much noise about it; I am sure I had much better let a flounder that can talk swim away." With these words he put him back again into the shining water, and the flounder sank to the bottom. Then the fisherman got up, and went home to his wife in the hut.

*I*f we are not accustomed to taking time to gaze into the waters—to become quiet and let our thoughts and feelings rise to the surface—we may become frightened by what we see. If our thoughts and fantasies seem unacceptable, and we feel uncomfortable or ashamed, we may not want to look at them.

Repressing our thoughts and feelings without trying to understand them can cut us off from valuable sources of creativity and inspiration. If we are disturbed by our dreams and fantasies, we can share them with a sponsor or someone else with whom we feel comfortable. Discussing our innermost thoughts with another person can reassure us that we are not so different from other people after all.

I need not be frightened or ashamed of my thoughts and feelings. If they make me uncomfortable, I will ask for help in understanding them.

"Husband," said his wife, "have you caught nothing today?" "No," said the man. "I caught a flounder who said he was an enchanted prince, so I let him swim away again." "Did you wish nothing from him?" said his wife. "No," said the man, "what should I have wished from him?" "Ah!" said the woman, "it's dreadful to have to live all one's life in this hut that is so small and dirty. Go now and call him; say to him that we choose to have a cottage, and he will certainly give it to you." The man did not like going at all, but he went down to the sea.

*I*f only life were so easy! If only we could sit around all day gazing into the water waiting for an enchanted flounder to rescue us from all our difficulties! While this doesn't happen in real life, wishful thinking can serve a useful purpose by making us aware of things we'd like to change and suggesting some goals we might choose to work toward.

Making a "wish-list" is one way of getting in touch with our dreams. Then we can begin to examine them realistically to decide whether or not they are within our reach. We can ask ourselves if they are things we can achieve easily or things we must ask for help in attaining. We can determine what we will have to sacrifice and what risks we must take in order to make them come true. Our dreams become a reality when we learn to break them down into small, achievable pieces and remember to move towards them one day at a time.

I will dare to dream today and I will explore ways to make my dreams come true.

When he came there the sea was quite green and yellow, and was no longer shining. Then the flounder came swimming up. "Alas!" said the man, "my wife does not want to live any longer in the hut; she would like a cottage." "Go home, then," said the flounder, "she has it." So the man went home, and there was his wife no longer in the hut, but in its place was a beautiful cottage. "See," said the wife, "isn't this nice?" "Yes," answered her husband; "here we shall remain and live very happily." "We will think about that," said his wife.

*W*hen the sea no longer shines—when we feel uncomfortable about what we want and about how we're going to get it—it is time to reconsider our approach. We may be trying to take shortcuts that will only impede our progress.

Instant success has certain drawbacks. If we haven't learned to be comfortable in our current surroundings, we may not be content when we reach the next rung on the ladder. We may think for awhile, "This is nice! I can live very happily here," but it's likely that it won't be long before our mind begins to race again. Learning to relax and enjoy what we have is one of recovery's gifts.

Am I able to be content with what I have today? It's impossible to be happy if I'm always thinking about things I don't have.

All went well for a week or a fortnight, then the wife said: "Go down to the flounder and tell him to send us a castle." The fisherman's heart was very heavy. He said to himself, "It is not right." Still, he went down. When he came to the sea, the water was all violet and dark blue, and dull and thick, but it was still smooth. "What does she want now?" said the flounder. "Ah!" said the fisherman, half-ashamed, "she wants to live in a great stone castle." "Go home; she is standing before the door," said the flounder.

*W*e may not have been aware of the conflicting parts of ourselves before we came into the program. Our addictions and compulsive behaviors may have isolated us from the inner turmoil that often accompanies wanting things that are out of our reach.

When we participate in a twelve-step program, it is more difficult to ignore our conflicts. We become more aware of the gap between what we want and what we have. If we are developing realistic ways to achieve our goals, our serenity will not be disturbed. If we convince ourselves that we're entitled to everything we want just because we're making an effort to change our lives, we may intensify the problem. Remembering to practice Step Seven and ask for removal of this shortcoming helps us get back into constructive action to restore our serenity.

If my inner seas are dull or thick today, I will stop and look for the source of my inner conflict.

The fisherman went home. There stood a great stone palace. Inside the castle were heaps of servants who threw open the great doors, and the best of food and drink was set before them when they wished to dine. "Now," said the wife, "isn't this beautiful?" "Yes, indeed," said the fisherman. "Now we will stay here and live in this beautiful castle, and be very happy." "We will consider the matter," said his wife, and they went to bed.

*A*h, the luxury of never having to work again—having heaps of servants to open doors for us and having the best food and drink whenever we wish to dine! What more could we possibly desire? At first we may say, "Nothing," but then another voice may intrude, saying, "Surely there must be something more!"

Learning to appreciate what we have is not always easy. A history of unfulfilled expectations may have left us feeling seriously deprived. We may have repressed our frustration, deciding it was better not to want or expect anything than it was to risk being disappointed. When we dare to dream we may find it difficult to maintain realistic expectations.

Taking time to make a gratitude list and thank our Higher Power for the many gifts we have already received helps us feel less deprived and tempers our craving for more. Remembering how our lives used to be and reviewing the progress we have made often revives our satisfaction with the present.

Today I can be grateful for what I've been given without worrying about what is still to come.

The next morning the wife woke up and looked out of the bed at the beautiful country stretched before her."Husband," she said, "could we not become the king of all this land? "Ah, wife!" replied her husband," why should we be king? I don't want to be king." "Well," said his wife, "if you don't want to be king, I will be king. Go down to the flounder." So the fisherman went. When he came to the sea, the water was a dark-grey color, and it was heaving against the shore. "What does she want now?" asked the flounder. "She wants to be king." "Go home; she is that already," said the flounder.

*A*t some point in recovery, we begin to realize how much we try to control others to achieve predictability in our lives. We avoid feeling vulnerable by trying to dominate people and events in subtle ways. If we have not developed skills to take care of ourselves properly, we may become expert at manipulating others to get our needs met.

As we become less dependent on those around us for our happiness, our need for control lessens. When we prepare a list of the people we have harmed in Step Eight and reflect on our past behavior, we are confronted with the truth about how we have injured people by our efforts to manipulate them. When we complete Step Eight and make amends in Step Nine, we can honor these amends by relating to others as partners and friends rather than authoritative, domineering monarchs.

I am learning that trying to manipulate and control others is as harmful to me as it is to those I am trying to influence.

The fisherman went home, and when he came near the palace he saw a sentinel standing before the gate. Then the doors of the hall flew open, and there stood the whole Court round his wife, who was sitting on a high throne. When he had looked for some time, he said: "Let that be enough, wife, now that you are king!" "Nay, husband," said his wife restlessly, "my wishing powers are boundless. King I am, now I must be emperor."

*W*hen we take advantage of other people's authority or position to get what we want, we may lose confidence. If we haven't achieved our present status through our own efforts, our feelings of powerlessness may increase with each new level of prestige. We become like the fisherman's wife, where each gain creates a hunger for more. We stop thinking, "Wouldn't it be nice?" and begin seeing things in terms of "must have" and "must be."

This puts us in a no-win situation. If we cannot be happy until we reach some distant goal, we can never take pleasure in the present. When we begin to see how self-defeating this vicious circle is, we begin to let go of our "boundless wishing powers." By surrendering in Step One, we admit our powerlessness and start the process of changing our lives. We learn to focus on the present moment and free ourselves from this endless cycle of always wanting what we don't have.

Rather than allowing grandiose fantasies to dominate me, I will use my wishing powers as inspiration to take positive action.

"Ah, wife," he said, "the flounder cannot make you emperor." "What!" said his wife. "If he can make king, he can make emperor, and emperor I must be. Go!" So he had to go. But he felt quite frightened. The sea was quite black and thick, and it was breaking high on the beach; the foam was flying about, and the wind was blowing. The fisherman was chilled with fear. "What does she want now?" asked the flounder. "Alas! flounder," he said, "my wife wants to be emperor." "Go home," said the flounder; "she is that already."

Most of us have moments when we are frustrated by our current position in life and wish we had more. We recognize these moments of internal crisis when our inner winds blow high, our sparkling sea of serenity turns black and the child within us shivers with fear. To continue to persevere in the face of such strong inner strife may not be the wisest thing to do. It may be a sign that unrealistic, grandiose thinking is dominating our lives.

We will never be entirely free of inner conflicts. Looking at more than one side of an issue and considering several possible courses of action gives us an opportunity to make choices in creative ways. Being dominated by illusions of grandeur is a sign that our lives have gotten out of balance again. When we practice Step Ten on a daily basis, we keep in touch with our behavior and can take prompt action to correct our wrongs.

I will use Step Ten to take a daily inventory and monitor my behavior. If I am wrong, I will promptly admit it.

So the fisherman went home, and he saw his wife upon a throne which was made out of a single block of gold. She had a great golden crown and many princes and dukes were standing before her. He stood looking at her magnificence, and when he had watched her for some time, said: "Ah, wife, let that be enough, now that you are emperor." "Husband," said she, "why are you standing there? I am emperor now, and I want to be pope too."

*I*t is hard to imagine anything more grandiose than wanting to become both emperor and pope—ruler of both the material and the spiritual worlds. When we look below the surface of such daydreams, we often discover that we are feeling weak and powerless again.

When we regain our self-esteem, we no longer need fantasies of people bowing and scraping before us to compensate for our lack of inner security. As our self-confidence increases, we begin to deal with those in authority without feeling diminished by their status. When we become more comfortable with our own achievements and abilities, we have less need to look to others for approval. We are content to be who we are.

By attending meetings and working the Steps, I can regain my inner authority and let go of my desire to dominate others.

"Alas! wife," said the fisherman, "you cannot be pope. "Husband," she said, I will be pope. I am emperor and you are my husband. Will you be off at once?" So he was frightened and went out, but he felt quite faint, and trembled and shook, and his knees and legs began to give way under him. The water was foaming and seething and dashing upon the shore. "Well, what does she want now?" asked the flounder. "She wants to be pope." "Go home, then; she is that already," said the flounder.

*W*e are most arrogant when the words, "I want" become "I must have." Intentionally causing others to tremble and shake in the turmoil we create is a signal that we are determined to have things our own way no matter what the cost or consequences. When we are out of control, we may be tempted to return to our old, self-destructive behaviors to relieve the inner tension.

We avoid crises like these by learning to stop pinning our hopes on any particular outcome. We learn through hindsight that what we want isn't necessarily what's best for us, and that what seem to be overwhelming disappointments can lead to great success. Remembering to practice Step Three and turn our lives over to our Higher Power helps us to be serene in these situations. Having the faith and courage to keep going despite temporary setbacks is one of the gifts of recovery.

Turning my will and my life over to my Higher Power, as Step Three suggests, frees me to do my best without needlessly worrying about the outcome.

Then he went home, and there he saw a large church surrounded by palaces. The interior was lit up with thousands of candles, and his wife wore three great golden crowns. All the emperors and kings were on their knees before her, and were kissing her foot. When he had watched her for some time he said: "Wife, be content now that you are pope. You cannot become anything more." "We will think about that," said his wife.

What is left to wish for after you have become pope and the world's rulers worship at your feet? The idea that we could still be discontent at the summit of such power suggests the degree of discomfort we can cause ourselves by indulging in grandiose fantasies without taking action to achieve our goals.

As part of recovery, we discover that true satisfaction comes from developing our own competencies, making choices based on our inner values and personal authority, and building relationships that increase our self-worth. When we experience the satisfaction of feeling neither "better than" nor "less than" others and realize we have become an equal among equals, we no longer need to be perfect or in absolute control.

I accept myself as an equal among equals
and am learning to make choices
based on my inner values.

With these words they went to bed. But the woman was not content; her greed would not allow her to sleep, and she kept on thinking what she could still become. Then the sun began to rise, and she thought, "Ha! could I not make the sun and man rise?" "Husband," said she, poking him in the ribs, "wake up. Go down to the flounder; I will be a god. I shall never have a quiet moment till I can make the sun and man rise."

*I*t is hard to be content with who we are if all we do is yearn to become more powerful. It is difficult to rest if we are continually driven to conquer new and greater challenges. A constant need to interfere with the natural course of things only results in endless frustrations and constant turmoil. Many of us remember times when we were so frantic to be in control that we even played "God."

Life gets easier when we let go of the fantasy that we can control everything that goes on around us. Learning to "go with the flow" doesn't mean abdicating responsibility for our own choices or going along with the crowd. It simply means learning to accept life as it unfolds, secure in the knowledge that our Higher Power will never send us more than we can handle at one time.

I will pay attention to my behavior today and look for indications that I am playing "God."

He looked at her in horror, and a shudder ran over him. "Alas! wife," said the fisherman, falling on his knees before her, "I implore you, be content and remain pope." Then she flew into a passion, and screamed: "I am not contented and I shall not be contented! Will you go?" So he hurried on his clothes as fast as possible, and ran away as if he were mad.

All of us experience occasional feelings of aggression and rage. Sometimes they are useful to us because they bring us in touch with things that are bothering us. They help us defend or remove ourselves from situations that are harmful to us. More often, these feelings occur because we are not getting what we want or what we think we should have. Expressing our emotions spontaneously in these situations may only get us in further trouble, and cause us to wish we had remained silent and not expressed ourselves.

When we can detach from our anger and examine what is causing it, we have an opportunity to be more rational. Our minds become free to analyze different approaches to reaching our goals and solving our problems. Sometimes we find that we are at fault because we expect too much of others and become angry when they don't perform to our standards.

Bringing our expectations in line with reality frees us from unnecessary frustration and helps us find satisfaction in who we are and what we have.

But the storm was raging so fiercely that he could scarcely stand. Houses and trees were being blown down, the mountains were being shaken, and pieces of rock were rolling in the sea. The sky was as black as ink, it was thundering and lightening, and the sea was tossing in great waves as high as church towers and mountains. "Well, what does she want now?" asked the flounder. "Alas!" said he, "she wants to be a god." "Go home, then; she is sitting again in the hut." And there they are sitting to this day.

We are not required to achieve positions of power and authority in order to acknowledge and value ourselves. We can decide instead to accept the fact that we are human beings, with our own special strengths and talents, fears and insecurities. We become godlike whenever we can simply be ourselves—as comfortable alone as we are with others—at home in a humble hut or a palace.

Although we gain satisfaction and pleasure in the things we accomplish, we achieve the greatest serenity when we come to understand that we are acceptable the way we are—that we are loved, that we have a place in the universe and that we have access to a calm, inner wisdom that gives meaning to our lives. The spiritual awakening at the end of the Steps relieves us of the need to impress others and frees us to live loving, healthy lives.

Remaining in touch with my Higher Power helps me be content with myself and know that I am loved.

The Selfish Giant

THE SELFISH GIANT

very afternoon, a group of children would stop and play in the giant's garden on the way home from school. The giant had been visiting his friend the ogre for seven years and when he returned, his peace of mind was disturbed by the boisterous children. He built a high wall around the garden to deny them entrance, and the children were left with no place to play but a dusty road full of hard stones. When the seasons changed and spring came to the country, winter remained in the giant's garden. Since the garden was devoid of laughter or joy, the trees forgot to blossom and the birds did not care to sing. Hail and cold winds raged continually about the giant's house. He wondered why spring did not follow winter, but could only hope for a change in the weather.

In time, the children discovered a small crack in the wall and climbed through to resume their play in the garden. As a result, spring returned and the flowers and trees bloomed again. One day, the giant noticed a little boy wandering around a big tree, unhappily crying because he was too small to climb it. The giant's heart went out to the child. "How selfish I have been," he thought, "I will put that poor little boy on the top of the tree, and then I will knock down the wall and my garden shall be the children's playground forever." He immediately accomplished these tasks and joined the children in their play, whereupon the seasons resumed their normal course. He had many happy years with them until the little boy he had helped returned to take him to paradise.

Every afternoon, as they were coming from school, the children used to go and play in the Giant's garden. It was a large lovely garden, with soft green grass. The birds sat on the trees and sang so sweetly that the children used to stop their games in order to listen to them. "How happy we are here!" they cried to each other.

We all have visions of some kind of paradise where we can be at peace with ourselves, the people we love and the world. Some of us remember such a place, where we were once protected from the harsher realities of life. If not, we may construct our ideal worlds from fantasies rather than memories. Whether or not our state of childhood innocence was real or imagined, we resent its loss if we haven't learned to recapture moments of childlike pleasure in the midst of our busy lives.

It is unlikely that we will ever live on the grounds of a castle like the Giant did, but we can create our own opportunities to play in beautiful gardens. Walking barefoot in the grass, rolling down a hill, running through the rain or listening to a bird sing can reunite us with our inner child. Being able to relax and enjoy ourselves is one of the joys of recovery.

I will find a time and place to stop and play today. Pleasurable activity refreshes me and renews my spirit.

One day the Giant came back. He had been to visit his friend the Cornish ogre, and had stayed with him for seven years. After the seven years were over he had said all that he had to say, for his conversation was limited, and he determined to return to his own castle. When he arrived, he saw the children playing in the garden. "What are you doing here?" he cried in a very gruff voice, and the children ran away.

When we assume adult responsibilities, many of us lose touch with the joys of life and forget how to play. As children, we may have experienced abuse and neglect, been faced with problems that required adult skills, or been expected to devote all our energies to making ourselves and the world a better place. We may have felt ashamed of our desire for pleasure or clumsy in our attempts to find it. As a result, we still carry the gruff voices of giants inside us who challenge our intentions.

In Step Two, we learn that trust in a power greater than ourselves can bring harmony to our lives. When we release our shame, we free ourselves from old inhibitions and give ourselves permission to play. The help of others who have fought monsters of their own and learned to live spontaneously can help us subdue the critical giants inside us.

I will turn away from gruff voices that discourage childlike behavior. Freeing myself from my inhibitions helps to restore my lost childhood.

The poor children had now nowhere to play. They tried to play on the road, but the road was very dusty and full of hard stones, and they did not like it. They used to wander round the high walls when their lessons were over, and talk about the beautiful garden inside. "How happy we were there!" they said to each other.

*T*he loss of our childhood security—our garden— can be devastating to us. Some of us wander around its high walls and remember how happy and safe we felt while playing inside. Others try to retrieve the feelings experienced while in the garden by entering into fantasy worlds or addictive behaviors that numb the pain of reality. We may even force ourselves to stay on the dusty road because we think we don't deserve any better—that a happy life is something we will never have.

In Step One, when we admit our powerlessness and recognize the unmanageability of our lives, we come to terms with the loss of our ideal worlds. We can turn to our Higher Power to give us security in the midst of life's variety and inconsistency. We can then begin to develop the adult skills we need to cultivate and maintain our garden and still retain the childlike spirit that allows us to revel in its beauty.

*I will continue to work the Steps knowing
that I can achieve peace and serenity
while learning to cultivate
my own garden.*

Then the Spring came, and all over the country there were little blossoms and little birds. Only in the garden of the Selfish Giant it was still winter. The birds did not care to sing in it as there were no children, and the trees forgot to blossom. The Spring never came, nor the Summer. The Autumn gave golden fruit to every garden, but to the Giant's garden she gave none.

*T*he walls we construct around ourselves to control our emotions actually isolate us from the joys of spring and force us to exist solely in the winter of self-repression. What we thought was a warm, protective wall becomes a cold dark prison where we are unable to connect with others and the world. In this frozen universe, we form superficial relationships based solely on outward appearances. When we restrain our natural vitality, our lives become empty and meaningless.

When we make a commitment to work the Steps, miraculous changes occur in our lives. We become willing to tear down our protective wall and allow the joys of spring into our world. In Step Three, when we turn our will and our lives over to the care of our Higher Power, we indicate that we are ready to be guided safely through the seasons of life. Our hope is strengthened, the spell of frozen life is broken and we begin to look forward to springtime.

I will have faith that spring cannot be far away.
I will prepare for its return by breaking
down my walls of isolation.

The only people who were pleased were the Snow and the Frost. "Spring has forgotten this garden," they cried, "so we will live here all the year round." The Snow covered up the grass with her great white cloak, and the Frost painted all the trees silver. They invited the North Wind to stay with them, and he came. He was wrapped in furs, and he roared all day about the garden, and blew the chimney-pots down.

*B*efore entering recovery, many of us found temporary comfort from a white cloak of denial. Although we were protected from the effects of our negative feelings and emotions, it kept us from experiencing warmth and spontaneity in our lives. The isolation and depression that resulted were sometimes very difficult to manage, but still we were shielded from the world around us.

As we work the Steps and attend meetings, we are able to halt winter's destructive process by examining our anger and resentment. When we get in touch with the negative behaviors that influence our lives, we remove the cloak of denial that we have worn for so long. We become acquainted with our true emotions and come to realize that healing is possible once we accept our true selves.

*I have shed my white cloak of winter and
am experiencing my true feelings.*

"This is a delightful spot," the North Wind said, "we must ask the Hail on a visit." So the Hail came. Every day for three hours he rattled on the roof of the castle till he broke most of the slates, and then he ran round and round the garden as fast as he could go. He was dressed in grey, and his breath was like ice.

Some of us learned to shut out people emotionally even though we were in close contact with them. This was the only way we could avoid being overwhelmed by their needs and feelings. We may have thought that being close to others meant we had to take responsibility for their lives. If so, we would sometimes experience their crises and demands as if they were our own. Other people came to represent hailstones beating on our roofs instead of sunlight offering us renewed energy.

Step Eight consists of listing all persons we have harmed and becoming willing to make amends to them all. This begins the process whereby we take responsibility for our own lives. We are freed to develop honest relationships in which we no longer have to fear being dominated by other people or compelled to assume control of their lives. Learning the difference between taking care of others and caring for others brings us closer to true intimacy.

Living my own life and allowing other people to live theirs enables me to establish healthy and mutually loving relationships.

"I cannot understand why the Spring is so late in com-
ing," said the Selfish Giant, as he sat at the window and
looked out at this cold, white garden. "I hope there will
be a change in the weather."

*H*oping for a change in the weather is a sign that
the first two Steps are working in our lives. Having
discovered that we are prisoners in our cold, white
gardens, we dare to hope that a power greater than
ourselves can release us from bondage. The anger,
boredom or pain that we feel is a signal that we might
need to make some changes in our lives. Hope for a
brighter future and faith in our ability to survive the
winter can lead us to embrace the new seasons willingly, in spite of our fears.

Change continues to be uncomfortable for many of
us. Its possibilities are obscured by the fear of losing
a part of ourselves in order to gain something new. It
is sometimes easier to hold on to winter than to risk
having the unfamiliar feelings that spring and new
growth may stimulate in us. When we learn that these
feelings are signs of progress and that our discomfort
is temporary, we become more accepting of new
beginnings and the many gifts that change can bring.

I am ready to make changes in my life, in
spite of the fear I have of the future.

One morning the Giant was lying awake in bed when he heard some lovely music. It sounded so sweet to his ears that he thought it must be the King's musicians passing by. It was really only a little linnet singing outside his window, but it was so long since he had heard a bird sing in his garden that it seemed to him to be the most beautiful music in the world.

*I*t seems like a miracle when we can relax and listen to the birds singing outside our window. We wake up slowly to the sights and sounds of the old world made new. Gradually we become less inhibited and more animated as we experience some of the pleasures we have denied ourselves for so long. We learn to enjoy the gentle breezes of a summer day, the bright color of a kite high in the sky, the surprise of spring's first flower or the joy of shared laughter.

When we give up our fear of loss and stop expecting the things we love to vanish, our concept of the basic goodness of the world widens. Our fear of never having enough or losing what we already have slowly diminishes. We stop worrying about the future, rejoicing in the abundance of the present moment and taking pleasure in each day.

Each day brings fresh miracles. I will open my eyes and ears so that I can see and hear them.

"I believe the Spring has come at last," said the Giant; and he jumped out of bed and looked out. Through a little hole in the wall the children had crept in, and they were sitting in the branches of the trees. And the trees were so glad to have the children back again that they had covered themselves with blossoms.

*T*hrough our program of recovery, the tools and inspiration we need to implement change in our lives are available to us. When we admit our powerlessness in Step One and begin to rely on our Higher Power in Step Two, we make a crack in the wall that has kept us separated from reality. Step Three helps us to overcome our fear of the unknown by trusting that our Higher Power will lead us through the changing seasons.

When we are honest with ourselves and others in Steps Four and Five, the crack in our wall widens into a small hole. When spring enters our garden through this portal, it brings fair weather so the trees of our self-esteem can blossom. Even if the walls we erected around ourselves were thick, it is possible to escape our prisons of unhealthy feelings, attitudes and responses if we faithfully follow the Twelve Steps, one day at a time.

I can trust my Higher Power to guide me through the pain and the joy of the changing seasons.

It was a lovely scene, only in one corner it was still winter. It was the farthest corner of the garden, and in it was standing a little boy. He was so small that he could not reach up to the branches of the tree, and he was wandering all round it, crying bitterly.

There are small, undernourished parts of the lost child within us that need help to reach the branches of the tree of life. Our shame at being unable to grasp the limbs sometimes causes us to conceal the damaged parts of ourselves so that others will not be aware of our inadequacies. We begin to grow when we can value ourselves enough to put our legitimate needs ahead of our shame and ask others for help.

Becoming closer to our lost child creates a new awareness within us. We recognize that life includes some degree of pain, but we are more willing and able to experience it in order to move forward. We see the need to pay attention to the child at the center of our lives. Practicing the principles of the program in relationships with ourselves and others helps us to gain the freedom we need that eventually leads us to wholeness and peace.

My self-worth depends on my ability to accept and nurture the vulnerable child inside me today.

And the Giant's heart melted as he looked out. "How selfish I have been!" he said. "Now I know why the Spring would not come here. I will put that poor little boy on top of the tree, and then I will knock down the wall, and my garden shall be the children's playground for ever and ever."

*W*orking the Steps involves having a spiritual awakening that allows us to establish a new relationship with ourselves and the world around us. Taking full responsibility for our behavior in Step Eight gives us an opportunity to allow others back into our garden. Making a list of those we have harmed is an important strategy in the process of learning to forgive. By forgiving ourselves and other people for prior mistakes, and taking action to correct the situation, we lessen our resentment and free ourselves from the past.

When we participate in a twelve-step program, we begin to let go of unhealthy attitudes and experiment with new ways of thinking and behaving. When we acknowledge and nurture the undeveloped aspects of our personalities, we can knock down the walls that isolate us from life and gradually learn to appreciate our childlike spirit of fun and adventure.

I will not limit myself to adult concerns and obligations. A playful and childlike spirit adds balance to my life.

And the other children when they saw that the Giant was not wicked any longer, came running back, and with them came the Spring. "It is your garden now, little children," said the Giant, and he took a great axe and knocked down the wall. And when the people were going to market at twelve o'clock they found the Giant playing with the children in the most beautiful garden they had ever seen.

*W*hen we become totally absorbed in the seriousness of life, we miss the whole point of recovery: to be able to engage fully and freely in life at whatever stage we happen to be. While we are responsible for our adult behavior, we still have the need to respond playfully when the situation warrants it. Thinking only in terms of demands and obligations stifles our creativity and our ability to love.

When we make amends in Step Nine, surprising changes begin to happen. Some of our relationships are repaired as dramatically as the Giant's were when he made the decision to knock down the wall and invite the children into his garden. Other relationships may not change at all if the people involved choose not to accept our amends. This does not mean our effort has been wasted. If we are sincere and honest in our approach, making restitution to the best of our ability is sufficient to free us from the obligation to do so.

*Today I will look for opportunities to express
my playful and childlike spirit.*

Every afternoon, when school was over, the children came and played with the Giant. But the little boy whom the Giant loved was never seen again. The Giant was very kind to all the children, yet he longed for his little friend, and often spoke of him. "How I would like to see him!" he used to say.

*L*ike the giant who longed for his little friend, we miss our lost child. Rediscovering the world through the eyes of a child restores wonder and delight to our lives. Taking care of ourselves requires us to nourish our playful spirit. This means learning to accept the things we cannot change without giving in to hopelessness and despair. It also means enjoying the things we can change.

We cannot have everything in life just the way we want it. We cannot constantly maintain the euphoria of peace and harmony with ourselves, the universe and the people we love. Life is a daily process of taking in and letting go—of giving and receiving. Our goal is to develop the ability to live happily, despite fear of the unknown, loneliness or loss. When we are able to accept life, we can enjoy whatever happiness and joy come our way.

I can find ways to acknowledge and mourn past losses without destroying my serenity. I will take advantage of opportunities for happiness today.

Years went over, and the Giant grew very old and feeble. One Winter morning he looked out of his window as he was dressing. He did not hate the Winter now, for he knew that it was merely the Spring asleep, and that the flowers were resting.

*L*iving comfortably with each season of life becomes easier once we accept the world as constantly changing. When we become confident in our ability to benefit from fluctuations in our lives, we no longer fear new beginnings. Our attitudes improve as we resolve our conflicts and find that we can have joy, peace and serenity in every season of the year.

One of the greatest rewards of recovery is being comfortable with change. Rather than dread our winters, we can look forward to spring, knowing that the flowers are resting. We can take pleasure in solitude and activity, work and play, teaching and learning. We can experience the benefits of being alone as well as being with others, of choosing when to give and when to receive, of recognizing our differences and our similarities. Being willing to explore new solutions leads to a wider repertoire of choices with which to meet life's challenges. Trusting that our Higher Power is available to guide us through changes in our lives is the basis of true serenity.

Am I experiencing the rewards of change in my life? New situations provide opportunities for growth and fulfillment.

Suddenly he rubbed his eyes in wonder and looked and looked. In the farthest corner of the garden was a tree quite covered with lovely white blossoms. Its branches were golden, and silver fruit hung down from them, and underneath it stood the little boy he had loved.

*P*art of having a spiritual awakening is recovering the little child we once loved and renewing our connection with our deepest self. If we were wounded as children, uncovering buried memories and feelings that still have the power to hurt us takes courage and persistence. Our willingness to expose the vulnerable parts of ourselves to trusted friends enables us to break through the denial that impedes our full development.

Remembering that we journey one day at a time helps us give ourselves permission to travel at our own pace. We don't have to wait until we are whole to reach out to other people. Each of us in recovery has experience, strength and hope to share with others. When we pass on what we've learned to those around us, we begin to build relationships based on mutual respect and equality. The close friendships we establish in the program enhance our connection with the precious golden branches and silver fruit from the richest parts of our being.

*I will facilitate my recovery by allowing
it to proceed at its own pace. I know
that my spiritual awakening will
come when I am ready.*

Downstairs ran the Giant in great joy, and out into the garden. He hastened across the grass and came near to the child. His face grew red with anger, and he said, "Who hath dared to wound thee?" "These are the wounds of Love," answered the child. And the child smiled on the Giant, and said to him, "You let me play once in your garden, today you shall come with me to my garden, which is Paradise." And when the children ran in that afternoon, they found the Giant lying dead under the tree, all covered with white blossoms.

*R*ecovery is a process of transformation. When we begin the journey, we are exhausted by the anger, fear or depression that occurs when we seek to avoid pain by engaging in self-destructive behaviors. As we proceed on our journey, we learn to accept suffering as an inevitable part of life without letting it dominate us and without engaging in it unnecessarily. Through faith in our Higher Power, we gain the strength to flourish during difficult times as we do in times of joy.

We gain vitality and lessen our fear of the unknown each time we allow our Higher Power to lead us into and through a new experience. Even the fear of death loses its hold over us. The power that has directed us through each of our life's transitions will help us through the final one, just as the child helped the Giant to reach Paradise.

I am facing new experiences with confidence. I meet them serenely, knowing that my Higher Power is there to guide me.

PRAYER FOR SERENITY

God, grant me the serenity
to accept the things I cannot change,
the courage to change the things I can,
and the wisdom to know the difference.

Amen

Reinhold Niebuhr

THE TWELVE STEPS OF ALCOHOLICS ANONYMOUS*

1. We admitted we were powerless over alcohol—that our lives had become unmanageable.

2. Came to believe that a Power greater than ourselves could restore us to sanity.

3. Made a decision to turn our will and our lives over to the care of God as we understood Him.

4. Made a searching and fearless moral inventory of ourselves.

5. Admitted to God, to ourselves, and to another human being the exact nature of our wrongs.

6. Were entirely ready to have God remove all these defects of character.

7. Humbly asked Him to remove our shortcomings.

8. Made a list of all persons we had harmed, and became willing to make amends to them all.

9. Made direct amends to such people wherever possible, except when to do so would injure them or others.

10. Continued to take personal inventory and when we were wrong promptly admitted it.

11. Sought through prayer and meditation to improve our conscious contact with God as we understood Him, praying only for knowledge of His will for us and the power to carry that out.

12. Having had a spiritual awakening as the result of these steps, we tried to carry this message to alcoholics, and to practice these principles in all our affairs.

---

*The Twelve Steps of Alcoholics Anonymous are taken from Alcoholics Anonymous, 3rd ed., published by A.A. World Services, Inc., New York, N.Y., 59-60. Reprinted with permission of A.A. World Services, Inc.

REFERENCES

Many authors have contributed to my understanding of the Twelve Steps. Because publications concerning recovery are numerous and readily available, I have not referenced them here.

The following books that concern the interpretation of fairy tales, mythology or other relevant literature have been especially helpful to me in the course of writing this book.

Bettelheim, Bruno, *The Uses of Enchantment: The Meaning and Importance of Fairy Tales*. New York: Vintage Books, 1977.

Birkhauser-Oero, Sibylle, *The Mother: Archetypal Image in Fairy Tales*. Toronto: Inner City Books, 1988.

Bolen, Jean Shinoda, *Gods in Everyman: A New Psychology of Men's Lives & Loves*. New York: Harper & Row, 1984.

Bolen, Jean Shinoda, *Goddesses in Every Woman: A New Psychology of Women*. New York: Harper & Row, 1984.

Chervin, Rhonda and Neill, Mary, *The Woman's Tale: A Journal of Inner Exploration*. New York: The Seabury Press, 1981.

Chinen, Allan B., *In the Ever After: Fairy Tales and the Second Half of Life*. Wilmette, Illinois: Chiron Publications, 1989.

Dieckmann, Hans, *Twice-Told Tales: The Psychological Use of Fairy Tales*. Wilmette, Illinois: Chiron Publications, 1986.

Mallet, Carl-Heinz, *Fairy Tales and Children: The Psychology of Children Revealed through Four of Grimm's Fairy Tales*. New York: Schocken Books, 1984.

Pearson, Carol, *The Hero Within: Six Archetypes We Live By*. San Francisco: Harper & Row, 1986.

Seifert, Theodor, *Snow White: Life Almost Lost*. Wilmette, Illinois: Chiron Publications, Wilmette, 1983.

Young-Eisendrath, Polly, and Wiedemann, Florence, *Female Authority: Empowering Women Through Psychotherapy*. New York: The Guilford Press, 1987.

The quotations from fairy tales in this book have been abstracted from the following:

Lang, Edward, Ed., *The Blue Fairy Book*. New York: Dover Publications, Inc. 1965:

Prince Hyacinth and the Dear Little Princess

East of the Sun and West of the Moon

Cinderella; or, The Little Glass Slipper

Rumpelstiltzkin

Beauty and the Beast

The Story of Pretty Goldilocks

Hansel and Grettel

The Princess on the Glass Hill

Lang, Andrew, Ed., *The Red Fairy Book*. New York: Dover Publications, Inc., 1965:

The Twelve Dancing Princesses

Rapunzel

Snow Drop

Lang, Andrew, Ed., *The Yellow Fairy Book*. New York: Dover Publications, Inc., 1966:

Story of the Emperor's New Clothes

Lang, Andrew, Ed., *The Pink Fairy Book*. New York: Dover Publications, Inc., 1967:

The Fir-Tree

Lang, Andrew, Ed., *The Green Fairy Book*. New York: Dover Publications, Inc., 1965:

The Story of the Fisherman and His Wife

Wilde, Oscar, *The Fairy Stories of Oscar Wilde*. New York: Peter Bedrick Books, 1986:

The Selfish Giant

TWELVE-STEP MESSAGES

MONTH	STEP ONE	STEP TWO	STEP THREE	STEP FOUR	STEP FIVE	STEP SIX
JANUARY	2	7	8	12	14	17, 19
FEBRUARY	3, 14	21	27	5	19	—
MARCH	25, 28	21, 28	2, 18, 22, 28	7, 11	7, 11	—
APRIL	25, 29	23, 25	10	11	11	13
MAY	11,19	11	11	11	5	21
JUNE	15, 22, 26	8	4, 14	3, 10, 16	7, 10, 18	17
JULY	2	4	3, 15	1, 9, 19	1, 9, 19	9, 11
AUGUST	1, 13	2, 16	—	6, 12, 18	7, 18	18
SEPTEMBER	2, 14	14	6	1, 18, 27	12, 25, 27	4, 25, 27
OCTOBER	—	6	16	24	12, 23	—
NOVEMBER	21	4, 20	5, 24	6, 15, 16	1, 15	8
DECEMBER	8, 18, 24	17, 24	11, 19, 24	24	24	—

TWELVE-STEP MESSAGES

STEP SEVEN	STEP EIGHT	STEP NINE	STEP TEN	STEP ELEVEN	STEP TWELVE	MONTH
17, 18, 19	—	25	26	28	—	JANUARY
—	—	—	6	—	28	FEBRUARY
—	10	10	12, 29	15, 29	29	MARCH
13	—	—	8	21	—	APRIL
21	23, 30	23, 30	11, 16	11	30	MAY
—	—	—	23	—	28	JUNE
9	9, 18	9, 18	16	8, 16	28	JULY
21	9, 23	9, 12	—	—	25, 26	AUGUST
27	—	—	—	16	—	SEPTEMBER
—	—	18	24	26	21	OCTOBER
8	8, 11	8, 28	9	13	29, 30	NOVEMBER
5	7, 21, 26	7, 27	9	1	—	DECEMBER

INDEX

ORDER FORM

CODE	TITLE	QTY	UNIT	TOTAL
9906	New Clothes from Old Threads	_____	$15.95	_____
9901	The 12 Steps—A Way Out	_____	$14.95	_____
9902	The 12 Steps For Adult Children	_____	$ 7.95	_____
9903	The Twelve Steps— A Spiritual Journey	_____	$14.95	_____
9904	The Twelve Steps For Christians	_____	$ 7.95	_____
9905	When I Grow Up... I Want To Be An Adult	_____	$12.95	_____
			Subtotal	_____
			*Sales Tax	_____
			**Shipping & Handling	
			TOTAL	_____

Please send a free catalog listing
additional titles.
Yes ☐   No ☐

To order by phone: (800) 873-8384
To order by FAX: (619) 275-5729
All other inquiries: (619) 275-1350

To order by mail:

Send this order form and a check or
money order for the total to:

RECOVERY PUBLICATIONS, INC.
1201 Knoxville Street
San Diego, CA 92110

*California residents add
   applicable sales tax.
**COD orders—add $3.30 to
   shipping cost.
Shipping & Handling:
   Minimum Charge $3.00
   Orders over $25.00—$5.00
   Orders over $50.00 Add 10%
      of Subtotal
Shipments Outside USA:
   Double shipping charges, U.S.
   funds only.

Name: _____

Address: _____

City, State, Zip: _____

Phone: (   )_____

Visa and **MasterCard** Accepted

Bankcard No.:_____

Expiration Date:_____

Signature: _____

Allow 2-3 Weeks for delivery—UPS